Penguin Books

The Penguin *Sun* Crossword Key

D1325219

The Penguin *Sun* Crossword Key

PENGUIN BOOKS
IN ASSOCIATION WITH
THE LONGMAN GROUP LTD

Penguin Books Ltd, Harmondsworth, Middlesex, England
Viking Penguin Inc., 40 West 23rd Street, New York, New York 10010, U.S.A.
Penguin Books Australia Ltd, Ringwood, Victoria, Australia
Penguin Books Canada Limited, 2801 John Street, Markham, Ontario, Canada L3R 1B4
Penguin Books (N.Z.) Ltd, 182–190 Wairau Road, Auckland 10, New Zealand

Published in Penguin Books in association with the Longman Group Ltd 1985
Copyright © The Longman Group Ltd, 1985
All rights reserved

Made and printed in Great Britain by
Richard Clay (The Chaucer Press) Ltd,
Bungay, Suffolk
Typeset in Times

Introduction

What do countless Britons do every day of the week (except Sunday) – in bed, lounging on a beach, down at the boozer, during a tea-break, sitting at home, travelling on a bus, tube or train – in fact, anywhere and at any time?

There may be more than one answer to the clue, so here's another: Britain's hottest verbal puzzle! (3,3,9).

The answer, of course, is the SUN crossword, which has proved so spectacularly popular. It's really two crosswords in one: both have the same answers, but the clues are different. The Coffee-Time clues are straightforward but not necessarily easier, while the Cryptic clues are the mind-bending ones to tackle when the grey matter needs a challenge. You can go for whichever set you want, depending on your mood – or you could even mix'n'match them and, either way, it's great fun.

But there's nothing more irritating than being stumped for an answer or two on those occasions when your mind goes blank. That's where the Penguin-SUN Crossword Key comes in. It contains many thousands of words and phrases arranged in order of their length. Three-letter words come first, in A–Z order; then four letter words (but not *those* ones, thank you!); and so on, up to eight-letter words. So it's a great help for finding those elusive answers, getting even more enjoyment from your SUN crossword and you can impress your family and friends by showing them a completed puzzle every day!

How to use the Key

The Penguin-SUN Crossword Key contains approximately 40,000 words and phrases arranged in sections according to length (from three to eight letters) and then in alphabetical order within each section. Thus all three-letter words are grouped together alphabetically, then all four-letter words and so on, up to eight letters. Phrases are listed according to the total number of letters, so **be a sport**, for example, can be found in the eight-letter section following **bearskin**.

To find the word or phrase you want, simply turn to the appropriate length section and start looking. In most cases at least one letter will already be known. If the first letter is known your search will be greatly reduced and if the first and one other are known you will very quickly be able to find the word you want.

For instance, if you want a six-letter word meaning 'to confine' that has 'i' as its first letter and 't' as its third, turn to the words beginning with 'i' in the six-letter section and run your eye down the third-letter column until you find – **intern**.

Even if only, say, the third or fourth letter is known, a rapid glance down the appropriate column will soon give you a number of words that fit. The skill then lies in deciding which is the right one.

3 letter words

aba	art	bob	cot	dog	eon	foe
ABC	ash	bod	cow	doh	era	fog
abo	ask	bog	cox	Dom	ere	fop
aby	asp	bok	coy	don	erf	for
ace	ass	boo	coz	dop	erg	fou
act	ate	bop	cru	dor	erk	fox
add	auk	bot	cry	dot	ern	foy
ado	ave	bow	cub	dow	err	Fra
adz	awe	box	cud	dry	ess	fro
aft	awl	boy	cue	dso	eta	fry
aga	awn	bra	cum	dub	eth	fug
age	axe	bub	cup	dud	eve	fun
ago	aye	bud	cur	due	ewe	fur
aha	azo	bug	cut	dug	eye	gab
aid	baa	bum	cwm	dun	fab	gad
ail	bad	bun	dab	duo	fad	gag
aim	bag	bur	dad	dup	fag	gal
ain	bah	bus	dag	dux	fah	gam
air	bam	but	dak	dye	fan	gan
ait	ban	buy	dal	dzo	far	gap
ala	bap	bye	dam	ear	fat	gar
alb	bar	cab	dan	eat	fay	gas
ale	bat	cad	dap	eau	fed	gat
all	bay	cam	daw	ebb	fee	gay
alp	bed	can	day	ecu	fen	gee
alt	bee	cap	deb	edh	feu	gel
ama	beg	car	dee	eel	few	gem
amp	bel	cat	den	een	fey	gen
ana	ben	caw	dew	eff	fez	get
and	bet	cay	dey	eft	fib	gey
ane	bey	chi	dib	egg	fid	ghi
ani	bib	cob	did	ego	fie	gib
ant	bid	cod	die	eke	fig	gid
any	big	cog	dig	eld	fin	gie
ape	bin	col	dim	elf	fir	gig
apt	bio	con	din	elk	fit	gin
arc	bis	coo	dip	ell	fix	git
are	bit	cop	dit	elm	flu	gnu
ark	biz	cor	div	emu	fly	Goa
arm	boa	cos	doe	end	fob	gob

god	hit	Jat	law	map	nim	ore
goo	hob	jaw	lax	mar	nip	ort
got	hod	jay	lay	mat	nit	our
gov	hoe	jet	lea	maw	nix	out
goy	hog	jeu	led	may	nob	ova
gum	hon	Jew	leg	men	nod	owe
gun	hop	jib	lei	met	nog	owl
gup	hot	jig	Leo	meu	Noh	own
gut	how	job	let	mew	non	oxy
guv	hoy	jog	leu	mho	nor	pad
guy	hub	jot	lev	mid	not	pah
gym	hue	jow	lex	mil	now	pal
gyp	hug	joy	ley	mir	nth	pam
had	huh	jug	lib	mix	nub	pan
hae	hum	jut	lid	moa	nun	pap
hag	Hun	kai	lie	mob	nut	par
hah	hup	kat	lip	mod	oaf	pas
ham	hut	kea	lis	mog	oak	pat
han	Ibo	ked	lit	mol	oar	paw
hap	ice	kef	lob	mom	oat	pax
has	icy	keg	log	moo	obi	pay
hat	Ido	ken	loo	mop	oca	pea
haw	ilk	key	lop	mor	och	ped
hay	ill	kid	lor	mot	odd	peg
heh	imp	kif	lot	mow	ode	pen
hem	Ind	kin	low	Mrs	oer	pep
hen	ink	kip	lox	mud	off	per
hep	inn	kit	loy	mug	oft	pet
her	ion	koa	lud	mum	ohm	pew
het	ire	kob	lug	nab	oho	phi
hew	irk	kop	lum	nae	oil	pie
hex	ism	lab	lur	nag	oke	pig
hey	ita	lac	lux	nap	old	pin
hic	its	lad	luz	nay	one	pip
hid	ivy	lag	lye	neb	oof	pit
hie	jab	lah	mac	nee	ooh	pix
him	jag	lam	mad	net	ope	ply
hin	jam	lap	mag	new	opt	pod
hip	Jap	lar	mam	nib	orb	poe
his	jar	lat	man	nil	orc	poi

pom	ret	sec	sri	tit	veg	won
pon	rev	see	sty	tod	vet	woo
pop	Rex	sei	sub	toe	vex	wop
pot	rho	sen	sue	tog	via	wot
pow	ria	set	sum	tom	vie	wow
pox	rib	sew	sun	ton	vim	wry
pro	rid	sex	sup	too	vis	wud
pry	rig	sez	tab	top	voe	wye
psi	rim	she	tag	tor	vow	yah
pub	rip	shy	tai	tot	vug	yak
pud	rob	sib	taj	tow	wad	yam
pug	roc	sic	tam	toy	wae	yap
pun	rod	sin	tan	try	wag	yaw
pup	roe	sip	tap	tub	wan	yea
pur	rom	sir	tar	tug	wap	yen
pus	rot	sis	tat	tui	war	yep
put	row	sit	tau	tum	was	yes
puy	rub	six	taw	tun	waw	yet
pye	rue	ski	tax	tup	wax	yew
pyx	rug	sky	tea	tut	way	yin
qua	rum	sly	tec	tux	web	yip
rad	run	sob	ted	twa	wed	yob
rag	rut	soc	tee	Twi	wee	yod
rah	rye	sod	teg	two	wen	yon
raj	sac	soh	ten	ufo	wet	you
ram	sad	sol	tew	ugh	wey	zap
ran	sag	son	the	ule	who	zax
rap	sai	sop	tho	ure	why	zed
rat	sal	sot	thy	urn	wig	zee
raw	sap	sou	tic	use	win	zel
ray	sat	sow	tie	vac	wis	Zen
red	saw	sox	tig	van	wit	zho
ref	sax	soy	til	vas	wiz	zip
rem	say	spa	tin	vat	woe	zoa
rep	sea	spy	tip	vee	wog	zoo

4 letter words

abba	akin	aria	bael	beau	blab	bora
abbe	alae	arid	bail	beck	blae	bore
abed	alar	aril	bait	Beeb	blah	born
able	alas	arms	bake	beef	blat	bort
ably	alee	army	bald	been	bleb	bosh
abut	alfa	arty	bale	beep	bled	bosk
abye	alga	arum	balk	beer	blew	boss
ache	ally	aryl	ball	beet	blin	both
achy	alms	asci	balm	bell	blip	bott
acid	aloe	ashy	band	belt	blob	bout
acme	alow	Asti	bane	bema	bloc	bowl
acne	also	atom	bang	bend	blot	boxy
acol	alto	atop	bank	bent	blow	boyo
acre	alum	auld	bant	bere	blub	bozo
Acts	amah	aunt	barb	berg	blue	brad
acyl	ambo	aura	bard	berk	blur	brae
Adam	amen	auto	bare	berm	boar	brag
Adar	amid	aver	bark	best	boat	bran
adit	amir	avid	barm	beta	bock	brat
adze	ammo	avow	barn	bevy	bode	braw
aeon	amok	away	base	bias	body	bray
aero	amyl	awed	bash	bice	Boer	bred
aery	anew	awny	bask	bide	bogy	bree
afar	anil	awry	bass	bier	boil	bren
Afro	ankh	axel	bast	biff	boko	brer
agar	anna	axes	bate	bigg	bold	brew
aged	anoa	axil	bath	bike	bole	Brie
agin	anon	axis	bats	bile	boll	brig
agio	anta	axle	batt	bilk	bolt	brim
agog	ante	axon	baud	bill	bomb	brio
agon	anti	ayah	bawd	bind	bond	brit
ague	apex	baas	bawl	bine	bone	brow
ahem	apod	baba	bawn	bint	bong	brut
ahoy	apse	babe	bays	bird	bony	bubo
aide	aqua	Babi	bead	birk	boob	buck
aine	Arab	babu	beak	birl	book	buff
Ainu	arak	baby	beam	bise	boom	buhl
airy	arch	bach	bean	bisk	boon	bulb
ajar	area	back	bear	bite	boor	bulk
akee	Ares	bade	beat	bitt	boot	bull

bumf	cane	chop	coed	cowl	czar	deft
bump	cang	chou	coho	coxa	dace	defy
buna	cant	chow	coif	coxy	Dada	deil
bund	cape	chub	coil	coze	dado	dele
bung	capo	chug	coin	crab	daff	delf
bunk	card	chum	coir	crag	daft	dell
bunt	care	chut	coke	cram	dago	deme
buoy	cark	ciao	cola	cran	dahl	demo
burd	carl	cine	cold	crap	Dail	demy
burg	carp	cire	cole	craw	dais	dene
burk	cart	cist	colt	cree	dale	dent
burl	case	cite	coma	crew	dame	deny
burn	cash	city	comb	crib	damn	derm
burp	cask	clad	come	crit	damp	derv
burr	cast	clam	comp	crop	Dane	desk
bury	cate	clan	cone	crow	dang	dewy
bush	caul	clap	conk	crud	dank	dhal
busk	cavy	claw	conn	crux	dare	dhow
buss	cede	clay	cony	cube	darg	dial
bust	cedi	clef	cook	cuff	dark	dice
busy	ceil	cleg	cool	cuit	darn	dick
butt	cell	clem	coon	cull	dart	dido
buzz	celt	clew	coop	culm	dash	diet
byre	cent	clip	coot	cult	data	dike
byte	cere	clod	cope	cups	date	dill
cade	cert	clog	Copt	curb	daub	dime
cadi	cess	clop	copy	curd	dawk	dine
cafe	chad	clot	cord	cure	dawn	ding
caff	chap	clou	core	curl	daze	dink
cage	char	cloy	corf	curn	dead	dint
cagy	chat	club	cork	curt	deaf	dire
cake	chaw	clue	corm	cush	deal	dirk
calf	chef	coal	corn	cusk	dean	dirl
calk	chew	coat	cosh	cusp	dear	dirt
call	chic	coax	cost	cuss	debt	disc
calm	chid	coca	cosy	cute	deck	dish
calp	chin	cock	cote	cyan	deed	disk
calx	chip	coco	cott	cyma	deem	diss
came	chit	coda	coup	cyme	deep	diva
camp	choc	code	cove	cyst	deer	dive

divi	doxy	dupe	else	face	fete	flex
dixy	doze	dura	emeu	fact	feud	fley
doat	dozy	durn	emir	fade	fiat	flic
dock	drab	duro	emit	fado	fico	flip
dodo	drag	dusk	Emmy	faff	fido	flit
doer	dram	dust	enow	fail	fief	floc
does	drat	duty	envy	fain	fife	floe
doff	draw	dyad	epee	fair	file	flog
doge	dray	Dyak	epha	fake	fill	flop
dogy	dree	dyer	epic	fall	film	flow
do it	dreg	dyke	epos	falx	fils	flub
dojo	drew	dyne	ergo	fame	find	flue
dole	drey	each	Erin	fane	fine	flux
doll	drib	earl	erne	fang	fink	flys
dolt	drip	earn	Eros	fard	Finn	foal
dome	drop	ease	Erse	fare	fino	foam
domy	drub	east	erst	farl	fire	foci
dona	drug	easy	esne	farm	firm	fogy
done	drum	eath	espy	faro	firn	fohn
dong	Druz	eats	esse	fash	fisc	foil
dont	duad	ebon	etch	fast	fish	foin
dook	dual	echo	etna	fate	fisk	fold
doom	duce	echt	etui	faun	fist	folk
door	duck	ecru	euro	fawn	fitz	fond
dope	duct	Edam	even	faze	five	font
dopy	dude	Edda	ever	fear	fizz	food
dorm	duds	eddy	evil	feat	flab	fool
dorp	duel	Eden	ewer	feck	flag	foot
dorr	dues	edge	exam	feed	flak	ford
dort	duet	edgy	exes	feel	flam	fore
dory	duff	edit	exit	feet	flan	fork
dose	duke	eery	exon	feis	flap	form
doss	dull	egad	expo	fell	flat	fort
dost	duly	egal	eyas	felt	flaw	foss
dote	duma	eger	eyed	feme	flax	foul
doth	dumb	eggy	eyne	fend	flay	four
do up	dump	egis	eyot	fere	flea	fowl
dour	dune	ekka	eyra	fern	fled	foxy
dove	dung	elan	eyre	fess	flee	frae
down	dunk	elmy	eyry	fest	flew	frap

frat	gang	gink	goof	gust	hash	hick
Frau	gaol	gird	gook	guts	hasp	hide
fray	gape	girl	goon	gybe	hast	hi fi
free	garb	girn	goop	gymp	hate	high
fret	garn	giro	gory	gyre	hath	hike
frit	gash	girt	Goth	gyri	haul	hila
froe	gasp	gist	gout	gyro	have	hill
frog	gast	give	gowk	gyve	hawk	hilt
from	gate	glad	gown	haaf	haze	hind
frow	gaud	glam	grab	hack	hazy	hint
fuci	Gaul	glee	graf	hade	head	hire
fuel	gaum	gleg	gram	hadj	heal	hiss
full	gaup	glen	gran	haem	heap	hist
fume	gaur	gley	grat	haet	hear	hive
fumy	gave	glia	gray	haft	heat	hoar
fund	gawk	glib	gree	haha	heck	hoax
funk	gawp	glim	grew	haik	heed	hobo
furl	gaze	glob	grey	hail	heel	hock
fury	gean	glop	grid	hair	heft	hoer
fuse	gear	glow	grig	hajj	heil	hogg
fuss	geat	glue	grim	haka	heir	hoho
fuze	geck	glum	grin	hake	held	hold
fuzz	Geez	glut	grip	hale	hele	hole
fyrd	geld	G man	gris	half	hell	holm
gaby	gelt	gnat	grit	hall	helm	holp
gade	gene	gnaw	grog	halm	help	hols
gadi	gens	goad	grot	halo	heme	holt
Gael	gent	goal	grow	halt	hemp	holy
gaff	germ	goat	grub	hame	hent	home
gaga	gest	goby	guan	hand	herb	homo
gage	geum	goer	guar	hang	herd	homy
gain	ghat	goes	guff	hank	here	hone
gait	ghee	gogo	gula	hard	herl	hong
gala	gibe	go in	gulf	hare	herm	honk
gale	gift	gold	gull	hark	hern	hood
gall	gila	golf	gulp	harl	hero	hoof
gamb	gild	gone	gump	harm	Herr	hook
game	gill	gong	gunk	harn	hers	hoop
gamp	gilt	gonk	guru	harp	hest	hoot
gamy	gimp	good	gush	hart	hewn	hope

horn	ikon	jerk	kale	kite	lamb	less
hose	ilea	jess	kali	kith	lame	lest
hoss	ilex	jest	kame	kiwi	lamp	Lett
host	ilia	jete	kana	knag	land	leva
hour	ilka	jibe	kaon	knap	lane	levy
hove	illy	jiff	kart	knar	lang	lewd
howl	imam	jill	kava	knee	lank	liar
hued	impi	jilt	kayo	knew	Lapp	Lias
huff	inby	jimp	keck	knit	lard	lice
huge	Inca	jink	keek	knob	lark	lich
hula	inch	jinn	keel	knop	larn	lick
hulk	info	jinx	keen	knot	lase	lido
hull	inky	jive	keep	know	lash	lied
hump	inly	jock	kelp	knur	lass	lief
hung	into	joey	Kelt	knut	last	lien
hunk	iota	john	kemp	koan	late	lier
hunt	iris	join	kent	koel	lath	lieu
hurl	iron	joke	kepi	kohl	laud	life
hurt	isle	joky	kept	kola	lava	lift
hush	isnt	jolt	kerb	kolo	lave	like
husk	itch	josh	kerf	kook	lawk	lilo
huss	item	joss	kern	koto	lawn	lilt
hwyl	iwis	jota	khan	kris	laze	lima
hyle	jack	jowl	khat	kudu	lazy	limb
hymn	jade	juba	kibe	Kurd	lead	lime
hype	jail	judo	kick	kyat	leaf	limn
hypo	Jain	judy	kier	kyle	leak	limo
iamb	jake	juju	kill	lace	lean	limp
ibex	jamb	July	kiln	lack	leap	limy
ibid	jane	jump	kilo	lacy	leat	line
ibis	jape	June	kilt	lade	leek	ling
icky	jarl	junk	kind	lady	leer	link
icon	jato	Juno	kine	laic	lees	linn
idea	Java	jury	king	laid	leet	lino
idem	jazz	just	kink	lain	left	lint
ides	jean	jute	kino	lair	lehr	liny
idle	jeep	kadi	kiri	lake	lend	lion
idly	jeer	kago	kirk	lakh	leno	lira
idol	jehu	kail	kiss	laky	lens	lire
iffy	jell	kaka	kist	lama	Lent	lisp

list	luce	mall	melt	mitt	muon	newt
live	luck	malm	memo	moan	mure	next
load	ludo	malt	mend	moat	murk	nice
loaf	lues	mama	menu	mock	muse	nick
loam	luff	mana	meow	mode	mush	nide
loan	luge	mane	mere	mods	musk	nidi
lobe	lull	Manx	mesa	moho	muss	niff
loch	lulu	many	mesh	moil	must	nigh
loci	lump	marc	mess	moke	mute	nill
lock	lune	mare	mete	moko	mutt	nine
loco	lung	mark	mewl	mole	myna	nipa
lode	lunt	marl	mews	moll	myth	nisi
loft	lure	marm	mica	mome	Naga	nixy
loge	lurk	Mars	mice	mona	naif	nock
logo	lush	mart	mick	monk	nail	node
loin	lust	mash	midi	mono	name	nodi
loir	lute	mask	mien	mood	nana	noel
loll	luxe	mass	miff	moon	nape	noil
lone	lyam	mast	mike	moor	nard	nome
long	lych	mate	mild	moot	nark	none
look	lyme	math	mile	mope	nary	non U
loom	lynx	matt	milk	mora	nave	nook
loon	Lyon	maty	mill	more	navy	noon
loop	lyre	maud	milt	morn	naze	nope
loot	lyse	maul	mime	Moro	Nazi	norm
lope	maam	maun	mina	mort	neap	nose
lord	mace	maxi	mind	moss	near	nosh
lore	Mach	maya	mine	most	neat	nosy
lorn	mack	maze	Ming	mote	neck	note
lory	made	mazy	mini	moth	need	noun
lose	mage	mead	mink	moue	neem	nous
loss	magi	meal	mint	move	neer	nova
lost	maid	mean	minx	mown	nene	nowt
loth	mail	meat	mire	moxa	neon	nude
loud	maim	Mede	mirk	much	ness	null
loup	main	meed	miry	muck	nest	numb
lour	make	meek	mise	muff	nett	nuts
lout	mako	meet	miss	mule	neum	oary
love	male	meld	mist	mull	neve	oast
luau	mali	mell	mite	mump	news	oath

oats	orts	park	phot	ploy	pout	quad
obey	oryx	parr	pica	plug	poxy	quag
oboe	otic	part	pice	plum	pram	quay
obol	otto	pash	pick	plus	prat	quid
odds	ouch	pass	Pict	pock	prau	quin
odea	ouph	past	pied	poco	pray	quip
odic	ours	pate	pier	poem	prep	quit
ogam	oust	path	pika	poet	prex	quiz
ogee	ouzo	paua	pike	pogo	prey	quod
ogle	oval	paul	pile	poke	prig	rabi
ogre	oven	pave	pili	poky	prim	race
oily	over	pawl	pill	pole	proa	rack
oink	ovum	pawn	pimp	poll	prod	racy
okay	oxen	peak	pine	polo	prof	raff
okra	oxer	peal	ping	poly	prog	raft
oleo	oyer	pean	pink	pome	prom	raga
olio	oyes	pear	pint	pomp	prop	rage
olla	oyez	peat	piny	pond	prow	ragi
omen	paca	peck	pion	pone	puce	raid
omer	pace	peek	pipe	pong	puck	rail
omit	pack	peel	pipy	pons	puff	rain
once	pact	peen	pirn	pony	puja	raja
oner	page	peep	pise	pood	puke	rake
only	paid	peer	pish	poof	pule	raki
onto	pail	peke	piss	pooh	pull	rale
onus	pain	pelf	pita	pool	pulp	rami
onyx	pair	pelt	pith	poon	puma	ramp
oont	pale	pent	pity	poop	pump	rand
oops	Pali	peon	pixy	poor	puna	rang
ooze	pall	pepo	plan	pope	punk	rani
oozy	palm	peri	plat	pore	punt	rank
opah	palp	perk	play	pork	puny	rant
opal	paly	perm	plea	porn	pupa	rape
open	pane	pern	pleb	port	pure	rapt
opus	pang	pert	pled	pose	purl	rare
oral	pant	peso	plie	posh	purr	rase
orfe	papa	pest	plod	post	push	rash
orgy	para	phew	plop	posy	puss	rasp
orle	pard	phiz	plot	pouf	putt	rata
orra	pare	phon	plow	pour	pyre	rate

rath	rimy	rude	sass	sere	Sikh	slim
rave	rind	ruff	sate	serf	sild	slip
raze	ring	ruin	sati	seta	silk	slit
razz	rink	rule	save	sett	sill	slob
read	riot	rump	sawn	sewn	silo	sloe
real	ripe	rune	saxe	sext	silt	slog
ream	rise	rung	scab	sexy	sima	slop
reap	risk	runt	scad	shad	sine	slot
rear	rite	ruse	scan	shag	sing	slow
reck	rive	rush	scar	shah	sinh	slub
redd	road	rusk	scat	sham	sink	slue
rede	roam	Russ	scot	Shan	Sion	slug
redo	roan	rust	scow	shaw	sire	slum
reed	roar	ruth	scry	shay	site	slur
reef	robe	ryal	scud	shea	sith	slut
reek	rode	ryot	scug	shed	Siva	smew
reel	roil	rype	scum	shew	size	smit
refs	role	sack	scup	shim	sizy	smog
reft	roll	safe	scut	shin	skat	smug
rein	romp	saga	seal	ship	skaw	smut
reis	rood	sage	seam	shiv	skep	snag
rely	roof	sago	sear	shod	skew	snap
rend	rook	said	seat	shoe	skid	sned
rent	room	sail	sect	shog	skim	snib
repp	root	sain	seed	shoo	skin	snip
rest	rope	sake	seek	shop	skip	snob
rete	ropy	saki	seel	shot	skit	snog
rhea	rose	sale	seem	show	skua	snot
rial	rosy	salt	seen	Shri	slab	snow
rice	rota	same	seep	shun	slag	snub
rich	rote	samp	seer	shut	slam	snug
rick	rotl	sand	self	sial	slap	soak
ride	roue	sane	sell	sice	slat	soap
rife	roup	sang	semi	sick	Slav	soar
riff	rout	sank	send	side	slaw	sock
rift	roux	sans	sent	sift	slay	soda
rile	rove	sard	seps	sigh	sled	sofa
rill	ruby	sari	sept	sign	slew	soft
rima	ruck	sark	sera	sika	sley	soho
rime	rudd	sash	Serb	sike	slid	soil

soke	spue	sure	tapa	thee	toff	trap
sola	spun	surf	tape	them	toft	tray
sold	spur	swab	taps	then	tofu	tree
sole	stab	swag	tara	thew	toga	trek
soli	stag	swam	tare	they	togs	tret
solo	stap	swan	tarn	thin	toil	trey
soma	star	swap	taro	thir	toko	trig
some	stay	swat	tarp	this	tola	trim
sone	stem	sway	tart	thou	told	trio
song	sten	swig	tash	thro	tole	trip
soon	step	swim	task	thud	toll	trod
soot	stet	swiz	tass	thug	tolu	tron
soph	stew	swob	ta ta	thus	tomb	trot
sora	stir	swop	taut	tick	tome	trow
sorb	stoa	swot	taws	tide	tone	troy
sore	stob	swum	taxa	tidy	tong	true
sori	stop	syce	taxi	tied	tony	trug
sorn	stot	sync	teak	tier	took	tsar
sort	stow	syne	teal	tiff	tool	Tshi
soso	stub	taal	team	tike	toom	tuan
souk	stud	tabu	tear	tiki	toon	tuba
soul	stum	tace	teat	tile	tope	tube
soup	stun	tach	teem	till	topi	tuck
sour	stye	tack	teen	tilt	tops	tufa
sown	such	taco	teff	time	torc	tuff
soya	suck	tact	tegg	tine	tore	tuft
spae	sudd	tael	tele	ting	tori	tule
span	suds	tahr	tell	tint	torn	tump
spar	suer	tail	temp	tiny	torr	tuna
spat	suet	take	tend	tire	tort	tune
spay	Sufi	tala	tent	tirl	Tory	tung
spec	suit	talc	term	tiro	tosh	Tupi
sped	sulk	tali	tern	titi	toss	turf
spew	sumo	talk	test	tizz	tote	Turk
spin	sump	tall	text	toad	tour	turn
spit	sung	tame	Thai	toby	tout	tush
spiv	sunk	tamp	than	toco	town	tusk
spot	sunn	tana	thar	to do	towy	tutu
spry	sura	tang	that	tody	trad	twae
spud	surd	tank	thaw	toed	tram	twee

twig	vary	volt	ways	whiz	word	yogh
twin	vasa	vote	weak	whoa	wore	yogi
twit	vase	Waac	weal	whom	work	yoke
tyke	vast	Waaf	wean	whop	worm	yolk
type	veal	wade	wear	wick	worn	yond
typo	Veda	wadi	weed	wide	wort	yoni
tyre	veer	wady	week	wife	wost	yore
tyro	vehm	waff	ween	wild	wove	york
tzar	veil	waft	weep	wile	wrap	your
ugli	vein	wage	weet	will	wren	yowl
ugly	vela	waif	weft	wilt	writ	yoyo
ulna	veld	wail	weir	wily	wynd	yuan
umbo	vena	wain	weka	wind	Xmas	yuca
unci	vend	wait	weld	wing	X ray	yuga
unco	vent	wake	well	wink	yack	yule
undo	verb	wale	wels	wino	yang	yurt
unit	vert	walk	welt	winy	yank	ywis
unto	vest	wall	wend	wipe	yapp	zack
upas	veto	wame	went	wire	yard	zany
upon	vial	wand	wept	wiry	yare	zati
Urdu	vice	wane	were	wise	yarn	zeal
urea	vide	want	wert	wish	yaup	zebu
urge	view	ward	west	wisp	yawl	zein
uric	vile	ware	wham	wist	yawn	Zend
urim	vill	warm	whap	wite	yaws	zero
urus	vina	warn	what	with	yeah	zest
used	vine	warp	whee	wits	yean	zeta
user	vino	wart	when	wive	year	zinc
uvea	vint	wary	whet	woad	yegg	zing
vagi	viny	wash	whew	woes	yeld	Zion
vail	viol	wasp	whey	woke	yell	zoea
vain	visa	wast	whid	wold	yelp	zoic
vair	vise	watt	Whig	wolf	yerk	zone
vale	viva	waul	whim	womb	yeti	zoom
vali	vive	wave	whin	wont	yeuk	zoon
vamp	vlei	wavy	whip	wood	yill	zoot
vane	void	wawl	whir	woof	ylem	zori
vang	vole	waxy	whit	wool	yoga	Zulu
vara						

5 letter words

abaca	adapt	aging	alkyl	amnia	apish
abaci	addax	agist	Allah	among	apode
aback	adder	aglet	allay	amort	aport
abaft	addle	agley	alley	amour	appal
abase	add up	aglow	all in	ample	apple
abash	adept	agogo	allot	amply	apply
abask	ad hoc	agone	allow	amuck	appro
abate	adieu	agony	alloy	amuse	appui
abaya	adios	agora	allyl	anele	appuy
abbey	ad lib	agree	aloft	anent	April
abbot	adman	agued	aloha	angel	apron
abeam	admit	ahead	alone	anger	apsis
abele	admix	ahold	along	angle	aptly
abhor	adobe	ahull	aloof	Anglo	Araby
abide	adopt	aider	aloud	angst	arbor
ablow	adore	aioli	alpha	anigh	areal
abode	adorn	airer	altar	anile	areca
aboil	adown	aisle	alter	anima	arena
A bomb	adoze	aitch	alway	anion	argil
abort	adult	alack	amain	anise	argol
about	adust	alarm	amass	anker	argon
above	adyta	alary	amaze	ankle	argot
abrim	aegis	alate	amban	annal	argue
abuse	aerie	album	amber	annex	Argus
abuzz	affix	alder	ambit	annoy	Arian
abysm	afire	aleph	amble	annul	ariel
abyss	afoot	alert	ambos	anode	arise
acari	afore	algae	ambry	anomy	armed
acerb	Afric	algal	ameer	antic	aroid
acini	afrit	algid	amend	antra	aroma
ackee	after	algin	ament	antre	arose
acock	again	Algol	amice	anvil	arrah
acold	agami	alias	amide	Anzac	arras
acorn	agape	alibi	amido	aorta	array
acred	agate	alien	amigo	apace	arris
acrid	agave	align	amine	apart	arrow
actin	agaze	alike	amino	apeak	arsis
actor	agent	aline	Amish	aphid	arson
acute	aggro	alive	amiss	aphis	artel
adage	agile	alkyd	amity	apian	arval

Aryan	auxin	baler	beady	berry	blade
ascus	avail	balky	beamy	berth	blain
asdic	avast	bally	beano	beryl	blame
ashen	avens	balmy	beard	beset	bland
ashet	avert	balsa	beast	besom	blank
Asian	avian	banal	beaus	besot	blare
aside	avoid	banco	beaut	betel	blase
asker	await	bandy	beaux	bet on	blast
askew	awake	banjo	bebop	bevel	blaze
aspen	award	banns	bedad	bezel	bleak
aspic	aware	Bantu	bedel	bhang	blear
assai	awash	barbe	bedew	bible	bleat
assay	awful	bardy	bedim	biddy	bleed
asset	awned	barge	beech	bidet	bleep
aster	awoke	baric	beefs	bifid	blend
astir	axial	barky	beefy	bight	blent
aswim	axile	barmy	beery	bigot	bless
ataxy	axiom	baron	befit	bijou	blest
atilt	ayrie	barre	befog	biker	blimp
atlas	azoic	basal	begad	bilbo	blimy
atman	azote	basan	began	bilge	blind
atoll	azoth	bases	begat	bilgy	blink
atomy	Aztec	basic	beget	billy	bliss
atone	azure	basil	begin	bimbo	blitz
atony	babel	basin	begot	binge	bloat
atria	baboo	basis	begum	bingo	block
atrip	babul	bassi	begun	biome	bloke
attar	bacca	basso	beige	biota	blond
attic	baccy	baste	being	biped	blood
audio	bacon	batch	belay	bipod	bloom
audit	baddy	bated	belch	birch	blown
auger	badge	bathe	belga	birth	blowy
aught	badly	baths	belie	bison	blude
augur	bagel	batik	belle	bitch	blues
aulic	baggy	baton	belly	biter	bluet
aunty	Bahai	batty	below	bitsy	bluey
aurae	bairn	baulk	bench	bitts	bluff
aural	baize	bawdy	bends	bitty	blunt
auras	baker	bayou	bendy	bivvy	blurb
auric	balas	beach	beret	black	blurt

blush	bossy	bread	bubby	butch	candy
board	bosun	break	bucko	butte	canna
boast	botch	bream	buddy	butty	canny
bobby	botel	brede	budge	butyl	canoe
boche	bothy	breed	buffi	buxom	canon
bodge	bough	brent	buffo	buyer	canst
bogey	boule	breve	buggy	bwana	canto
boggy	boult	briar	bugle	by gum	canty
bogie	bound	bribe	build	bylaw	caper
bogle	bourg	brick	built	byway	capon
bogus	bourn	bride	bulge	cabal	carat
bohea	bouse	brief	bulgy	cabby	carer
bolas	bousy	brier	bulky	caber	caret
bolus	bowed	brill	bulla	cabin	cargo
bombe	bowel	brine	bully	cable	Carib
bonce	bower	bring	bumph	cabob	carob
boned	bowls	brink	bumpy	caboc	carol
boner	bowse	briny	bunch	cacao	carom
boney	boxer	brisk	bunco	cache	carpi
bongo	boyar	brize	bunia	cacti	carry
bonne	brace	broad	bunko	caddy	carve
bonny	brach	broch	bunny	cadet	caste
bonus	bract	brock	bunty	cadge	catch
bonze	braid	broil	bunya	cadre	cater
booby	brail	broke	buran	caeca	cates
booed	brain	bronc	burgh	cagey	catty
boost	brake	brood	burin	caird	cauli
booth	braky	brook	burka	cairn	caulk
boots	brand	broom	burke	calid	cause
booty	brank	brose	burly	calif	caver
booze	brant	broth	burnt	calix	cavil
boozy	brash	brown	burro	calla	cease
borax	brass	bruin	burry	calpa	cedar
borer	brava	bruit	bursa	calve	cello
boric	brave	brule	burse	calyx	cense
borne	bravo	brume	burst	camas	cento
boron	brawl	brunt	busby	camel	ceorl
bosky	brawn	brush	bused	cameo	cesti
bosom	braxy	brute	bushy	campy	chafe
boson	braze	bubal	busty	canal	chaff

chain	chimp	civic	cluck	conge	covey
chair	china	civil	clump	conic	covin
chalk	chine	civvy	clung	conky	cowed
champ	chink	clack	clunk	conte	cower
chant	chirk	claim	coach	cooee	cowry
chaos	chirp	clamp	coact	cooey	coxae
chape	chirr	clang	coapt	cooky	coxal
chaps	chivy	clank	coast	cooly	coyly
chard	chizz	clary	coati	coomb	coypu
chare	chock	clash	cobby	coopt	cozen
charm	choir	clasp	coble	copal	crack
charr	choke	class	Cobol	coper	craft
chart	choky	clave	cobra	cop it	crake
chary	choli	clean	cocky	copra	cramp
chase	chomp	clear	cocoa	copse	crane
chasm	chops	cleat	coder	copsy	crank
cheap	chord	cleek	codex	coral	crape
cheat	chore	cleft	codon	cords	craps
check	chose	clepe	cogue	corer	crash
cheek	choux	clerk	cohoe	corgi	crass
cheep	chuck	click	coign	corky	crate
cheer	chuff	cliff	coley	corno	crave
cheka	chump	climb	colic	cornu	crawl
chela	chunk	clime	colly	corny	craze
chert	churl	cline	colon	corps	crazy
chess	churn	cling	colza	corse	creak
chest	churr	clink	comae	coset	cream
chevy	chuse	cloak	comal	costa	credo
chewy	chute	clock	combe	cotta	creed
chiao	chyle	cloke	combo	couch	creek
chick	chyme	clone	comer	coude	creel
chide	cider	clonk	comet	cough	creep
chief	cigar	cloot	comfy	could	creme
chiel	cilia	close	comic	count	crepe
child	cimex	cloth	comma	coupe	crept
chile	cinch	cloud	compo	court	cress
chili	circa	clout	compt	couth	crest
chill	cirri	clove	conch	coven	crick
chimb	cissy	clown	coney	cover	crier
chime	civet	clubs	conga	covet	cries

crime	cully	damar	demon	disco	dotty
crimp	cumin	dance	demos	dishy	Douay
crisp	cupel	dandy	demur	disme	doubt
croak	Cupid	darky	denim	ditch	douce
Croat	cuppa	darts	dense	ditto	dough
crock	curch	dated	depot	ditty	douse
croft	curds	dater	depth	divan	dowdy
crone	curdy	datum	derby	diver	dowed
cronk	curer	daunt	derma	Dives	dowel
crony	curia	davit	desex	divot	dower
crook	curie	dealt	deter	divvy	downy
croon	curio	deary	deuce	dixie	dowry
crore	curly	death	devil	dizzy	dowse
cross	curry	debag	dewan	djinn	doyen
croup	curse	debar	dhobi	dobby	dozen
crowd	curst	debit	dhole	docht	dozer
crown	curve	debug	dhoti	dodge	Draco
cruck	curvy	debut	Diana	dodgy	draff
crude	cusec	decal	diary	dodos	draft
cruel	cushy	decay	dicer	doest	drail
cruet	cutey	decor	dicey	doeth	drain
crumb	cutie	decoy	dicky	doggo	drake
crump	cutis	decry	dicot	doggy	drama
cruse	cycad	deedy	dicta	dogie	drank
crush	cycle	defer	didst	dogma	drape
crust	cyclo	degas	dight	doily	drawl
crwth	cyder	degum	digit	doing	drawn
cryer	Cymry	deice	diker	dolce	dread
crypt	cynic	deify	dilly	dolly	dream
Cuban	Czech	deign	dimer	domed	drear
cubby	dacha	deism	dimly	donah	dregs
cubeb	daddy	deist	dinar	donee	dress
cubic	daffy	deity	diner	donga	dried
cubit	dagga	dekko	dingo	donna	drier
cuddy	dagos	delay	dingy	donor	drift
Cufic	daily	delft	dinky	donut	drill
cuish	dairy	delta	diode	doper	drily
culch	daisy	delve	dippy	dopey	drink
culet	dalek	demit	dirge	Doric	drive
culex	dally	demob	dirty	doter	droit

droll	durra	elate	entry	evoke	farci
drome	durst	elbow	enure	exact	farcy
drone	durum	elder	envoi	exalt	farle
drool	dusky	elect	envoy	excel	fatal
droop	dusty	elegy	Eolic	exeat	fated
drops	dutch	elfin	epact	exert	fatly
dross	duvet	elide	ephod	exile	fatso
drove	dwale	elite	ephor	exine	fatty
drown	dwarf	elope	epoch	exist	faugh
druid	dwell	elude	epode	expel	fault
drunk	dwelt	elute	epoxy	extol	fauna
drupe	dying	elvan	equal	extra	favus
druse	eager	elver	equip	exude	fawny
Druze	eagle	elves	erase	exult	fayre
dryad	eagre	embay	erect	exurb	feast
dryer	eared	embed	ergot	eye up	fed up
dryly	early	ember	erica	eying	feeze
dry up	earth	embow	Ernie	eyrie	feign
ducal	easel	embus	erode	fable	feint
ducat	eaten	emcee	erose	faced	fella
duchy	eater	emeer	error	facer	felly
ducks	eaves	emend	eruct	facet	felon
ducky	ebony	emery	erupt	facia	femur
duddy	eclat	emmer	esker	faddy	fence
dulia	Eddic	emmet	essay	faery	fenny
dully	edged	emote	ester	fagin	feoff
dulse	edict	empty	estop	fagot	feral
dumka	edify	enact	ether	faint	ferly
dumky	educe	enate	ethic	fairy	fermi
dummy	educt	ended	ethos	faith	ferny
dumps	eerie	endow	ethyl	faker	ferry
dumpy	egest	endue	etude	fakir	fesse
dunce	eggar	end up	etwee	falls	fetal
dungy	egger	enema	evade	false	fetch
dunno	egg on	enemy	evens	famed	fetid
dunny	egret	enjoy	event	fancy	fetor
duomo	eider	ennui	evert	fanny	fetus
duper	eight	enrol	every	Fanti	fever
duple	eject	ensue	evict	farad	fibre
duppy	eland	enter	evite	farce	fiche

fichu	flamy	flyer	frisk	gaily	genre
field	flank	foamy	frith	Galla	gents
fiend	flare	focal	fritz	gally	genus
fiery	flash	focus	frizz	galop	geode
fifer	flask	foehn	frock	gamba	geoid
fifth	flaxy	fogey	frond	games	germy
fifty	fleck	foggy	front	gamic	gesso
fight	fleer	foist	frost	gamin	geste
filch	fleet	folio	froth	gamma	get up
filet	flesh	folly	frown	gammy	Ghazi
fille	flews	foots	froze	gamut	ghost
filly	flick	footy	fruit	ganja	ghoul
filmy	flied	foray	frump	gaper	giant
filth	flier	forby	fryer	gappy	giber
final	flimp	force	fryup	garth	giddy
finch	fling	fordo	fubsy	gassy	gigot
fines	flint	forge	fucus	gaudy	gigue
finis	flirt	forgo	fudge	gauge	gimme
finny	float	forme	fugal	gaumy	ginny
fiord	flock	forte	fuggy	gaunt	gipsy
firer	flood	forth	fugle	gauss	girly
firry	floor	forty	fugue	gauze	giron
first	flora	forum	fully	gauzy	girth
firth	floss	fossa	fumet	gavel	gismo
fishy	flour	fosse	funds	gawky	given
fitch	flout	found	fungi	gawsy	giver
fitly	flown	fount	funky	gazer	glace
fit up	fluff	fovea	funny	gecko	glade
fiver	fluid	foyer	furor	geese	glady
fives	fluke	frail	furry	geist	glair
fixed	fluky	frame	furze	gelid	gland
fixer	flume	franc	furzy	gelly	glare
fizzy	flump	frank	fusee	gemma	glary
fjord	flung	fraud	fusil	gemmy	glass
flack	flunk	freak	fussy	gemot	glaze
flail	fluor	freer	fusty	genet	glazy
flair	flush	fresh	fuzzy	genic	gleam
flake	flute	friar	gabby	genie	glean
flaky	fluty	frier	gable	genii	glebe
flame	flyby	frill	gaffe	genoa	glede

gleed	gorge	grise	guppy	harry	hexad
gleek	gorse	grist	gushy	harsh	hight
gleet	gorsy	grits	gusto	haste	hiker
glial	gotta	groan	gusty	hasty	hilar
glide	Gouda	groat	gutsy	hatch	hillo
glint	gouge	groin	gutta	hater	hilly
gloat	gourd	groom	gutty	haugh	hilum
globe	gouty	grope	guyot	haulm	Hindi
gloom	goyim	gross	gypsy	haunt	Hindu
glory	grace	group	gyral	Hausa	hinge
gloss	grade	grout	gyron	haven	hinny
glove	graft	grove	gyrus	haver	hippo
gloze	grail	growl	habit	havoc	hippy
gluey	grain	grown	hadal	hawse	hirer
glume	grand	gruel	Hades	hazel	hitch
glyph	grant	gruff	hadji	hazer	hives
gnarl	grape	grume	hadst	H bomb	hoard
gnarr	graph	grump	haick	heady	hoary
gnash	grapy	grunt	haiku	heard	hobby
gnawn	grasp	guana	haily	heart	hocus
gnome	grass	guano	hairy	heath	hodge
goaty	grate	guard	hajji	heave	hogan
godet	grave	guava	hakim	heavy	hoick
godly	gravy	Guelf	halal	hedge	hoise
goest	graze	guess	hallo	hefty	hoist
goeth	great	guest	halma	heigh	hokey
going	grebe	guide	halos	heist	hokum
golem	greed	guild	halva	helix	holey
golly	Greek	guile	halve	hello	holla
gonad	green	guilt	hamal	helot	hollo
goner	greet	guimp	hammy	helve	holly
gonna	grief	guise	handy	he man	homer
goody	griff	gular	hanky	hence	homey
gooey	grift	gulch	Hanse	henge	honey
goofy	grike	gules	haply	henry	honky
goopy	grill	gully	happy	herby	hooch
goose	grime	gumbo	haram	herma	hooey
go out	grimy	gummy	hardy	heron	hooky
gopak	grind	gunge	harem	hertz	hoots
goral	gripe	gunny	harpy	hewer	horal

horde	hydro	inert	jaded	juice	kiang
horme	hyena	infer	jaggy	juicy	kiddy
horny	hying	infix	Jaina	julep	kinin
horse	Hykos	infra	jakes	jumbo	kinky
horst	hyoid	ingle	jalap	jumpy	kiosk
horsy	hypha	ingot	jammy	junky	kitty
hosta	hyrax	injun	japan	junta	kloof
hotch	ichor	inker	jaspe	junto	knack
hotel	icily	inkle	jaunt	jural	knave
hotly	icing	inlaw	jazzy	jurat	knead
hot up	ictus	inlay	jeans	juror	kneed
hough	ideal	inlet	jehad	Kaaba	kneel
hound	idiom	inner	jelly	kabob	knell
houri	idiot	in off	jemmy	Kafir	knelt
house	idler	input	jenny	kalif	knife
hovel	idyll	inset	jerky	kalpa	knish
hover	igloo	inter	Jerry	kapok	knock
howdy	ileac	intro	Jesse	kappa	knoll
howff	ileum	inure	jetty	kaput	knout
hubby	ileus	inurn	jewel	karma	known
huffy	iliac	iodic	Jewry	karoo	knurl
hullo	Iliad	ionic	jibba	karst	knurr
human	ilium	irade	jiber	kauri	koala
humic	image	Iraqi	jiffy	kayak	koine
humid	imago	irate	jingo	kazoo	kooky
humph	imaum	Irish	jinks	kebab	kopek
humpy	imbed	irony	jinni	kebob	kopje
humus	imbue	Islam	jocko	kedge	kotow
hunch	impel	islet	joint	kefir	kraal
hunks	imply	issei	joist	kelpy	krait
hunky	inane	issue	joker	kempt	krans
hurly	inapt	istle	jokey	kenaf	kraut
hurry	inarm	itchy	jolly	kendo	krill
hurst	incur	ivied	jolty	kerne	krona
husky	incus	ivory	Jonah	kerry	krone
hussy	index	ixtle	jorum	ketch	kudos
hutch	Indic	izard	joule	keyed	kudzu
huzza	indri	izzat	joust	khadi	Kufic
huzzy	indue	jabot	judas	khaki	kukri
hydra	inept	jacks	judge	Khmer	kulak

kulan	lauds	let on	liven	loris	lymph
kumis	laugh	letup	liver	lorry	lynch
kvass	laura	levee	lives	losel	lyric
kyang	laver	level	livid	loser	lysis
kylin	lawks	lever	livre	lotto	lythe
kyrie	lawny	levin	llama	lotus	macaw
label	laxly	lewis	llano	lough	macer
labia	layby	lexis	loach	louis	macho
labra	layer	liana	loamy	loupe	macle
lacet	lay up	liang	loath	loury	Macon
lacey	lazar	libel	lobar	louse	macro
laded	leach	liber	lobby	lousy	madam
laden	leads	libra	lobed	loved	madge
Ladin	leady	licht	lobus	lover	madly
ladle	leafy	licit	local	lovey	Mafia
lagan	leaky	liege	locum	lower	magic
lager	leant	liein	locus	lowly	magma
laird	leapt	lifer	loden	lowne	magus
lairy	learn	ligan	lodge	loyal	Mahdi
laity	lease	liger	loess	Lucan	mains
lance	leash	light	lofty	lucid	maize
lanky	least	liken	logan	lucky	major
lapel	leave	lilac	logia	lucre	makar
lapse	ledge	limbo	logic	luffa	maker
larch	ledgy	limen	Logos	lumen	malar
lardy	leech	limey	lolly	lumme	Malay
lares	leery	limit	loner	lumpy	malty
large	lefty	linen	longa	lunar	mamba
largo	legal	liner	longe	lunch	mambo
larky	leger	lines	looby	lunge	mamma
larum	leges	lingo	loofa	lungi	mammy
larva	leggy	links	looks	lupin	maned
laser	legit	linny	loony	lupus	manes
lasso	leman	lipid	loopy	lurch	mange
latch	lemma	lippy	loose	lurid	mango
lated	lemon	lisle	loppy	lushy	mangy
laten	lemur	lists	loral	lusty	mania
latex	lento	lithe	loran	lyart	manic
lathe	leper	litho	lordy	lycee	manly
Latin	lepta	litre	lorel	lying	manna

manor	medal	mimer	monte	muddy	naive
manse	media	mimic	month	mudir	naked
manta	medic	mince	mooch	mufti	naker
manus	Medoc	miner	moody	muggy	namer
Maori	meiny	mingy	moola	mujik	nancy
maple	melee	minim	moony	mulch	nanna
march	melon	minor	moose	mulct	nanny
mares	mense	minty	moped	muley	nappe
maria	mercy	minus	moper	mulga	nappy
marly	merge	mirky	mop up	mulla	narky
marry	meril	mirth	moral	multi	nasal
marsh	merit	misdo	moray	mummy	nasty
maser	merle	miser	morel	mumps	natal
mashy	merry	missy	mores	munch	nates
mason	mesel	misty	moron	mungo	natty
masse	mesic	mitre	morph	mural	naval
massy	mesne	mixed	morra	murex	navel
match	meson	mixen	morse	murky	navvy
mater	messy	mixer	mosey	murra	nawab
matey	metal	mix up	mossy	murre	neath
maths	meter	mizen	motel	muser	necks
matin	meths	mobby	motet	mushy	neddy
matte	metic	mocha	mothy	music	needs
matzo	metif	modal	motif	musky	needy
maund	metis	model	motor	mussy	Negro
mauve	metre	modus	motte	musth	negus
mavis	metro	mogul	motto	musty	neigh
maxim	mezzo	mohur	mould	mutch	neive
Mayan	miaow	moire	moult	muted	nelly
maybe	micky	moist	mound	muzzy	nerve
mayor	micro	moksa	mount	myall	nervy
mayst	middy	molal	mourn	mynah	netty
mazer	midge	molar	mouse	myoma	neume
McCoy	midon	molly	mousy	myope	never
mealy	midst	molto	mouth	myrrh	newel
means	might	momma	mover	nabob	newly
meant	milch	monad	movie	nacre	newsy
meany	miler	monas	mower	nadir	nexus
meaty	milky	monde	mucky	naevi	niche
mecca	mille	money	mucus	naiad	nidus

niece	noser	ogham	ormer	paddy	pasta
nieve	nosey	ogive	orpin	padre	paste
niffy	notch	ogler	orris	paean	pasty
nifty	noted	ohmic	ortho	paeon	patch
night	notum	oidia	Osage	pagan	paten
nimbi	novae	oiled	Oscan	paint	pater
ninny	novel	oiler	Oscar	paisa	patio
ninon	no way	okapi	osier	palea	patsy
ninth	Nowel	olden	ossia	pally	patty
nippy	nudge	oldie	ostia	palmy	pause
nisei	nulla	oleic	otary	palsy	pavan
nisus	numen	olein	other	pampa	paver
nitid	nurse	oleum	otter	panda	pavid
nitre	nutty	olive	ought	pandy	pavis
nitro	nyala	ology	ounce	panel	pawky
nixie	nylon	omasa	ouphe	panga	payee
nizam	nymph	ombre	ousel	panic	payer
nobby	oaken	omega	outdo	panne	pay up
noble	oakum	oncer	outer	pansy	peace
nobly	oared	one up	outgo	panto	peach
nodal	oases	onion	outre	pants	peaky
noddy	oasis	onset	ouzel	panty	pearl
nodus	oaten	on tap	ovary	papal	peart
nohow	oaves	oomph	ovate	papaw	pease
noise	obeah	opera	overs	paper	peaty
noisy	obeli	opine	overt	pappy	pecan
nomad	obese	opium	ovine	parch	pedal
nomen	occur	optic	ovoid	parer	peeve
nonce	ocean	orach	ovolo	parge	peggy
nones	ochre	oracy	ovule	parka	pekan
nonet	ochry	orate	owing	parky	pekoe
nonny	octal	orbed	owner	parol	pelta
nooky	octet	orbit	oxbow	parry	penal
noone	oddly	order	oxeye	parse	pence
noose	odeum	oread	oxide	Parsi	penna
nopal	odium	organ	oxlip	parti	penny
noria	odour	oribi	oxter	party	peony
Norse	offal	oriel	ozone	Pasch	peppy
north	offer	Oriya	pacer	pasha	perai
	often	orlop	pacha	passe	perch

perdu	piney	plonk	potto	prose	pussy
peril	pinko	pluck	potty	prosy	put on
perky	pinky	plumb	pouch	proud	putti
perry	pinna	plume	poult	Provo	putto
perse	pinny	plump	pound	prowl	putty
pesky	pinon	plumy	pouty	proxy	put up
petal	pinta	plush	powan	prude	pygmy
peter	pinto	Pluto	power	prune	pylon
petit	pinup	poach	praam	pryer	pyxie
petri	pious	pocky	prang	psalm	pyxis
petty	pipal	poddy	prank	pseud	Q boat
pewit	piper	podge	prase	pshaw	quack
phage	pipit	podgy	prate	psoas	quaff
phase	pipul	podia	prawn	psora	quail
phial	pique	poesy	preen	psych	quake
phlox	piste	poilu	press	pubic	quaky
phone	pitch	poind	prest	pubis	qualm
phono	pithy	point	prexy	pucka	quark
phony	piton	poise	price	pudge	quart
photo	pitta	poker	prick	pudgy	quash
phyla	pivot	polar	pricy	puffy	quasi
phyle	pixie	polio	pride	puggy	quean
piano	pizza	polka	prier	pukka	queen
picky	place	polyp	prima	puler	queer
picot	plage	pommy	prime	pulpy	quell
piece	plaid	ponce	primo	pulse	quern
pieta	plain	poncy	primp	punch	query
piety	plait	pongo	prink	Punic	quest
piezo	plane	pooch	print	punty	queue
piggy	plank	pools	prior	pupae	quick
pigmy	plant	poppy	prise	pupal	quiet
piker	plash	popsy	prism	pupil	quiff
pilaf	plasm	porch	privy	puppy	quill
pilau	plate	porgy	prize	puree	quilt
pilaw	playa	porky	probe	purge	quins
pilea	plaza	porno	proem	Purim	quint
pilei	plead	Porte	prole	purin	quipu
pilot	pleat	poser	prone	purse	quire
pilus	plebs	posit	prong	pursy	quirk
pinch	plica	posse	proof	pushy	quirt

quite	ratio	Reich	ribes	roper	rusty
quits	ratty	reify	ricer	ropey	rutty
quoin	ravel	reign	rider	rorty	sable
quoit	raven	reins	ridge	roset	sabot
quota	raver	reive	ridgy	rosin	sabra
quote	ravin	rejig	rifle	rotor	sabre
quoth	rawly	relax	right	rouge	sacra
Quran	rayed	relay	rigor	rough	sadhu
rabbi	rayon	relet	rille	round	sadly
rabic	razee	relic	rinse	roupy	saggy
rabid	razor	relit	ripen	rouse	sahib
racer	reach	reman	risen	roust	saiga
races	react	remex	riser	route	saint
radar	ready	remit	rishi	routh	saith
radii	realm	renal	risky	rover	saker
radio	reams	renew	ritzy	rowan	Sakta
radix	rearm	rente	rival	rowdy	salad
radon	reata	repay	rived	rowel	salep
raggy	reave	repel	rivel	rowen	sales
rainy	rebec	reply	riven	rower	salic
raise	rebel	repot	river	royal	sally
rajah	rebid	repro	rivet	rubin	salmi
raker	rebus	reran	roach	ruble	salon
rally	rebut	rerun	roast	rubus	salse
ramus	recap	resat	robin	ruche	salts
ranch	recce	reset	robot	ruddy	salty
randy	recto	resin	rocks	rugby	salve
ranee	recur	resit	rocky	ruler	salvo
range	redan	retch	rodeo	rumba	samba
rangy	reddy	retry	roger	rumen	sandy
raper	redid	reuse	rogue	rumly	sapan
raphe	redly	revel	roily	rummy	sapid
rapid	redox	revet	rolls	rumpy	sapor
raspy	reedy	revue	roman	runic	sappy
rasse	reeky	rheum	Romeo	runny	saree
ratan	reeve	rhine	rondo	runty	sarge
ratch	refer	rhino	rooky	runup	sarky
ratel	refit	rhomb	roomy	rupee	saros
rater	regal	rhumb	roost	rural	sasin
rathe	regie	rhyme	rooty	rushy	sassy

Satan	scoff	sedum	setup	shewn	sidle
sated	scold	seedy	seven	Shiah	siege
satin	scone	seely	sever	shiel	sieve
satyr	scoop	seepy	sewer	shift	sight
sauce	scoot	segno	sexed	shill	sigla
saucy	scope	segue	sexto	shily	sigma
Saudi	score	seine	shack	shine	silex
sault	scorn	seise	shade	shiny	silks
sauna	Scots	seism	shady	shire	silky
saury	scour	seize	shaft	shirk	silly
saute	scout	sekos	shake	shirr	silty
saver	scowl	selah	shako	shirt	silva
savin	scrag	sells	shaky	Shiva	simar
savoy	scram	selva	shale	shoal	since
savvy	scran	semee	shall	shoat	sinew
Saxon	scrap	semen	shalt	shock	singe
sayer	scray	senna	shaly	shoer	Singh
say so	scree	senor	shame	shoji	sinus
scald	screw	sensa	shank	shone	Sioux
scale	scrim	sense	shant	shook	siren
scall	scrip	sepal	shape	shoon	sisal
scalp	scrod	sepia	shard	shoot	sissy
scaly	scrub	sepoy	share	shore	sitar
scamp	scrum	septa	shark	shorn	sit in
scant	scuba	serac	sharp	short	sit up
scape	scudi	serai	shave	shout	sixer
scare	scudo	seral	shawl	shove	sixte
scarf	scuff	serge	shawm	shown	sixth
scarp	scull	Seric	sheaf	showy	sixty
scart	sculp	serif	shear	shred	sizar
scary	scurf	serin	sheen	shrew	sizer
scaup	scuta	serow	sheep	shrub	skate
scena	scute	serra	sheer	shrug	skean
scend	seamy	serry	sheet	shuck	skeet
scene	sebum	serum	sheik	shunt	skein
scent	secco	serve	shelf	shush	skelm
schmo	sedan	servo	shell	shyer	skelp
schwa	Seder	setae	Sheol	shyly	skene
sci fi	sedge	set on	sherd	sibyl	skier
scion	sedgy	set to	sheva	sided	skiey

skiff	slope	snarl	sonar	spell	spree
skill	slops	snash	sonde	spelt	sprig
skimp	slosh	snath	sonic	spend	sprit
skink	sloth	sneak	sonny	spent	spume
skint	slubb	sneap	sonsy	sperm	spumy
skirl	sluit	sneck	sooth	spica	spunk
skirr	slump	sneer	sooty	spice	spurn
skirt	slung	snell	sophy	spick	spurt
skite	slunk	snick	sopor	spicy	sputa
skive	slurp	snide	soppy	spiel	squab
skoal	slush	sniff	sorel	spier	squad
skulk	slyer	snipe	sorgo	spike	squat
skull	slyly	snips	sorra	spiky	squaw
skunk	smack	snoek	sorry	spile	squib
skyer	small	snood	sorus	spill	squid
skyey	smalt	snook	sough	spilt	squit
slack	smarm	snoop	sound	spine	stack
slain	smart	snoot	soupy	spiny	staff
slake	smash	snore	souse	spire	stage
slang	smaze	snort	south	spirt	stagy
slant	smear	snout	sowar	spiry	staid
slash	smell	snowy	sower	spite	stain
slate	smelt	snuff	space	spitz	stair
slaty	smile	soapy	spade	splat	stake
slave	smirk	sober	spado	splay	stale
sleek	smite	socle	spahi	split	stalk
sleep	smith	sodic	spake	Spode	stall
sleet	smock	Sodom	spall	spoil	stamp
slept	smoke	softa	spank	spoke	stand
slice	smoko	softy	spare	spoof	stang
slick	smoky	soggy	spark	spook	stank
slide	smolt	solan	spasm	spool	stare
slily	smote	solar	spate	spoon	stark
slime	snack	soldi	spawn	spoor	start
slimy	snafu	soldo	speak	spore	stash
sling	snail	solfa	spean	sport	state
slink	snake	solid	spear	spout	stave
slips	snaky	solum	speck	sprag	stays
sloop	snare	solus	specs	sprat	stead
sloot	snark	solve	speed	spray	steak

steal	stool	Sudra	swayl	tacky	tawer
steam	stoop	sudsy	sweal	taffy	tawny
steed	stope	suede	swear	tafia	tawse
steek	store	suety	sweat	taiga	taxer
steel	stork	Sufic	swede	tails	taxis
steep	storm	sugar	sweep	taint	taxon
steer	story	suint	sweet	taken	taxus
stein	stoup	suite	swell	taker	tazza
stele	stour	sulci	swept	takin	teach
steno	stout	sulfa	swift	tales	teary
steps	stove	sulky	swill	tally	tease
stere	strad	sully	swine	talon	techy
stern	strap	sumac	swing	taluk	teens
stich	straw	summa	swink	talus	teeny
stick	stray	Sunna	swipe	tamer	teeth
sties	strep	Sunni	swirl	Tamil	tehee
stiff	strew	sunny	swish	tammy	teind
stile	stria	sun up	Swiss	tango	telex
still	strip	super	swizz	tangy	telic
stilt	strop	supra	swoon	tanka	telly
sting	strum	surah	swoop	tansy	tempi
stink	strut	sural	sword	taper	tempo
stint	stuck	surat	swore	tapir	tempt
stipe	study	surfy	sworn	tapis	tench
stirk	stuff	surge	swung	tardy	tenet
stirp	stull	surly	sybil	targe	tenne
stoat	stump	surra	sycee	tarok	tenon
stock	stung	sutra	sylph	tarot	tenor
stogy	stunk	swage	sylva	tarre	tense
stoic	stunt	swain	synch	tarry	tenth
stoke	stupa	swale	synod	tarsi	tenty
stola	stupe	swami	syrup	tarty	tepee
stole	sturt	swamp	tabby	tasse	tepid
stoma	styes	swank	tabes	taste	terai
stomp	style	sward	tabla	tasty	terce
stone	styli	swarf	table	Tatar	terms
stonk	suave	swarm	taboo	tater	terne
stony	suber	swart	tabor	tatty	terra
stood	sucre	swash	tache	taunt	terse
stook	sudor	swath	tacit	taupe	tesla

testa	thuja	Tokay	toxin	trout	tween
testy	thumb	token	trace	trove	tweet
tetra	thump	toman	track	truce	twere
texas	thyme	tommy	tract	truck	twerp
thane	tiara	tonal	trade	trull	twice
thank	tibia	tondi	tragi	truly	twill
thawy	tical	tondo	trail	trump	twine
theca	tidal	toner	train	trunk	twink
theft	tie in	tonga	trait	truss	twiny
thegn	tie up	tongs	tramp	trust	twirl
their	tiger	tonic	traps	truth	twirp
thema	tight	tonka	trash	tryon	twist
theme	tigon	tonne	trass	tryst	twite
there	tilde	tonus	trawl	tubal	twixt
therm	tiler	tooth	tread	tubby	tying
these	tilth	topaz	treat	tuber	typal
theta	timer	topee	treen	Tudor	typic
thews	times	toper	trend	tufty	Uboat
thewy	timid	tophi	tress	tuism	udder
thick	tinea	topic	trews	tulip	Ugric
thief	tined	topoi	triad	tulle	uhlan
thigh	tinge	topos	trial	tumid	ulcer
thill	tinny	top up	Trias	tummy	ulnae
thine	tinty	toque	tribe	tuner	ulnar
thing	tippy	Torah	trice	tunic	ultra
think	tipsy	torch	trick	tunny	umbel
third	tip up	torsk	tried	tuque	umber
thirl	titan	torso	trier	turbo	umbra
thole	tithe	torte	trike	turfy	umiak
tholi	title	torus	trill	Turki	umpty
thong	titre	total	trine	turps	unapt
thorn	tizzy	totem	tripe	tusky	unarm
those	toady	touch	trist	tutee	unbar
thraw	toast	tough	trite	tutor	unbed
three	today	touse	troll	tutti	uncap
threw	toddy	tousy	trona	tutty	uncle
throb	toffy	towel	trone	twain	uncus
throe	togue	tower	troop	twang	uncut
throw	toile	towny	trope	tweak	under
thrum	toils	toxic	troth	tweed	undid

undue	uveal	venue	vocal	wares	which
unfit	uvula	Venus	vodka	warty	whiff
unfix	Uzbeg	verge	vogue	washy	while
ungum	Uzbek	verse	voice	waste	whine
Uniat	vacua	verso	voile	watch	whiny
unify	vagal	verst	volar	water	whirl
union	vague	vertu	volet	waved	whirr
unite	vagus	verve	volta	waver	whish
unity	vails	vesta	volte	wavey	whisk
unlay	valet	vetch	volti	waxen	whist
unlit	valid	viand	volva	waxer	white
unman	valse	vibes	vomer	weald	whity
unpeg	value	vicar	vomit	weary	whizz
unpin	valve	Vichy	voter	weave	whole
unrig	vaned	video	vouch	webby	whoop
unrip	vapid	viewy	vouge	weber	whore
unsay	varec	vigil	vowel	wedge	whorl
unset	varix	villa	vrouw	weeds	whose
unsex	varus	villi	vuggy	weedy	whoso
untie	varve	vinal	vying	weeny	widen
until	vasal	vinca	wacke	weepy	widow
unzip	vasty	vinyl	wacky	weigh	width
upend	vatic	viola	waddy	weird	wield
upped	vault	viper	wader	welch	wigan
upper	vaunt	viral	wafer	wells	wight
upset	vealy	vireo	wager	welsh	wilco
urban	Vedda	vires	wages	wench	wilds
uredo	Vedic	virga	wagon	wetly	wiles
urger	veena	Virgo	wahoo	whack	willy
urial	veery	virid	waist	whale	wince
urine	vegan	virtu	waits	whang	winch
urubu	veiny	virus	waive	wharf	windy
usage	velar	visit	waken	wheal	winey
usher	veldt	visor	waker	wheat	winge
usual	velum	vista	wakes	wheel	wings
usurp	venae	vital	waler	wheen	wingy
usury	venal	vivat	wally	whelk	wiper
uteri	venge	vivid	waltz	whelm	wispy
utile	venin	vixen	waney	whelp	witan
utter	venom	vizor	wanly	where	witch

withe	woozy	wrapt	xenia	yippy	zebra
withy	words	wrath	xenon	yobbo	zesty
witty	wordy	wreak	xeric	yodel	zibet
wives	works	wreck	Xhosa	yokel	zinco
wizen	world	wrest	Xrays	yolky	zincy
wodge	worms	wrick	xylem	yonks	zingy
woful	wormy	wring	yacht	young	zinky
woken	worry	wrist	yahoo	yours	zippy
woman	worse	write	yapok	youth	zloty
women	worst	wrong	yauld	yucca	zombi
wonga	worth	wrote	yawny	yucky	zonal
wonky	would	wroth	yearn	yukky	zooid
woods	wound	wrung	years	yummy	zooks
woody	woven	wryly	yeast	zanza	zoril
wooer	wrack	xebec	yield		

6 letter words

abacus	acetyl	advert	agnise	allege	animal
abater	achene	advice	agonic	allele	animus
abatis	acidic	advise	agouti	allied	anklet
abbacy	acidly	adytum	aguish	allium	anlace
abbess	ackack	aedile	ahimsa	all out	anlage
abduce	acquit	Aegean	aikido	all set	annals
abduct	across	Aeolic	airbed	allude	anneal
abject	acting	aerate	airbus	allure	annexe
abjure	action	aerial	airgun	almond	annual
ablate	active	aerily	airily	almost	annuli
ablaut	actual	aerobe	airing	alpaca	anodal
ablaze	acuity	aether	airman	alpine	anodic
abloom	acumen	afeard	airsac	alsike	anoint
ablush	adagio	affair	airway	alulae	anomic
aboard	Adamic	affect	aisled	alumna	anomie
aboral	addend	affeer	akimbo	alumni	anorak
abound	addict	affine	alalia	always	anoxia
abrade	addled	affirm	alarum	amazon	anoxic
abroad	adduce	afflux	alated	ambler	answer
abrupt	adduct	afford	albedo	ambush	anthem
abseil	adenyl	affray	albeit	amends	anther
absent	adhere	Afghan	albert	amenta	antiar
absorb	adieus	afield	albino	amerce	anting
absurd	adieux	aflame	albite	amidst	antler
abulia	adipic	afloat	alcaic	amnion	antrum
abuser	adjoin	afraid	alcove	amoeba	anyhow
acacia	adjure	afreet	Aldine	amoral	anyone
acajou	adjust	afresh	aldose	amount	anyway
acarid	admass	afrite	aldrin	ampere	aorist
acarus	admire	afters	alegar	amulet	aortal
accede	adnate	agamic	A level	amuser	aortic
accent	adnexa	agamid	alevin	anabas	apache
accept	Adonic	agaric	alexia	ananas	apathy
access	Adonis	ageing	alexin	anchor	apexes
accord	adorer	agency	algoid	angary	aphony
accost	adrift	agenda	alight	angina	apiary
accrue	adroit	age old	alkali	angled	apical
accuse	adsorb	aghast	alkane	angler	apices
acetal	advent	agnail	alkene	angora	apiece
acetic	adverb	agnate	alkyne	anicut	aplomb

apnoea	armpit	assort	Aussie	badger	banter
apodal	arnica	assume	Austin	baffle	banyan
apogee	aroint	assure	author	bagful	banzai
appeal	around	astern	autism	bagged	baobab
appear	arouse	asthma	autumn	bagman	barbed
append	arpent	astral	avatar	bagnio	barbel
appose	arrack	astray	avaunt	bagwig	barber
Arabic	arrant	astute	avenge	bailee	barbet
arable	arrest	aswoon	avenue	bailer	bardic
arbour	arrive	asylum	averse	bailey	barege
arcade	arroba	ataman	Avesta	bailie	barely
Arcady	arrowy	ataxia	aviary	bailor	barfly
arcana	arroyo	ataxic	aviate	baiter	bargee
arcane	arsine	athome	avidly	bakery	barite
arched	artery	atomic	avocet	balata	barium
archer	artful	atonal	avouch	balboa	barker
archil	artist	atonic	avowal	baldly	barley
archly	ascend	atrial	avowed	baleen	barman
archon	ascent	atrium	avulse	balker	barony
arctic	aseity	attach	awaked	ballad	barque
ardent	ashbin	attack	awaken	ballet	barred
ardour	ashcan	attain	aweary	ballon	barrel
areola	ashlar	attend	aweigh	ballot	barren
areole	ashore	attest	awheel	balsam	barret
argali	ashpan	attire	awhile	Baltic	barrio
argent	ashram	attorn	awmous	bamboo	barrow
Argive	askant	attune	awning	banana	barter
argosy	askari	aubade	awoken	bandit	barton
arguer	aslant	auburn	axilla	bandog	baryon
argufy	asleep	audile	ayeaye	banger	baryta
argyle	aslope	Augean	azalea	bangle	basalt
aright	aspect	augite	azonal	banian	basely
ariosi	aspire	augury	azotic	banish	basher
arioso	assail	august	Baalim	banjax	basics
arisen	assent	auklet	babble	banjos	basket
arista	assert	aumbry	babbly	banker	basnet
armada	assess	auntie	baboon	banket	Basque
armful	assign	aurist	backer	banned	basset
armlet	assist	aurora	backup	banner	bassos
armour	assize	aurous	baddie	bantam	baster

Basuto	becket	belief	bibbed	bistro	bobble
Basutu	beckon	belike	bibber	bitchy	bobcat
bataba	become	belive	biceps	biting	boblet
bateau	bedaub	bellow	bicker	bitted	bobwig
bather	bedaze	belong	bidden	bitten	bocage
bathos	bedbug	belted	bidder	bitter	bodega
bating	bedded	belt up	bieldy	bizone	bodger
batman	bedder	beluga	biffin	bladed	bodice
batted	bedeck	bemire	biform	blanch	bodily
batten	bedell	bemoan	bigamy	blanky	boding
batter	bedlam	bemock	big end	blazer	bodkin
battle	bedpan	bemuse	bigger	blazes	boffin
battue	bedsit	bender	biggin	blazon	bogged
bauble	beduin	benign	bigwig	bleach	boggle
bawbee	beeper	benumb	Bihari	bleary	bohunk
bawble	beetle	berate	bijoux	blench	boiler
bawdry	beeves	Berber	bikini	blende	boldly
bawler	befall	bereft	bilbos	blenny	bolero
bawley	befell	berlin	bilker	blight	bolide
bayard	befool	bertha	billet	blimey	bolshy
bazaar	before	beseem	billon	blintz	bolter
beachy	befoul	beside	billow	blithe	bomber
beacon	beggar	bested	billyo	blonde	bonbon
beadle	begged	bestir	binary	bloody	bonded
beagle	begird	bestow	binate	bloomy	bonder
beaked	begirt	betake	binder	blotch	bongos
beaker	begone	bethel	binful	blotto	bonito
beamer	behalf	betide	bionic	blouse	bonnet
beanie	behave	betony	biopsy	blowed	bonnie
bearer	behead	betook	biotic	blower	bonsai
bear up	beheld	betray	biotin	blowsy	bonxie
beaten	behest	betted	birdie	blowup	bonzer
beater	behind	better	bireme	blowzy	booboo
beat it	behold	bettor	birkie	bluing	boodle
Beaune	behoof	bewail	birler	bluish	boohoo
beauty	behove	beware	birsect	blurry	booing
beaver	belaud	bewray	bishop	boatel	booker
becall	beldam	beyond	bisque	boater	bookie
becalm	belfry	bezant	bister	bobbed	booksy
became	Belgic	bhisti	bistre	bobbin	boomer

booted	bowfin	brevet	buccal	bunter	butane
bootee	bowing	brewer	bucker	burble	butene
boozer	bowleg	brewis	bucket	burbly	butler
bopeep	bowler	briary	buckle	burbot	butter
bopped	bowman	briber	buckra	burden	butt in
bopper	bowsaw	bricky	budded	bureau	button
borage	bowtie	bridal	Buddha	burgee	buzzer
bordel	bowwow	bridge	budget	burger	byblow
border	bowyer	bridle	budgie	burgle	byebye
boreal	boxbed	briefs	buffer	burgoo	byelaw
Boreas	boxcar	briery	buffet	burhel	byform
boring	boxful	bright	bugged	burial	bygone
borrow	boxing	briner	bugler	burkha	by Jove
borsch	boyish	briony	bulbar	burlap	bylane
borzoi	bracer	Briton	bulbed	burler	byline
bosche	braces	broach	bulbil	Burman	byname
bosket	Brahma	broche	bulbul	burner	bypass
bosomy	Brahmi	brogue	Bulgar	burnet	bypast
boston	brains	broken	bulger	burnup	bypath
botany	brainy	broker	bulimy	burrel	byplay
botchy	braise	brolly	bulker	burrow	byroad
botfly	branch	bromic	bullae	bursae	byssus
bother	brandy	bronco	buller	bursar	byword
bothie	branle	bronze	bullet	bursas	bywork
bottle	brassy	bronzy	bumalo	burton	cabala
bottom	brawly	brooch	bumble	busbar	cabana
boucle	brawny	broody	bumkin	busboy	cabman
bought	brayer	browny	bummed	bushed	cachet
bougie	brazen	browse	bummer	bushel	cackle
boulle	brazil	bruise	bummle	busily	cacoon
bounce	breach	brumal	bumper	busing	cactus
bouncy	breast	brumby	bunchy	busker	caddie
bounds	breath	brunch	bunder	buskin	caddis
bounty	breech	brunet	bundle	busman	cadent
bourne	breeks	brushy	bungle	bussed	cadger
bourse	breese	brutal	bunion	busted	caecal
bovine	breeze	brutus	bunker	bustee	caecum
bovver	breezy	bryony	bunkum	buster	cafard
bowels	bregma	bubble	bunsen	bustle	Caffre
bowery	Breton	bubbly	bunted	bustup	caftan

cagily	candle	carney	caudex	chacma	chimer
cahier	canful	carpal	caudle	chafer	chintz
cahoot	cangue	carpel	caught	chaffy	chip in
caiman	canine	carper	caulis	chaise	chippy
caique	canker	carpet	causal	chalet	chirpy
cajole	canned	carpus	causer	chalky	chisel
calash	cannel	carrel	caveat	chance	chital
calces	canner	carrot	cavern	chancy	chitin
calcic	cannon	cartel	caviar	change	chiton
calico	cannot	carter	caving	chanty	chitty
caliph	canopy	carton	cavity	chapel	chives
calker	canter	carvel	cavort	chappy	chivvy
calkin	cantle	carven	cayman	charas	choice
caller	canton	carver	cayuse	charge	choker
callet	cantor	casbah	cecity	Charon	chokey
call in	cantus	casein	celery	chaser	choler
call on	Canuck	cashew	celian	chaste	choose
callow	canvas	casing	cellar	chatty	choosy
call up	canyon	casino	celled	chaunt	chopin
callus	capful	casket	Celtic	cheeky	choppy
calmly	caplin	casque	cement	cheers	choral
calory	capote	cassia	censer	cheery	chorea
calpac	capped	cassis	censor	cheese	choric
calque	capric	caster	census	cheesy	chorus
calves	capsid	castle	cental	chelae	chosen
calxes	captor	castor	centre	chemic	chough
camber	carafe	casual	centum	cheque	chouse
camera	carbon	catalo	cereal	cherry	chrism
camion	carboy	catchy	cereus	cherty	Christ
camise	carder	catena	ceriph	cherub	chroma
camlet	careen	catgut	cerise	chesil	chrome
camper	career	Cathar	cerium	chesty	chromo
campus	caress	cation	cermet	chevet	chuffy
canape	carfax	catkin	ceruse	chiasm	chukar
canard	carful	catnap	cervix	chichi	chukka
canary	caries	catnip	cesser	chicle	chummy
cancan	carina	catsup	cestus	chield	chunky
cancel	carman	cattle	cesura	chigoe	church
cancer	carnal	caucus	cetane	chilli	chypre
candid	carnet	caudal	chacha	chilly	cicada

cicala	clinic	cocoon	comedo	coolie	corymb
cicely	clip on	coddle	comedy	coolly	coryza
cigala	clique	codger	comely	cooper	cosher
cilice	cliquy	codify	come on	cootie	cosily
cilium	cloaca	codlin	come to	copeck	cosine
cinder	cloche	coelom	comfit	copier	cosmic
cinema	cloddy	coerce	coming	coping	cosmos
cineol	cloggy	coeval	comity	copita	cosset
cinque	clonal	coffee	commie	copout	costae
cipher	clonic	coffer	commis	copped	costal
circle	clonus	coffin	commit	copper	costar
circus	closed	coffle	commix	Coptic	coster
cirque	closet	cogent	common	copula	costly
cirrus	clothe	cogged	comose	coquet	cottar
cistus	cloudy	cogito	comous	corban	cotted
cither	clough	cognac	compel	corbel	cotter
citric	cloven	coheir	comply	corbie	cotton
citron	clover	cohere	comsat	corded	coucal
citrus	clumpy	cohort	concha	corder	cougar
civics	clumsy	coigne	conchy	cordon	coulee
claggy	clunch	coiner	concur	corked	county
clammy	clutch	coinop	condor	corker	couple
claque	clypei	coital	confab	cornea	coupon
claret	coaita	coitus	confer	corned	course
classy	coarse	coldly	congee	cornel	cousin
clause	coated	coleus	conger	corner	covert
claver	coatee	collar	congou	cornet	coving
clayey	cobalt	collet	conics	cornua	cowage
cleave	cobber	collie	conker	corody	coward
clench	cobble	collop	conman	corona	cowboy
clergy	cobnut	colony	conned	corozo	cowish
cleric	cobweb	colour	conner	corpse	cowled
clever	coccal	colter	conoid	corpus	cowman
clevis	coccid	colugo	consul	corral	cowpat
cliche	coccus	column	convex	corrie	cowpea
client	coccyx	colure	convey	corsak	cowpox
cliffy	cochin	comate	convoy	corset	cowrie
climax	cocked	combat	cooker	cortex	coyote
clinch	cocker	combed	cookie	corvee	crabby
clingy	cockle	comber	cooler	Corvus	cradle

craggy	croppy	cumuli	cyanic	Daniel	debris
crambo	crotch	cunner	cycler	Danish	debtor
crania	croton	cupful	cyclic	dankly	debunk
cranky	crouch	cupola	cygnet	daphne	decade
cranny	croupy	cupped	cymbal	dapper	decamp
crappy	cruces	cupric	cymose	dapple	decant
cratch	cruddy	cuptie	Cymric	daring	deceit
crater	cruise	cupule	cypher	darken	decent
cravat	cruive	curacy	cyprid	darkey	decide
craven	crumby	curare	cystic	darkie	decker
craver	crummy	curate	cystid	darkle	deckle
crawly	crunch	curdle	dabbed	darkly	decoct
crayon	crural	curfew	dabber	darned	decode
crazed	crusty	curiae	dabble	darnel	decoke
creaky	crutch	curial	dacoit	darner	decree
creamy	cruxes	curium	dactyl	darter	deduce
crease	crying	curler	daedal	dartle	deduct
create	crypto	curlew	daemon	dartre	deejay
creche	cubage	currie	daftly	dasher	deepen
credal	cubism	cursed	dagger	dassie	deeply
credit	cubist	cursor	dagoes	datary	deface
creeps	cuboid	cursus	dahlia	dative	defame
creepy	cuckoo	curtal	daimio	datura	defeat
creole	cuddie	curtly	daimon	dauber	defect
cresol	cuddle	curtsy	dainty	dawdle	defend
Cretan	cuddly	curule	damage	daybed	defier
cretic	cudgel	curvet	damask	dazzle	defile
cretin	cueing	cuscus	dammar	deacon	define
crewel	cueist	cushat	dammed	deaden	deform
crikey	cuesta	cusped	damned	deadly	defray
crimpy	cuffed	cuspid	dampen	deafen	deftly
cringe	cuisse	cussed	damper	deafly	defuse
cripes	culler	custom	damply	dealer	degree
crises	cullis	cutely	damsel	dearie	degust
crisis	cultch	cutler	damson	dearly	dehorn
crispy	cultic	cutlet	dancer	dearth	deicer
crista	cultus	cutoff	dander	deasil	deject
critic	culver	cutout	dandle	debark	delate
croaky	cumber	cutter	danger	debase	delete
crocus	cummer	cuttle	dangle	debate	delict

delude	desalt	dicker	direct	dogear	dotted
deluge	descry	dickey	direly	dogend	dottle
deluxe	desert	dictum	dirham	dogfox	douane
delver	design	diddle	dirhem	dogged	double
demand	desire	didoes	dirndl	dogger	doubly
demark	desist	diesel	disarm	doggie	douche
demean	desman	dieses	disbar	dogleg	dought
dement	desmid	diesis	disbud	do good	doughy
demise	desorb	dieter	discal	dolium	dourly
demist	despot	differ	discus	dollar	douser
demode	detach	digest	diseur	dollop	do well
demote	detail	digger	dismal	dolman	dowlas
demure	detain	diglot	dismay	dolmen	downer
denary	detect	dikdik	disown	dolour	dowser
dengue	detent	diktat	dispel	domain	doyley
denial	detest	dilate	distal	domino	dozily
denier	detour	dilute	distil	donate	drably
denims	deuced	dimity	disuse	done up	drachm
denote	devest	dimmed	dither	donjon	drafty
dental	device	dimmer	dittos	donkey	dragee
dentel	devise	dimple	divers	donned	draggy
dentil	devoid	dimply	divert	doodad	dragon
denude	devoir	dimwit	divest	doodah	drag up
deodar	devote	dingey	divide	doodle	draper
depart	devour	dinghy	divine	doolie	drawee
depend	devout	dingle	diving	dopant	drawer
depict	dewily	dingus	djinni	Dopper	draw in
deploy	dewlap	dining	doable	dorado	draw on
deport	dexter	dinkum	dobbin	Dorian	dreamt
depose	dharma	dinned	docent	dormer	dreamy
depute	dhooti	dinner	docile	dormie	dreary
deputy	dhurra	diplex	docker	dorsal	dredge
derail	diacid	diploe	docket	dorsum	dreich
derate	diadem	diplon	doctor	dorter	drench
deride	diaper	dipnet	dodder	dosage	dressy
derive	diatom	dipody	doddle	dossal	drifty
dermal	dibbed	dipole	dodgem	dossel	drippy
dermic	dibber	dipped	dodger	dosser	drivel
dermis	dibble	dipper	dodoes	dotage	driven
derris	dicast	dirdum	dogate	dotard	driver

droger	dunite	edgily	embank	englut	eonian
drogue	Dunker	edging	embark	engram	Eozoic
droich	dunlin	edible	embers	engulf	Eozoon
drolly	dunned	editor	emblem	enhalo	epical
drongo	dupery	eerily	emblic	enigma	epimer
droopy	duplet	efface	embody	enisle	epizoa
drop in	duplex	effect	emboli	enjoin	epodic
dropsy	durbar	effete	emboss	enlace	eponym
drossy	duress	effigy	embryo	enlist	epopee
drouth	durgan	efflux	emerge	enmesh	equate
drover	Durham	effort	emeses	enmity	equine
drowse	durian	effuse	emesis	ennead	equity
drowsy	during	Egeria	emetic	enosis	eraser
drudge	durned	egesta	emeute	enough	erbium
drupel	durrie	eggcup	empery	enrage	eremic
drybob	duster	eggler	empire	enrapt	erenow
dryfly	dust up	eggnog	employ	enrich	ergate
dryish	duyker	egoism	empusa	enrobe	ermine
dryrot	dyadic	egoist	emulge	enroll	erotic
dryrun	dybbuk	egress	enable	enroot	errand
dually	dyeing	eidola	enamel	ensign	errant
dubbed	dynamo	eighth	encage	ensile	errata
dubbin	dynast	eighty	encamp	ensoul	ersatz
ducker	eaglet	either	encase	ensure	eryngo
dudeen	earful	ejecta	encash	entail	escape
dudish	earing	elapse	encode	entice	escarp
duello	earner	elated	encore	entire	eschar
duende	earthy	elater	encyst	entity	eschew
duenna	earwax	eldest	endear	entoil	escort
duffel	earwig	eleven	ending	entomb	escrow
duffer	easily	elevon	endive	entrap	escudo
duffle	easter	elfish	endure	entree	Eskimo
dugong	eatery	elicit	energy	envier	espial
dugout	eating	elixir	enface	enwind	esprit
duiker	echoer	elodea	enfold	enwomb	Essene
dukery	echoic	eloign	engage	enwrap	estate
dulcet	eclair	eloper	engild	enzyme	esteem
dumbly	eczema	elvish	engine	Eocene	etcher
dumdum	Eddaic	elytra	engird	eolian	ethane
dumper	Edenic	embalm	engirt	eolith	ethics

ethnic	extasy	family	fawner	fetter	finish
etymon	extend	famine	fealty	fettle	finite
euchre	extent	famish	feckly	feudal	finnan
eulogy	extern	famous	fecula	fezzed	finned
eunuch	extort	famuli	fecund	fezzes	finner
eureka	eyalet	fandom	fedora	fiacre	Finnic
evader	eyecup	fanged	feeble	fiance	fipple
evener	eyeful	fanion	feebly	fiasco	firing
evenly	eyeing	fanjet	feeder	fibbed	firkin
evilly	eyelet	fanned	feeing	fibber	firmly
evince	eyelid	fanner	feeler	fibred	fiscal
evolve	Eyetie	fantan	feirie	fibril	fisher
evzone	Fabian	Fantee	feisty	fibrin	fitful
exceed	fabled	fantod	feline	fibula	fitted
except	fabler	fantom	fellah	fickle	fitter
excess	fabric	faquir	feller	fiddle	fixate
excide	facade	fardel	felloe	fiddly	fixity
excise	facete	farfel	fellow	fidget	fizgig
excite	facial	farina	felony	fierce	fizzle
excuse	facies	farmer	female	fiesta	flabby
exedra	facile	far off	femora	figged	flacon
exempt	facing	far out	fencer	figure	flagon
exequy	factor	farrow	fender	filfot	flambe
exeunt	facula	fasces	Fenian	filial	flanch
exhale	fade in	fascia	fenman	filing	flange
exhort	faerie	fasten	fennec	filler	flappy
exhume	fagend	faster	fennel	fillet	flashy
exilic	fagged	fathen	ferial	fillip	flatly
exodus	faggot	father	ferine	filmic	flatus
exotic	failed	fathom	ferret	filter	flaunt
expand	faille	fatted	ferric	filthy	flaxen
expect	fainly	fatten	ferula	fimble	fleche
expend	fairly	fatter	ferule	finale	fledge
expert	fakery	fauces	fervid	finals	fleece
expire	falcon	faucet	fescue	finder	fleech
expiry	fallen	faulty	festal	finely	fleecy
export	fall in	faunae	fester	finery	flench
expose	fallow	faunal	fetial	finger	fleshy
exsert	falsie	faunas	fetich	finial	fletch
extant	falter	favour	fetish	fining	fleury

flexor	fogged	forrit	frisky	fusser	galosh
flight	foible	forsay	frizzy	fustic	gambir
flimsy	foiled	fossae	froggy	futile	gambit
flinch	foison	fossil	frolic	future	gamble
flinty	folder	foster	frosty	fylfot	gambol
flirty	foliar	fother	frothy	gabbed	gamely
flitch	folium	fought	frowst	gabber	gamete
floaty	folksy	foully	frowsy	gabble	gamily
flocci	follow	foulup	frowzy	gabbro	gamine
floozy	foment	fourth	frozen	gabion	gaming
floppy	fondle	foveae	frugal	gabled	gammer
florae	fondly	foveal	fruity	gablet	gammon
floral	fondue	fowler	frumpy	gadded	gander
floras	fontal	fracas	frusta	gadder	ganger
floret	fooler	fraena	fuddle	gadfly	gangly
florid	footed	fraise	fugato	gadget	gangue
fiorin	footer	framer	fugged	Gadhel	gannet
flossy	footle	frappe	fuhrer	gadoid	ganoid
floury	foozle	fratch	fulcra	Gaelic	gantry
flower	forage	frater	fulfil	gaffer	gaoler
fluent	forbad	Frauen	fulgid	gagged	gapped
fluffy	forbid	freaky	fulham	gagger	garage
flukey	forbye	freely	fullam	gaggle	garbed
flunky	forced	freest	fuller	gagman	garble
flurry	forcer	freeze	fulmar	gaiety	garcon
fluted	fordid	french	fumble	gainer	garden
fluter	forego	frenum	fundus	gainly	garget
flying	forest	frenzy	fun fur	gainst	gargle
flyman	forger	fresco	fungal	gaited	garial
flysch	forget	friary	fungus	gaiter	garish
flyway	forgot	Friday	funned	galago	garlic
fobbed	forint	fridge	funnel	galaxy	garner
focsle	forked	friend	fun run	galena	garnet
fodder	formal	frieze	furfur	galiot	garret
foeman	format	fright	furore	galley	garrot
foetal	formed	frigid	furred	Gallic	garter
foetid	former	frijol	furrow	gallon	gasbag
foetus	formic	frilly	fusain	gallop	Gascon
fogbow	fornix	fringe	fusile	galoot	gasify
fogdog	forrad	fringy	fusion	galore	gasket

gaskin	get off	glairy	goggle	gradus	groats
gasman	get out	glaive	goggly	grainy	grocer
gassed	getter	glance	goglet	gramme	groggy
gasser	gewgaw	glassy	go home	Grammy	groove
gateau	geyser	glazer	Goidel	gramps	groovy
gather	gharry	gleamy	goitre	grange	groper
gauche	ghetto	gleety	gokart	granny	grotto
gaucho	ghosty	glibly	golden	Granth	grotty
gauger	giaour	glider	golfer	grappa	grouch
gavage	gibber	glitch	gollop	grassy	ground
gavial	gibbet	global	golosh	grater	grouse
gazebo	gibbon	gloomy	goober	gratin	grovel
gazump	giddap	gloria	goodie	gratis	grower
geckos	gifted	glossy	goodly	graved	growly
geegee	gigged	glover	googly	gravel	growth
geezer	giggle	glower	googol	graven	groyne
geisha	giggly	glumly	gooier	graver	grubby
gelled	giglet	glumpy	gooney	Graves	grudge
Gemara	giglot	gluten	gooses	gravid	grugru
Gemini	gigman	gnarly	gopher	grazer	grumly
gemmae	gigolo	gnawer	goramy	grease	grumps
gemmed	gilder	gneiss	gorget	greasy	grumpy
gender	gilled	gnomic	gorgio	greave	grutch
genera	gillie	gnomon	gorgon	greedy	guddle
geneva	gimbal	gnosis	gorily	greens	Guelph
genial	gimlet	goalie	goslow	greeny	guenon
genius	gimmal	goanna	gospel	greyly	guffaw
genned	gimmer	goatee	gossan	grieve	guggle
genome	gingal	go away	gossip	grigri	guider
gentes	ginger	gobang	Gothic	grille	guilty
gentle	gingko	gobbet	gotten	grilse	guinea
gently	ginkgo	gobble	gourde	grimly	guiser
gentoo	ginned	goblet	govern	gringo	guitar
gentry	ginner	goblin	gowany	griper	gulden
geodic	girder	gocart	goyish	grippe	Gullah
George	girdle	goddam	gozzan	grippy	gullet
gerbil	girlie	godown	grabby	grisly	gulley
gerent	give up	godson	graben	grison	gummed
german	glacis	godwit	grader	gritty	gundog
gerund	gladly	goffer	gradin	grivet	gunman

gunned	halloa	hasten	heehaw	heyday	holily
gunnel	halloo	hatbox	heeled	hiatus	holism
gunner	hallow	hatful	heeler	hiccup	holler
gunsel	hallux	hatpeg	hegira	hickey	holloa
gunshy	haloes	hatpin	heifer	hidden	hollow
gunter	halter	hatred	height	hiding	holpen
gunyah	halvah	hatted	hejira	hieing	homage
gurgle	halves	hatter	helium	higgle	hombre
Gurkha	hamate	hauler	heller	higher	homely
gurnet	Hamite	haunch	helmet	highly	homily
gurrah	hamlet	Havana	helper	hijack	homing
gusset	hammal	havers	hemmed	hinder	hominy
guttae	hammam	hawhaw	hempen	Hindoo	honest
gutted	hammed	hawked	hen run	hinged	honied
gutter	hammer	hawker	henrys	hipped	honour
guvnor	hamper	hawser	hepcat	hippie	hooded
guzzle	handed	haybox	heptad	hirple	hoodie
gypped	handle	haymow	herald	hispid	hoodoo
gypsum	hangar	hazard	herbal	hisser	hoofed
gyrate	hanged	hazily	herder	hither	hoofer
habile	hanger	headed	herdic	hitman	hookah
hacker	hang on	header	hereat	hoarse	hooked
hackle	hangup	headon	hereby	hoaxer	hooker
hackly	hanker	healer	herein	hobbit	hookey
haddie	hankie	health	hereof	hobble	hookup
hadron	hansel	hearer	hereon	hobnob	hooper
haemal	hansom	hearse	heresy	hocker	hoopla
haemin	happed	hearth	hereto	hockey	hoopoe
haffet	happen	hearty	heriot	hodden	hooray
haffit	haptic	heated	hermit	hodman	hootch
hagbut	harass	heater	hernia	hoeing	hooter
haggis	harden	heathy	heroic	hogged	hooves
haggle	hardly	heat up	heroin	hogget	hopped
hailer	hardup	heaven	herpes	hogtie	hopper
hairdo	harken	heaver	Herren	hoicks	hopple
haired	harlot	Hebrew	hetero	hoised	horary
haleru	harper	heckle	hetman	holden	horned
halide	harrow	hectic	hexact	holder	horner
halite	haslet	hector	hexane	hold on	hornet
hallal	hassle	hedger	hexose	holdup	horrid

horror	hurter	immesh	indign	inrush	ironer
horsey	hurtle	immune	indigo	insane	ironic
hosier	husker	immure	indite	insect	irrupt
hostel	hussar	impact	indium	insert	Isabel
hotbed	hustle	impair	indole	inside	ischia
hotdog	hutted	impala	indoor	insist	island
hotpot	huzoor	impale	induce	insole	isobar
hotter	hyaena	impark	induct	instal	isomer
hourly	hybrid	impart	infamy	instar	isopod
housel	hybris	impawn	infant	instep	italic
housey	hydric	impede	infare	instil	itself
howdah	hymnal	impend	infect	insult	izzard
howler	hymnic	impish	infelt	insure	jabbed
hoyden	hyphae	impone	infest	intact	jabber
hubbub	hyphal	import	infirm	intake	jabiru
hubcap	hyphen	impose	inflow	intend	jacana
hubris	hyssop	impost	influx	intent	jackal
huckle	iambic	impugn	infold	intern	jacket
huddle	iambus	impure	inform	intone	jaeger
hugely	ibexes	impute	infuse	in tray	jagged
hugged	ibices	inarch	ingest	intuit	jagger
humane	ibidem	inborn	ingulf	invade	jaguar
humble	iceaxe	inbred	inhale	invent	jailer
humbly	icebag	incase	in hand	invert	jailor
humbug	icebox	incept	inhere	invest	jalopy
humify	icecap	incest	inhume	invite	jammed
hummed	iceman	inches	inject	invoke	jammer
hummel	icicle	incise	injure	inward	jangle
hummer	iconic	incite	injury	inwick	jarful
humour	ideaed	income	inkpot	inwove	jargon
humped	ideate	incubi	inlaid	inwrap	jarrah
hunger	idiocy	incult	inland	iodate	jarred
hungry	idolum	incuse	inlaws	iodide	jarvey
hunker	ignite	indaba	inlier	iodine	jasper
hunter	ignore	in debt	in love	iodise	jaunce
hurdle	iguana	indeed	inmate	Ionian	jaunty
hurler	illume	indene	inmost	ionise	jeerer
hurley	illuse	indent	innate	ionium	jejune
hurrah	imbibe	Indian	inning	ireful	jennet
hurray	imbrue	indict	inroad	irenic	jerbil

jerboa	jotted	karmic	kipper	laches	lapsed
jerker	jotter	karroo	kirsch	lacing	lapsus
jerkin	jounce	kasbah	kirtle	lackey	larder
jersey	jouncy	keenly	kismet	lactic	lardon
jester	jovial	keeper	kisser	lacuna	lariat
Jesuit	Jovian	kelpie	kitbag	ladder	larker
jetlag	joyful	kelson	kitsch	laddie	larrup
jetsam	joyous	kelter	kitten	ladify	larvae
jet set	Judaic	Keltic	kittle	lading	larval
jetted	judder	kelvin	klepht	ladino	larynx
Jewess	Judean	kenned	knaggy	ladyfy	lascar
Jewish	judger	kennel	knight	lagged	lasher
jibbah	jugate	kermes	knives	lagger	lashup
jibbed	jugful	kermis	knobby	lagoon	lassie
jibber	jugged	kerned	knotty	laguna	lassos
jigged	juggle	kernel	knower	laical	laster
jigger	jujube	kersey	koodoo	lallan	lastly
jiggle	Julian	ketone	kookie	lambda	lateen
jiggly	jumbal	kettle	kopeck	lamber	lately
jigsaw	jumble	kewpie	koppie	lamely	latent
jilter	jumbly	keyway	Korean	lament	latest
jingly	jumper	kiaugh	kosher	lamina	lather
jinnee	jungle	kibble	kowhai	lamish	latish
jitney	jungly	kibitz	kowtow	Lammas	latten
jitter	junior	kibosh	kraken	lammed	latter
joanna	junker	kicker	krantz	lancer	launch
jobber	junket	kidded	kronen	lancet	laurel
job lot	junkie	kidder	kroner	landau	lavabo
jockey	jurist	kiddie	kronor	landed	lavage
jocose	justly	kidnap	kronur	lander	lavish
jocund	Jutish	kidney	kultur	langue	lawful
jogged	jutted	kiekie	kumiss	langur	lawman
jogger	kabala	killer	kummel	lankly	lawyer
joggle	Kaffir	kilted	kurgan	lanner	laxity
johnny	kaftan	kilter	laager	lanugo	layday
joiner	kaiser	kimono	labial	lapdog	layman
jolter	kakapo	kincob	labile	lapful	layoff
josher	kaolin	kindle	labium	lapped	layout
josser	kaputt	kindly	labour	lappet	lazily
jostle	karate	kingly	laceup	lappie	lazuli

leaden	lessen	limner	lizard	lopper	lupine
leader	lesser	limper	loaded	loquat	lurker
lead in	lesson	limpet	loader	lordly	lushly
lead up	lessor	limpid	loafer	lorica	lustra
leafed	lethal	limply	loaner	lotion	lustre
league	let off	limuli	loathe	lotted	luteal
lealty	letter	linage	loaves	louche	lutein
leanly	Lettic	linden	lobate	louden	luting
leanto	levant	lineal	lobbed	loudly	luxate
leaper	Levite	linear	lobose	lounge	luxury
leaved	levity	lineup	lobule	loupen	lyceum
leaven	lewdly	linger	locale	louver	lychee
leaver	liable	lingua	locate	louvre	Lydian
leaves	liaise	lining	lochan	lovage	lyrate
lecher	libber	linkup	locker	lovein	lyrics
lector	libido	linnet	locket	lovely	lyrism
ledged	Libyan	linney	lockup	loving	lyrist
ledger	lichee	linsey	loculi	lowboy	lysine
leeway	lichen	lintel	locust	lowery	macaco
legacy	lictor	lintie	lodger	lowing	mackle
legate	lidded	lionel	lofter	lowish	macron
legato	lieder	lipase	logged	lowkey	macula
leg bye	lie low	lipped	logger	lubber	macule
legend	lierne	liquid	loggia	lubric	Madame
legged	lifter	liquor	logion	lucent	madcap
legion	liftup	lisper	logjam	lucern	madden
legist	ligate	lissom	loiter	luetic	madder
legman	ligger	listed	loller	lugged	madman
legume	lights	listen	lollop	lugger	madras
lemony	lignin	lister	loment	luggie	maduro
lender	ligula	litany	lonely	lumbar	maenad
length	ligule	litchi	longan	lumber	maggot
lenity	likely	lithic	loofah	lummox	Magian
lensed	liking	litmus	looker	lumpen	magnet
Lenten	lilied	litter	look in	lumper	magnum
lentil	limbed	little	look up	lunacy	magpie
Leonic	limber	live in	looper	lunate	maguey
lepton	limbic	lively	loosen	lunger	Magyar
lesion	limbus	livery	looter	lunula	mahout
lessee	liming	living	lopped	lunule	maidan

maiden	manner	marshy	meadow	merest	mildew
maigre	manque	marten	meagre	merger	mildly
mailed	mantel	martin	mealie	merino	milieu
mainly	mantid	martyr	meanie	merlin	milker
Majlis	mantis	marvel	meanly	merlon	milled
make do	mantle	mascle	measly	merman	miller
make up	mantra	mascon	meddle	merrie	millet
making	mantua	mascot	mediae	mescal	milord
Malaga	manual	masher	medial	mesial	milter
malate	manuka	mashie	median	messan	mimosa
maleic	manure	masker	medick	Messra	mincer
malice	Maoism	maslin	medico	metals	minded
malign	Maoist	Masora	medium	meteor	minder
malism	mapped	masque	medlar	method	mingle
malkin	mapper	massif	medley	methyl	minify
mallee	maquis	masted	medusa	metier	minima
mallei	maraca	master	meekly	metope	mining
mallet	maraud	mastic	meetly	metred	minion
mallow	marble	matico	megilp	metric	minium
maltha	marbly	matins	megohm	mettle	minnow
mammae	marcel	matlow	megrim	mezuza	Minoan
mammal	margay	matrix	mellow	miasma	minter
mammee	margin	matron	melody	mickey	minuet
mammer	marina	matted	melton	mickle	minute
mammon	marine	matter	member	micron	miosis
manage	marish	mature	memoir	midair	miotic
manana	Marist	matzoh	memory	midday	mirage
manche	marked	maugre	menace	midden	mirror
Manchu	marker	maundy	menage	middle	miscue
man day	market	maxima	mender	midget	misdid
manege	mark up	maxixe	menhir	midgut	misere
manful	marlin	maybug	menial	midoff	misery
mangel	marmot	mayday	meninx	midrib	misfit
manger	maroon	mayest	mensal	midway	mishap
mangle	marque	mayfly	menses	miffed	mishit
mangos	marram	mayhap	mental	mighty	mishmi
maniac	marred	mayhem	mentor	mignon	Mishna
manila	marron	maying	mentum	mikado	mislay
manioc	marrow	mazard	mercer	milady	misled
manned	marrum	mazily	merely	milage	missal

missel	monger	mostly	musing	namely	nether
missis	Mongol	motett	muskeg	nanism	netted
missus	monial	mother	musket	napalm	nettle
mister	monied	motile	muskox	napkin	neural
mistle	monies	motion	Muslim	napped	neuron
misuse	monism	motive	muslin	narrow	neuter
mitral	monist	motley	mussel	nastic	new age
mitten	monkey	mottle	muster	natant	new era
mizzen	monody	mouldy	mutant	nation	newish
mizzly	moocow	moulin	mutate	native	newton
moaner	mooing	mouser	mutely	natron	niacin
moated	moolah	mousse	mutiny	natter	nibbed
mobbed	mopish	mouthy	mutism	nature	nibble
mobcap	mopoke	moving	mutter	naught	nicely
mobile	mopped	mucous	mutton	nausea	nicety
mocker	mopper	muddle	mutual	nautch	nicish
mockup	moppet	muesli	muumuu	Nazify	nickel
modena	morale	muffin	muzhik	Nazism	nicker
modern	morals	muffle	muzzle	neaped	nidget
modest	morass	muflon	myelin	nearby	nidify
modify	morbid	mugged	myopia	nearer	nielli
modish	morbus	mugger	myopic	nearly	niello
module	moreen	mukluk	myosin	neaten	nigger
moduli	morgen	mulish	myosis	neatly	niggle
modulo	morgue	mullah	myotic	nebula	nighty
moggie	morion	muller	myriad	nectar	nignog
mohair	morish	mullet	myrica	needle	nilgai
Mohawk	Mormon	mulley	myrtle	neednt	nimble
Mohock	mornay	mumble	myself	negate	nimbly
mohole	morose	mummer	mystic	nekton	nimbus
moider	morpho	mundic	mythic	nelson	Nimrod
moiety	morris	Munich	mythos	Nepali	ninety
moiler	morrow	muntin	my word	nephew	nipped
molest	morsel	murder	myxoma	nereid	nipper
mollie	mortal	murmur	nabbed	nerine	nipple
Moloch	mortar	murphy	naevus	nerite	nitric
molten	mosaic	murrey	nagana	neroli	nitwit
moment	moshav	muscat	nagged	nestle	nobble
Monday	Moslem	muscle	nagger	Nestor	nobbut
moneys	mosque	museum	nailer	netful	nobody

nocent	nuance	obtuse	O level	ordure	outsat
nodded	nubble	obvert	oliver	orfray	outset
noddle	nubbly	occult	omasum	orgasm	outsit
nodose	nubile	occupy	omelet	orgeat	outwit
nodule	nuchal	ocelot	omenta	orient	ovally
noggin	nuclei	ochone	onager	origin	overdo
no good	nudely	oclock	oncost	oriole	overly
no hope	nudism	octane	oneoff	orison	ovisac
nomism	nudist	octant	oneway	ormolu	ovular
no more	nudity	octave	on foot	ornate	owlish
nonage	nugget	octavo	online	ornery	oxalic
nonary	nullah	octroi	onrush	orphan	oxalis
noncom	number	ocular	onside	orphic	oxbird
nonego	numbly	oddity	onward	orpine	oxford
nonfat	numina	oddjob	oocyte	orrery	oxhide
nonuse	nuncio	odds on	oodles	oscine	oxtail
noodle	nuncle	odious	oolite	osmium	oxygen
Nordic	nurser	oedema	oology	osprey	oyster
normal	nutant	oeuvre	oolong	ossify	ozonic
Norman	nutate	offend	oomiak	osteal	pacify
nosh up	nutmeg	office	opaque	ostler	packer
no side	nutria	offing	opener	otiose	packet
nosily	nutter	offish	openly	otitis	padded
nosing	nuzzle	offkey	ophite	ottava	paddle
nostoc	nympho	offset	opiate	ouster	paella
notary	oafish	ogamic	oppose	outact	paeony
notate	oarage	ogival	oppugn	outage	pagoda
notice	obeyer	ogress	optics	outbid	paid up
notify	object	ogrish	optime	outcry	pajama
notion	objure	oh dear	option	outdid	pakeha
not out	oblast	ohmage	orache	outfit	palace
nougat	oblate	oidium	oracle	outfox	palais
nought	oblige	oilcan	orally	outgun	palate
nounal	oblong	oilman	orange	outing	palely
novena	oboist	oilnut	orator	outlaw	paling
novice	obsess	old age	orcein	outlay	palish
Nowell	obtain	old hat	orchid	outlet	pallet
nowise	obtect	oldish	orchis	output	pallid
noyade	obtest	oleate	ordain	outran	pallor
nozzle	obtund	olefin	ordeal	outrun	palmar

palmer	parley	pavior	pelvic	peyote	pileum
palolo	parody	pavise	pelvis	peyotl	pile up
palpal	parole	pawnee	pencil	phatic	pileus
palter	parous	pawner	penman	phenol	pilfer
paltry	parpen	pawpaw	pennae	phlegm	pillar
pampas	parral	payday	penned	phloem	pillow
pamper	parrel	payoff	pennon	phobia	pilose
panada	parrot	payola	pentad	phobic	pilous
panama	parsec	peachy	pent up	phoebe	pilule
pander	Parsee	peahen	pentyl	phoney	pimple
pandit	parson	peaked	penult	phonic	pimply
panful	partan	peanut	penury	phonon	pincer
panned	partly	pearly	people	phooey	pineal
pantry	parvis	pebble	peplum	photoc	pinery
panzer	pascal	pebbly	pepped	photon	pineta
papacy	Pashto	pecker	pepper	phrase	pinger
papain	pass by	pecten	pepsin	phylum	pinion
papaya	passer	pectic	peptic	physic	pinkie
papers	passim	pectin	perdue	piaffe	pinnae
papery	pass on	pedalo	period	piazza	pinned
papism	pastel	pedant	perish	picker	pinner
papist	pastil	pedate	permit	picket	pinole
pappus	pastor	peddle	perron	pickle	pintle
papula	pastry	pedlar	person	pick up	piolet
papule	patchy	peeler	pertly	picnic	pionic
papyri	patent	peeper	peruke	picric	piping
parade	Pathan	peepul	peruse	piddle	pipkin
parang	pathos	peewit	pesade	pidgin	pipped
paraph	patina	pegged	peseta	piecer	pippin
parcel	patois	pegleg	pesewa	piedog	piquet
pardon	patrol	pegtop	pester	pieman	piracy
parent	patron	pelage	pestle	pierce	pirate
parget	patted	pelham	petara	piffle	piraya
pariah	patten	pellet	petard	pigeon	Pisces
parian	patter	pelmet	petite	pigged	pissed
paring	paunch	pelota	petrel	piggin	pistil
parish	pauper	peltae	petrol	piglet	pistol
parity	pavage	pelter	petted	pignut	piston
parkin	pavane	peltry	petter	pigsty	pitchy
parlay	paving	pelves	pewter	pilaff	pitman

pitsaw plough pommel potboy primer pug dog
pitted plover pommie poteen primly puisne
pitter plucky pompom potent primus puller
pizzle plumed poncho potful prince pullet
placed plummy ponder pother priory pulley
placer plumpy pongee potion prison pull in
placet plunge pontil potman prissy pull on
placid plural ponton potpie privet pull up
plagal plushy poodle potted prizer pulper
plague pluton pooped potter prober pulpit
plaguy pneuma poorly pottle probit pulque
plaice pocked popery pouchy profit pulsar
plaint pocket popgun pouffe proleg pulser
planar podded popish pounce prolix pumice
planer podite poplar pourer prompt pummel
planet podium poplin pouter pronto pumper
plaque podsol popped powder propel punchy
plashy podzol popper powwow proper puncta
plasma poetic poppet praise propyl pundit
platan poetry popple prance proser punily
platen pogrom popply prater prosit punish
plater pointe porgie praxis protea punkay
player points porism prayer proton punned
play on poison porker preach proven punner
pleach Polack porose precis pruina punnet
please polder porous prefab pruner punter
plebby police portal prefer prying pupate
pledge policy porter prefix pseudo pupped
plenty polish portly prelim psyche puppet
plenum polite posada premed psycho purdah
pleura polity poseur premix pterin purely
plexor pollan posset prepay ptisan purfle
plexus polled possum preset ptosis purger
pliant pollen postal presto public purify
pliers poller poster pretax pucker purine
plight pollex postil pretty puddle purism
plinth polony potage prewar puddly purist
plisse pomace potale pricey puffed purity
ploidy pomade potash priest puffer purler
plotty pomelo potato primal puffin purlin

purple	quiche	ragman	rarely	reborn	refill
purply	quince	ragout	raring	rebuff	refine
purser	quinol	ragtag	rarity	rebuke	reflex
pursue	quinsy	raider	rascal	recall	reflow
purvey	quinta	railer	rasher	recant	reflux
pusher	quirky	raiser	rashly	recast	reform
Pushtu	quitch	raison	rasper	recede	refuel
pushup	quiver	Rajput	raster	recent	refuge
put off	quoits	rakish	rasure	recess	refund
put out	quorum	ramate	ratbag	recipe	refuse
putrid	quotes	ramble	rather	recite	refute
putsch	rabbet	ramify	ratify	reckon	regain
puttee	rabbin	ramjet	ratine	recoil	regale
putter	rabbit	rammed	rating	recoin	regard
puttie	rabble	rammer	ration	record	regent
puzzle	rabies	ramose	ratite	recoup	reggae
pyedog	raceme	ramous	ratlin	rector	regime
pyknic	rachis	ramrod	ratoon	rectum	regina
pyrite	racial	rancho	rattan	rectus	region
pyrope	racily	rancid	rattat	redact	regius
python	racism	random	ratted	redcap	reglet
quagga	racist	ranger	ratter	redden	regnal
quaggy	racker	ranker	rattle	redder	regret
quahog	racket	rankle	ravage	reddle	regulo
quaich	racoon	rankly	ravine	redeem	rehash
quaigh	raddle	ransom	raving	redeye	rehear
quaint	radial	ranter	ravish	red fox	reheat
Quaker	radian	ranula	razzle	red hot	reheel
qualmy	radish	raphia	reader	redone	reject
quanta	radium	rapids	really	redraw	rejoin
quarry	radius	rapier	realty	Red Sea	relaid
quarte	radome	rapine	reamer	redtop	relate
quarto	radula	rapist	reaper	reduce	relent
quartz	raffia	rapped	rearer	reebok	relict
quasar	raffle	rappee	reason	reecho	relief
quaver	rafter	rappel	reaver	reedit	reline
queasy	ragbag	rapper	rebate	reefer	relish
queazy	ragged	raptly	rebato	reeler	relive
quench	raggle	raptor	rebeck	reface	reload
queuer	raglan	rarefy	rebore	refect	remade

remain	reship	revive	rifler	rodman	rubbed
remake	reside	revoke	rigged	roller	rubber
remand	resign	revolt	rigger	roll on	rubble
remark	resile	revved	righto	roll up	rubbly
remind	resist	reward	rigour	Romaic	rubefy
remint	resold	rewind	rigout	Romany	rubify
remise	resole	rewire	rillet	Romish	rubric
remiss	resorb	rewoke	rimmed	romper	ruched
remora	resort	reword	rimose	rondel	ruckus
remote	rester	rework	rimous	roofer	rudder
remove	result	rhaphe	ringed	rookie	ruddle
rename	resume	rhebok	ringer	roomer	rudely
render	retail	rhesus	ring up	rooted	rudish
renege	retain	rhetor	rinser	rooter	rueful
rennet	retake	rheumy	rioter	ropery	ruffed
renown	retard	rhinal	ripely	roping	ruffle
rental	retell	rhumba	ripoff	roquet	rufous
renter	retest	rhymer	ripped	rosace	rugged
reopen	retina	rhythm	ripper	rosary	rugger
repaid	retire	ribald	ripple	rosery	rugose
repair	retold	riband	ripply	rosily	ruiner
repass	retook	ribbed	riprap	rosiny	ruling
repast	retool	ribbon	ripsaw	roster	rumble
repeal	retort	ribose	rising	rostra	rumbly
repeat	retral	richen	risker	rotary	rumina
repent	retrod	riches	risque	rotate	rummer
replay	returf	richly	ritual	rotgut	rumour
report	return	ricker	rivage	rotted	rumple
repose	retuse	rickey	roadie	rotten	rumpus
repugn	revamp	ricrac	roamer	rotter	rundle
repute	reveal	rictal	roarer	rotund	runlet
reread	reverb	rictus	robalo	rouble	runnel
resale	revere	ridded	robbed	rouncy	runner
rescue	revers	ridden	robber	rouser	run off
reseat	revert	riddle	robust	router	run off
reseau	revery	rident	rochet	roving	runrig
resect	revest	ridged	rocker	rowing	runway
reseda	review	riding	rocket	royals	rupiah
resell	revile	rifely	rococo	rozzer	rusher
resent	revise	riffle	rodent	rubato	rushes

russet	saliva	sarape	scarry	scryer	seeker
russia	sallet	sarong	scathe	sculpt	seemly
rustic	sallow	sarsen	scatty	scummy	seesaw
rustle	salmon	sashay	scazon	scurfy	seethe
rutile	saloon	sateen	scenic	scurry	seiche
sabbat	saloop	satiny	schema	scurvy	seiner
Sabian	salter	satire	scheme	scutal	seisin
Sabine	saltus	satori	schism	scutch	seizer
sables	saluki	satrap	schist	scutum	seizin
sachem	salute	Saturn	schizo	scyphi	sejant
sachet	salver	satyra	schlet	scythe	seldom
sacque	salvia	saucer	school	sea air	select
sacral	salvor	sauger	schorl	seabed	Seljuk
sacred	salvos	saurel	schuss	seacow	seller
sacrum	samara	savage	scilla	sea dog	selves
sadden	sambar	savant	sclera	sea ear	semble
sadder	sambur	savate	scolex	sea fan	Semite
saddhu	Samian	saving	sconce	sea fog	semmit
saddle	samite	savory	scorch	sealer	sempre
sadism	samlet	savour	scorer	seaman	senary
sadist	Samoan	sawder	scoria	seamer	senate
safari	sampan	sawfly	scotch	sea mew	sendal
safely	sample	sawney	scoter	seance	sender
safety	Samson	sawpit	scotia	sea pen	sendup
sagely	sandal	sawset	Scotic	search	senega
saggar	sander	sawyer	scouse	season	senhor
sagged	sandhi	saxony	scouth	seater	senile
sagger	sanely	sayest	scrape	seaway	senior
saidst	sanies	saying	scrawl	secant	sennet
sailed	sanify	sayyid	screak	secede	sennit
sailer	sanity	scabby	scream	second	senora
sailor	sanjak	scalar	screed	secret	senses
saithe	sannup	scaled	screen	sector	sensor
salaam	santal	scaler	screwy	secund	sensum
salami	santir	scales	scribe	secure	sentry
salary	sapele	scampi	scrimp	sedate	sephen
Salian	sapota	scanty	script	sedile	sepsis
salify	sappan	scarab	scroll	seduce	septal
salina	sapped	scarce	scruff	seeder	septet
saline	sapper	scarer	scrump	seeing	septic

sequel	shader	sheugh	shucks	singer	skiver
sequin	shades	shield	shut in	single	skivvy
serang	shadow	shiest	shut up	singly	skylab
serape	shaggy	shifty	shyest	sinker	skyman
seraph	shaken	Shiite	sialic	sinned	skyway
serein	shaker	shikar	sicken	sinner	slacks
serene	Shakta	shiksa	sicker	sinnet	slaggy
serial	Shakti	shimmy	sickle	sinter	slalom
series	shalom	shindy	sickly	Siouan	slangy
seriph	shaman	shiner	siding	siphon	slap up
sermon	shammy	shinny	sienna	sipped	slater
serous	shamus	Shinto	sierra	sipper	slaver
serrae	shandy	shinty	siesta	sippet	slavey
serran	shanny	shirty	sifter	sircar	Slavic
serval	shanty	shiver	sigher	sirdar	slayer
server	shaped	shoaly	siglum	sirkar	sleave
sesame	shapen	shoddy	signal	sirrah	sleazy
seseli	shaper	shofar	signer	sirree	sledge
sestet	sharer	shogun	signet	siskin	sleepy
set off	sharif	shoran	signor	sissoo	sleety
setose	sharps	shorts	silage	sister	sleeve
set out	shaven	shorty	sileni	sistra	sleigh
settee	shaver	should	silent	sittar	sleuth
setter	shears	shovel	silica	sitter	slicer
settle	sheass	shover	silken	six gun	slider
sevens	sheath	shower	siller	sizing	slight
severe	sheave	shrank	silvan	sizzle	slimly
severy	sheeny	shrewd	silver	skater	slinky
Sevres	sheets	shriek	simian	skeely	slip on
sewage	sheikh	shrift	simile	skeigh	slippy
sewing	sheila	shrike	simmer	skerry	slip up
sexily	shekel	shrill	simnel	sketch	sliver
sexism	shelly	shrimp	simony	skewer	slogan
sexist	Shelta	shrine	simoom	skibob	sloppy
sexpot	shelty	shrink	simoon	skiddy	sloshy
sextan	shelve	shrive	simper	skiing	slough
sextet	sheoak	shroff	simple	skilly	Slovak
sexton	sherif	shroud	simply	skimpy	sloven
sexual	Sherpa	shrove	sinewy	skinny	slowly
shabby	sherry	shrunk	sinful	ski run	sludge

sludgy	sniffy	solver	specie	spouse	stalky
sluice	sniper	sombre	speech	sprain	stamen
sluicy	snippy	somite	speedo	sprang	stance
slummy	snitch	sonant	speedy	sprawl	stanch
slurry	snivel	sonata	speiss	spread	stanza
slushy	snobby	sonnet	spence	spring	stapes
slyest	snoopy	sonsie	spewer	sprint	staple
smalls	snooty	sooner	sphene	sprite	starch
smarmy	snooze	soothe	sphere	sprout	starer
smarty	snorer	sophic	sphery	spruce	starry
smeary	snotty	sopped	sphinx	spruit	starve
smeech	snouty	sorage	spider	sprung	stases
smelly	snubby	sorbet	spiffy	spryer	stasis
smilax	snuffy	sordid	spigot	spryly	stated
smiler	snugly	sorely	spilth	spunky	stater
smirch	soaker	sorgho	spinal	spurge	states
smirky	sobbed	sorner	spined	spurry	static
smiter	sobeit	sorrel	spinel	sputum	stator
smithy	socage	sorrow	spinet	squall	statue
smoggy	soccer	sorter	spiral	squama	status
smoker	social	sortes	spirit	square	stayer
smooch	socket	sortie	splash	squash	stay in
smooth	sodden	Sothic	spleen	squawk	steady
smouch	sodium	sotted	splent	squeak	steamy
smudge	sodomy	sought	splice	squeal	steely
smudgy	soever	souled	spline	squill	steeve
smugly	soffit	source	splint	squint	stemma
smutch	soften	sourly	splits	squire	stench
smutty	softie	souter	splosh	squirm	step in
snaggy	softly	soviet	spoffy	squirt	step on
snap at	soigne	sovran	spoilt	squish	steppe
snappy	soiree	spacer	spoken	stable	step up
snap up	solace	spadix	sponge	stably	stereo
snarer	solano	sparer	spongy	stacte	steric
snarly	soldan	sparge	spooky	stadia	sterna
snatch	solder	sparks	spoony	stager	sterol
snazzy	solely	sparry	sports	stagey	stewed
sneaky	solemn	sparse	sporty	stairs	sticky
sneeze	solids	spathe	spot on	stakes	stifle
sneezy	solute	spavin	spotty	stalag	stigma

stilly	stream	stylet	sun dog	swimmy	taking
stingo	streek	stylus	sundry	swinge	talbot
stingy	street	stymie	sun dry	swiper	talcky
stinko	stress	styrax	sun god	swipes	talcum
stipel	strewn	suable	sun hat	swirly	talent
stipes	striae	subbed	sunken	swishy	talion
stirps	strict	subdue	sunlit	switch	talker
stitch	stride	sublet	sunned	swivel	talkie
stithy	strife	submit	sunray	swoosh	tallow
stiver	strike	suborn	sunset	sylvan	Talmud
stocks	Strine	subset	suntan	symbol	tamale
stodge	string	subtil	superb	syndic	tamara
stodgy	stripe	subtle	supine	syntax	tamely
stogie	stripy	subtly	supped	syphon	taming
stoker	strive	suburb	supper	Syriac	tamper
stokes	strobe	subway	supply	Syrian	tampon
stolen	strode	sucker	surely	syrinx	tamtam
stolid	stroke	suckle	surety	syrupy	tandem
stolon	stroll	sudary	surfer	system	tangle
stoned	stroma	sudden	surrey	syzygy	tangly
stoner	stromb	suffer	surtax	tabard	tanist
stooge	strong	suffix	survey	tabbed	tanked
stop go	stroud	Sufism	suslik	tablet	tanker
storax	strout	sugary	sutile	tabour	tanned
stores	strove	suitor	sutler	tacker	tanner
storey	strown	sulcus	suttee	tacket	tannic
stormy	struck	sullen	suture	tackle	tannin
stound	strung	sultan	svelte	tactic	tanrec
stover	strunt	sultry	swaddy	taenia	tantra
strafe	Stuart	sumach	swampy	tagend	Taoism
strain	stubby	summae	swanky	tagged	Taoist
strait	stucco	summed	swaraj	tagrag	tapeta
strake	studio	summer	swarth	tahini	tapped
strand	stuffy	summit	swatch	tahsil	tapper
strass	stumer	summon	swathe	tailor	tappet
strata	stumpy	sunbow	swayer	taipan	tappit
strath	stupid	sundae	sweaty	takahe	target
strawy	stupor	Sunday	sweeny	take in	Targum
strays	sturdy	sunder	sweets	take on	tariff
streak	stylar	sundew	swerve	take up	tarmac

tarpan	tedium	termer	thoria	tidbit	tiptoe
tarpon	teemer	termly	thorny	tiddly	tiptop
tarras	teensy	termor	thoron	tidily	tirade
tarred	teepee	terret	thorpe	tied up	tisane
tarsal	teeter	testae	though	tie dye	tissue
tarsia	teethe	tester	thrall	tiepin	titbit
tarsus	tegmen	teston	thrash	tierce	titfer
tartan	tegula	tetany	thrawn	tiered	tither
tartar	teledu	tetchy	thread	tie rod	titian
tartly	teller	tether	threap	tiffin	titled
Tarzan	telson	tetrad	threat	tights	titter
tassel	Telugu	tetter	thresh	tiling	tittle
tassie	temper	Teuton	thrice	tiller	tittup
taster	temple	thaler	thrift	tilter	tmesis
tatami	tenace	thalli	thrill	timbal	tocher
tatted	tenant	thanks	thrips	timber	tocsin
tatter	tender	thatch	thrive	timbre	toddle
tattle	tendon	Theban	throat	timely	toecap
tattoo	tenner	thecae	throes	timing	toeing
taught	tennis	thecal	throne	tincal	toffee
Taurus	tenour	theine	throng	tinder	togaed
tautly	tenpin	theirs	throve	tinful	togged
tautog	tenrec	theism	thrown	tingle	toggle
tavern	tenson	theist	thrush	tingly	to heel
tawdry	tensor	thenar	thrust	tinily	toiler
tawery	tenter	thence	thulia	tinker	toilet
tawpie	tentie	theory	thwack	tinkle	Toledo
taxies	tenues	theses	thwart	tinkly	toluic
taxman	tenuis	thesis	thymus	tinman	toluol
teabag	tenure	thetic	thyrse	tinned	tomato
teacup	tenuto	thieve	thyrsi	tinner	tombac
teapot	tenzon	things	tibiae	tinpot	tombak
teapoy	tepefy	thingy	tibial	tinsel	tomboy
teasel	teraph	thinly	ticked	tinter	tomcat
teaser	tercel	thirst	ticker	tipcat	tomcod
teaset	tercet	thirty	ticket	tipoff	tomtit
teazel	teredo	tholoi	tickey	tipped	tomtom
teazle	terete	tholos	tickle	tipper	toneme
tedded	tergal	tholus	tickly	tippet	tongue
tedder	tergum	thorax	tictac	tipple	tonish

tonsil	toxoid	triste	tuffet	tutted	umbras
tooter	tracer	triton	tufted	tuxedo	umlaut
toothy	traces	triune	tufter	tuyere	umpire
tootle	tracks	trivet	tugged	twangy	unable
tootsy	trader	trivia	tuille	tweeds	unbend
Tophet	tragic	trocar	tulwar	tweedy	unbent
tophus	tragus	troche	tumble	tweeny	unbind
topman	trance	trogon	tumefy	twelve	unbolt
topped	trapan	troika	tumour	twenty	unborn
topper	trapes	Trojan	tumtum	twicer	unbred
topple	trappy	trolly	tumuli	twiggy	uncage
torero	trashy	trompe	tumult	twilit	uncial
Tories	trauma	trophy	tundra	twiner	uncini
toroid	travel	tropic	tuning	twinge	unclad
torose	treaty	troppo	tunnel	twirly	uncoil
torpid	treble	trough	tupelo	twisty	uncool
torpor	trebly	troupe	turban	twitch	uncork
torque	tremie	trouty	turbid	two ply	uncurl
torrid	tremor	trover	turbit	two way	undies
torsel	trench	trowel	turbot	tycoon	undine
torten	trendy	truant	tureen	tymbal	undock
torula	trepan	trudge	turgid	tympan	undoer
tosher	tressy	truism	turgor	typhus	undone
tosser	triage	trumps	turion	typify	unduly
tossup	tribal	trusty	turkey	typing	unease
tother	tricar	trying	Turkic	typist	uneasy
totted	tricky	tryout	turner	tyrant	uneath
totter	tricot	tsamba	tunr in	Tyrian	uneven
touche	trifid	tsetse	turnip	ubiety	unfair
touchy	trifle	Tshirt	turn on	uglify	unfold
toupee	trigon	tsotsi	turnup	uglily	unfurl
toupet	trilby	Tswana	turret	Ugrian	ungird
tourer	trimer	Tuareg	turtle	ugsome	ungirt
tousle	trimly	tubful	turves	ullage	unglue
touter	trinal	tubing	Tuscan	ulster	ungual
towage	triode	tubule	tusked	ultima	ungues
toward	triple	tuchun	tusker	ultimo	unguis
towery	triply	tucker	tussah	umbles	unhair
towhee	tripod	tucket	tusser	umbrae	unhand
townee	tripos	tuck in	tussle	umbral	

unholy	unripe	uphill	utopia	veloce	vetted
unhook	unrobe	uphold	uvulae	velour	viable
Uniate	unroll	upkeep	uvular	velvet	viands
unific	unroof	upland	vacant	vendee	viator
uniped	unroot	uplift	vacate	vender	vibist
unipod	unrope	upmost	vacuum	vendor	vibrio
unique	unruly	upping	vagary	vendue	victim
unisex	unsafe	uppish	vagile	veneer	victor
unison	unsaid	uppity	vainly	venery	vicuna
united	unseal	uprise	Vaisya	venial	vielle
uniter	unseam	uproar	valeta	venire	viewer
unjoin	unseat	uproot	valgus	Venite	vigour
unjust	unseen	uprush	valine	venose	Viking
unkind	unself	upshot	valise	venous	vilely
unking	unship	upside	valley	venter	vilify
unkink	unshod	uptake	valour	ventre	villus
unknit	unshoe	uptown	valuer	venule	vinery
unknot	unstop	upturn	valuta	verbal	vinous
unlace	unsung	upward	valved	verger	violet
unlade	untidy	upwind	vamper	verify	violin
unlaid	untied	uracil	vandal	verily	virago
unlash	untold	uraeus	vanish	verism	virgin
unless	untrue	Uralic	vanity	verist	virile
unlike	untuck	Urania	vapour	verity	virose
unlink	untune	uranic	varied	vermin	virtue
unload	unused	Uranus	variet	vernal	visage
unlock	unveil	uranyl	varved	versal	viscid
unmade	unwary	urbane	vassal	versed	viscus
unmake	unwell	urchin	vastly	verser	Vishnu
unmash	unwept	ureter	vatful	verset	vision
unmeet	unwind	urgent	vatted	versus	visual
unmoor	unwise	urinal	vaudoo	vertex	vitals
unnail	unworn	urnful	vaulty	vervet	vittae
unpack	unwrap	ursine	vector	vesica	vivace
unpaid	unyoke	usable	Vedist	vesper	vivers
unpick	upbear	usance	vegete	vessel	vivify
unread	upbeat	useful	veiled	vestal	vizard
unreal	upcast	usurer	veined	vested	vizier
unreel	update	uterus	veleta	vestee	vizsla
unrest	upheld	utmost	vellum	vestry	voiced

voided	wallop	waxily	whiles	willet	wombat
voider	wallow	waylay	whilom	willow	wonder
volant	walnut	wayout	whilst	Wilton	wonted
volley	walrus	weaken	whimsy	wimble	wonton
volume	wamble	weakly	whiner	wimple	wooded
volute	wambly	wealth	whinge	wincey	wooden
volvox	wampee	weaner	whinny	winded	woodsy
voodoo	wampum	weapon	whippy	winder	woofer
vortex	wander	wearer	whirly	window	wooled
votary	wangle	weasel	whisht	wind up	woolly
voting	wanted	weaver	whisky	winery	worker
votive	wanton	webbed	whited	winged	wormer
voyage	wapiti	wedded	whiten	winger	worrit
voyeur	wapper	weeder	whites	winker	worsen
vulcan	warble	weekly	whitey	winkle	worthy
vulgar	warcry	weeper	wholly	winner	wortle
vulgus	warden	weepie	whomso	winnow	woundy
wabble	warder	weever	whoops	winsey	wowser
wadded	wardog	weevil	whoosh	winter	wraith
waddie	wargod	weight	whydah	wintle	wrap up
waddle	warily	weirdo	wicked	wintry	wrasse
waders	warmer	weirdy	wicker	wirily	wrathy
wafery	warmly	welder	wicket	wiring	wreath
waffle	warmth	welkin	widely	wisdom	wrench
wafter	warm up	welter	widget	wisely	wretch
wagged	warped	Wendic	widish	wisent	wright
waggle	warper	wester	wieldy	wisher	writer
waggly	warred	wether	wiener	withal	writhe
waggon	warren	wetted	wifely	wither	wyvern
Wahabi	warsle	wetter	wigeon	within	xylene
wailer	warted	whacky	wigged	withit	xylose
waiter	washer	whaler	wiggle	witted	yabber
waiver	wasted	whatso	wiggly	wivern	yaffle
walker	waster	wheeze	wigwag	wizard	Yahvey
walk in	waters	wheezy	wigwam	wizier	Yahweh
walk on	watery	whenas	wilder	wobble	yammer
wallah	wattle	whence	wildly	wobbly	Yankee
walled	waught	wherry	wilful	woeful	yaourt
waller	wavery	wheyey	wilily	woggle	yapock
wallet	wavily	whidah	willed	wolves	yapped

yapper	yenned	yolked	zapped	zillah	zombie
yarely	yeoman	yonder	zarape	zinced	zonary
yarrow	yes man	yoohoo	zareba	zincky	zonate
yatter	yester	yorker	zariba	zinnia	zoning
yaupon	yipped	Yoruba	zealot	zipped	zonked
yclept	yippee	yumyum	zenana	zipper	Zouave
yearly	yippie	zaffer	zenith	zircon	zounds
yeasty	yogism	zaffre	zephyr	zither	zygoma
yellow	yogurt	zander	zeugma	zlotys	zygote
yelper	yoicks	zanily	zigzag	zodiac	zymase

7 letter words

abalone	abysmal	acronym	adviser	airhole
abandon	abyssal	acroter	advisor	airless
abashed	academe	acrylic	aeolian	airlift
abattis	academy	actinia	aeonian	airline
abaxial	Acadian	actinic	aerator	airlock
Abbasid	acantha	actinon	aerobic	airmail
abdomen	acarian	actress	aerosol	airmiss
Abelian	accidie	actuary	afeared	airport
abetted	acclaim	actuate	affable	airpost
abetter	account	acutely	affably	airship
abettor	accrete	acyclic	affaire	airsick
abeyant	accrual	adamant	affined	airwave
abiding	accurst	Adamite	afflict	ajutage
abigail	accusal	adapter	affront	akvavit
ability	accused	adaptor	African	alameda
abiotic	accuser	adaxial	against	a la mode
a bit off	acerbic	addable	agamous	alanine
abjurer	acerola	addenda	ageless	alation
ablator	acerose	addible	agelong	albumen
abolish	acetate	address	aggress	albumin
abomasa	acetify	adducer	agilely	alcaide
aborter	acetone	adenine	agility	alcalde
abought	acetous	adenoid	agitate	alcayde
aboulia	Achaean	adenoma	agitato	alcazar
abrader	Achaian	adeptly	agnatic	alchemy
abreact	Achates	adherer	agnomen	alcohol
abreast	achieve	adipose	agonise	Alcoran
abridge	acicula	adjoint	agonist	alembic
abroach	acidify	adjourn	agraffe	alertly
abscess	acidity	adjudge	agrapha	aleuron
abscise	acinous	adjunct	aground	A levels
abscond	ack emma	admiral	aiblins	alewife
absence	acolyte	admirer	aileron	alfalfa
absinth	aconite	adopter	ailment	algebra
absolve	acquest	adrenal	aimless	alidade
abstain	acquire	adulate	aircrew	alienly
abubble	acrasin	adultly	airdrop	aliform
abusive	acreage	advance	airfare	aliment
abutted	acridly	adverse	airflow	alimony
abutter	acrobat	advised	airglow	aliquot

alkalis	amatory	Ananias	annulet	aplasia
alkanet	amazing	anarchy	annulus	aplenty
Alkoran	ambient	anatase	anodise	apocope
all ears	amender	anatomy	anodyne	apodous
alleged	amenity	anchovy	anomaly	apogamy
allegro	amentia	ancient	anosmia	apogean
allelic	amentum	ancones	anosmic	apology
allergy	Amerind	ancress	another	apolune
allheal	Amharic	andante	antacid	apostil
allonge	amiable	andiron	ant bear	apostle
all over	amiably	android	antefix	apothem
allseed	ammeter	anemone	antenna	apparat
allstar	ammonal	aneroid	ant hill	apparel
alltime	ammonia	aneurin	anthrax	appease
alluvia	amnesia	angelic	antigen	applaud
almanac	amnesic	angelus	antilog	applied
almirah	amnesty	Angevin	antique	applier
almoner	amoebae	anginal	ant lion	appoint
almonry	amoebas	angioma	antonym	apprise
almsman	amoebic	Anglian	anurous	approve
alodial	amongst	anglice	anxiety	apraxia
alodium	amorist	angling	anxious	apricot
aloetic	amorous	Anglist	anybody	apropos
aloofly	amphora	angrily	anymore	apsidal
alphorn	amplify	anguine	anyroad	apsides
already	ampoule	anguish	anytime	apteryx
alright	ampulla	angular	anyways	aptness
also ran	amputee	aniline	anywise	aquaria
althaea	amusive	anility	apagoge	aquatic
alumina	amylase	animate	apanage	aquavit
alumnae	amyloid	animism	apatite	aqueous
alumnus	amylose	animist	aphasia	aquifer
alunite	anaemia	anionic	aphasic	aquiver
alveoli	anaemic	aniseed	aphelia	Arabian
alyssum	anagoge	annates	aphides	arabise
amalgam	anagogy	annatta	aphonia	Arabist
amanita	anagram	annatto	aphonic	Aramaic
amarant	analogy	annelid	aphotic	araneid
amateur	analyse	annuity	aphylly	Arapaho
amative	analyst	annular	apishly	arbiter

arbutus	arsenal	astride	auroral	babbler
arcaded	arsenic	asunder	auroras	babyish
arcadia	article	as usual	auspice	babysit
arcanum	artisan	at a loss	austere	baccara
archery	artiste	ataraxy	austral	baccate
archive	artless	atavism	autarky	bacchic
archway	artwork	atavist	autobus	bacilli
arc lamp	as a rule	atelier	autocar	backing
arctoid	ascarid	at fault	autocue	backlog
arcuate	ascaris	atheism	autopsy	back off
arcweld	ascesis	atheist	auxesis	backsaw
ardency	ascetic	athirst	auxetic	backset
arduous	ascidia	athlete	avarice	baddish
areally	ascribe	athwart	avenger	bad form
areaway	asepsis	atingle	average	badmash
areolae	aseptic	atomise	averred	badness
areolar	asexual	atomism	Avestan	bad news
areolas	ashamed	atomist	Avestic	baffler
aridity	ashtray	atresia	aviator	bagasse
arietta	Asiatic	atrophy	avidity	baggage
aristae	asinine	attaboy	avionic	baggily
aristas	askance	attache	avocado	bagging
armband	asocial	attaint	awarder	bagpipe
armfuls	asperse	attempt	aweless	Bahadur
armhole	asphalt	attract	awesome	Bahaism
armiger	aspirer	attrite	awfully	Bahaist
armless	aspirin	auction	awkward	Bahaite
armlike	asquint	audible	awnless	bailiff
armoire	assagai	audient	axially	baklava
Armoric	assault	auditor	axillae	balance
armoury	assayer	augment	axillar	balcony
armrest	assegai	augural	axolotl	balding
armsful	assizes	aurally	Azilean	baldish
arousal	assuage	aureate	azimuth	baldric
arraign	assured	aurelia	azurine	baleful
arrange	assurer	aureola	azurite	ballade
arrayer	astable	aureole	azygous	ballast
arrears	astatic	auricle	Baalism	ballboy
arrival	asteria	aurochs	babassu	balloon
arriver	astound	aurorae	babbitt	balmily

baloney	bascule	becloud	bellman	betoken
bambini	baseman	bedding	bellows	betroth
bambino	basenji	bedevil	beloved	betting
banally	bashful	bedfast	Beltane	between
bananas	basidia	bedight	belting	betwixt
bandage	basilar	bedizen	belying	bewitch
bandana	basinet	bedouin	bencher	bezique
bandbox	bassist	bedpost	beneath	bheesty
bandeau	bassoon	bedrock	benefic	bheetie
bandore	bastard	bedroll	benefit	Biafran
bandsaw	basting	bedroom	Benelux	biassed
baneful	bastion	bedside	Bengali	biaxial
banjoes	bateaux	bedsock	benison	bibbery
banking	bath bun	bedsore	benthic	bibbing
banksia	bathing	bedtime	benthos	bibcock
banning	bathtub	bee balm	benzene	bibelot
bannock	batiste	beechen	benzine	biblist
banquet	batsman	beehive	benzoic	bicycle
banshee	battels	beeline	benzoin	bidding
banteng	battery	beeswax	benzole	biennia
banting	batting	beggary	benzoyl	bifocal
baptise	Bauhaus	begging	bepaint	big deal
baptism	bauxite	begonia	bequest	biggest
baptist	bawcock	begorra	bereave	biggish
barbate	bawdily	begrime	berried	bighead
barbell	bay leaf	beguile	berserk	bighorn
barbule	bayonet	beguine	beseech	bigname
bargain	bay tree	behaver	beshrew	bigness
barilla	bazooka	behoove	besides	bigoted
barline	beading	beignet	besiege	bigotry
barmaid	beamish	bejewel	besmear	big time
barn owl	beanbag	beknown	bespeak	bilboes
baronet	bearded	belated	bespoke	biliary
baroque	bearing	belcher	bestead	bilious
barrack	bearish	beldame	bestial	billing
barrage	beastly	Belgian	best man	billion
barring	beatify	believe	bestrew	billowy
barroom	beating	bellboy	betaken	bilobar
barytes	beatnik	bellhop	bethink	bilobed
barytic	because	belljar	betimes	biltong

bimanal	blather	bluntly	bookend	bounden
bindery	blatter	blurred	bookful	bounder
binding	bleakly	blusher	booking	bouquet
biology	bleater	bluster	bookish	bourbon
biomass	bleeder	boarder	booklet	bourdon
bionics	bleeper	boarish	bookman	bourree
biotite	blemish	boaster	booksie	bowhead
bipedal	blender	boating	Boolean	bow legs
biplane	blesbok	boatman	boomlet	bowlful
bipolar	blessed	bobbery	boorish	bowline
birchen	blether	bobbing	booster	bowling
birddog	blewits	bobbish	bootleg	bowshot
birdman	blighty	bobeche	booze up	boxcalf
biretta	blinder	bobsled	boozily	box file
biriani	blindly	bobstay	bopping	boxhaul
biscuit	blinker	bobtail	boracic	boxkite
bismuth	blintze	bodeful	borazon	boxlike
bistort	blister	bogbean	bordure	boxroom
bistred	blither	boggler	boredom	boxseat
bit part	bloated	bogyman	borings	boxwood
bittern	bloater	bohemia	bornite	boycott
bitters	blocker	boiling	borough	boyhood
bitting	blooded	boletus	borscht	brabble
bittock	blossom	bolivar	borstal	bracing
bitumen	blotchy	bollard	bortsch	bracken
bivalve	blotted	bologna	boscage	bracket
bivouac	blotter	boloney	boskage	bradawl
bizarre	blouson	bolshie	bossism	bragged
blabbed	blowdry	bolster	Boswell	bragger
blabber	blowfly	bombard	botanic	Brahman
blacken	blowgun	bombast	botcher	Brahmin
blackly	blowout	bonanza	bottega	braille
bladder	blowzed	bondage	bottled	bramble
blandly	blubber	bondman	bottony	brambly
blanket	blueing	bone dry	botulin	branchy
blankly	blue sky	bonfire	bouchee	brander
blarney	bluffer	bongoes	boudoir	bransle
blasted	bluffly	bonkers	boulder	brantle
blaster	blunder	bonnily	boulter	brantub
blatant	blunger	boobook	bouncer	brashly

brassie	briquet	buckram	bunting	by and by
brattle	brisker	bucksaw	buoyage	byebyes
braunch	brisket	bucolic	buoyant	bygones
bravado	briskly	budding	burbler	Byronic
bravely	bristle	buffoon	burdock	by turns
bravery	bristly	bugaboo	bureaus	by way of
bravura	British	bugbane	bureaux	bywoner
brawler	brittle	bugbear	burette	cabaret
brazier	brittly	bugeyed	burgage	cabbage
breaded	broaden	bugging	burgeon	cabbagy
breadth	broadly	bugloss	burgess	cabbala
breaker	brocade	builded	burghal	cabinet
breakin	brocket	builder	burgher	cabling
breakup	broider	buildup	burglar	caboose
breathe	broiler	built in	Burmese	cabrank
breathy	brokage	built up	burning	cacanny
breccia	broking	bulbous	burnish	cachexy
breeder	bromate	bulimia	burnous	cacique
brevier	bromide	bulkily	bursary	cackler
brevity	bromine	bullace	burster	cacodyl
brewage	bromism	bullary	burthen	cacoepy
brewery	bronchi	bullate	burweed	cacumen
bribery	broncho	bullbat	bushido	cadaver
brickie	brooder	bulldog	bushman	caddice
brickle	brothel	bullion	bushtit	caddish
bricole	brother	bullish	busking	cadence
bridoon	brought	bullock	bussing	cadency
briefly	brownie	bullpen	bus stop	cadenza
brigade	browser	bulrush	bustard	Cadmean
brigand	bruhaha	bulwark	bustler	cadmium
brimful	bruiser	bumbler	butcher	caducei
brimmed	brumous	bumboat	buttend	caesium
brimmer	brusher	bummalo	buttery	caesura
brinded	brusque	bumming	buttock	cagoule
brindle	brutish	bumpily	buttons	cahoots
bringer	bruxism	bumpkin	buttony	caimans
bring in	Brython	bump off	butyric	caisson
bring up	bubonic	bungler	buyable	caitiff
brinjal	buckeye	bunk bed	buzzard	cajoler
brioche	buckler	bunraku	buzzsaw	cake tin

calamus	camelot	capital	carnage	catboat
calando	camelry	capitol	caroche	catcall
calcify	came off	caporal	carotid	catcher
calcine	came out	capping	carotin	catchup
calcite	cameral	caprice	carouse	catechu
calcium	camorra	caprine	car park	catenae
calculi	campbed	caprioc	carping	catenas
caldera	camphor	Capsian	carport	cateran
caldron	camping	capsize	carrack	caterer
calends	campion	capstan	carrier	catfish
calibre	camp out	capsule	carrion	Cathari
calices	camwood	captain	carroty	Cathars
caliche	canakin	caption	carryon	cathead
calicle	canasta	captive	carsick	cathode
calipee	candela	capture	cartage	cathood
caliper	candent	caracal	cartful	catlike
callant	candied	caracul	cartoon	catling
callbox	candour	caramel	carving	catmint
callboy	canikin	caravan	cascade	catseye
calling	cannery	caravel	cascara	catspaw
callous	cannily	caraway	caseous	catsuit
calomel	canning	carbide	caserne	cattalo
caloric	cannula	carbine	cash box	cattery
calorie	canonic	car bomb	cashier	cattily
calotte	canonry	carcase	cassata	catwalk
caloyer	Canopic	carcass	cassava	caudate
calpack	cantata	cardiac	cassino	caulker
caltrap	cantate	cardoon	cassock	caustic
caltrop	canteen	careful	castile	cautery
calumet	canthus	caribou	casting	caution
calumny	cantina	carinae	castled	cavally
calvary	canting	carinas	castoff	cavalry
calyces	cantrip	carioca	casuals	caveman
calypso	canvass	cariole	casuist	cavetti
calyxes	canzone	carious	Catalan	cavetto
camaron	canzoni	carking	catalos	caviare
cambist	capable	Carlism	catalpa	cayenne
cambium	capably	Carlist	catarrh	caymans
cambrel	capelin	carload	catawba	cedilla
cambric	caperer	carmine	catbird	ceilidh

ceiling	champak	cheddar	chinwag	ciboria
celadon	chancel	cheerer	chipped	cichlid
celesta	chancre	cheerio	chipper	cidaris
celeste	changer	cheer up	chirrup	ciliary
cellist	channel	cheetah	chitter	ciliate
cellule	chanson	chelate	chlamys	cimices
Celsius	chanter	chemise	chloral	cindery
censure	chantry	chemism	chloric	cineast
centaur	chaotic	chemist	choc ice	cineole
centavo	chapati	chequer	Choctaw	cingula
centime	chaplet	cherish	cholera	Circean
central	chapman	cheroot	choline	circler
centred	chapped	chervil	chooser	circlet
centric	chappie	chessel	choosey	circuit
centrum	chapter	chested	chopine	circusy
century	charade	cheviot	chopped	cirrose
cepheid	charger	chevron	chopper	cirrous
ceramic	charily	Chianti	chorale	cistern
cerebra	chariot	chiasma	chordal	citable
ceresin	charism	chibouk	chorine	citadel
certain	charity	chicane	chorion	cithara
certify	charley	Chicano	choroid	cithern
cerumen	charlie	chicken	chowder	citizen
cervine	charmer	chicory	chrisom	citrate
cession	charnel	chidden	christy	citrine
cesspit	charpoy	chiefly	chromic	cittern
cestode	charqui	chiffon	chronic	civilly
cestoid	charred	chigger	chuckle	civvies
Chablis	charter	chignon	chuddah	clabber
chaffer	chassis	childer	chudder	clacker
chagrin	chasten	childly	chuffed	cladode
chalaza	chateau	chiliad	chugged	claimer
Chaldee	chatted	chillum	chukker	clamant
chalice	chattel	chimera	chummed	clamber
challis	chatter	chimere	chunnel	clammed
chalone	cheapen	chimney	chunter	clamour
chamber	cheaply	chindit	chupati	clanger
chamfer	cheater	Chinese	churchy	clapped
chamois	checker	Chinook	chutney	clapper
champac	checkup	chintzy	chymous	clarify

clarion	clotted	coffers	comfort	concert
clarity	cloture	cogency	comfrey	conchae
clarkia	clubbed	cogging	comical	concise
classes	clubman	cognate	comitia	concoct
classic	clumber	cognise	command	concord
classis	Cluniac	cohabit	commend	concuss
clastic	clupeid	coherer	comment	condemn
clatter	cluster	coinage	commode	condign
clausal	clutter	coinbox	commons	condole
clavate	coacher	coition	commune	condone
clavier	coagula	coldish	commute	conduce
claypan	coal tit	cole tit	compact	conduct
cleaner	coaming	colicky	company	conduit
cleanly	coarsen	colitis	compare	condyle
cleanse	coastal	collage	compart	confect
cleanup	coaster	collard	compass	confess
clearly	coating	collate	compend	confide
cleaver	coaxial	collect	compere	confine
clement	cobbler	colleen	compete	confirm
clerisy	cocaine	college	compile	conflux
clerkly	coccoid	collide	complex	conform
clicker	cochlea	collier	complin	confuse
climate	cockade	collins	complot	confute
climber	cockeye	colloid	compony	congeal
clinker	cockily	collude	comport	congest
clipped	cockney	colobus	compose	conical
clipper	cockpit	cologne	compost	conidia
clippie	cockshy	colonel	compote	conifer
cliquey	coconut	colonic	compute	coniine
clivers	cocotte	colossi	comrade	conjoin
cloacae	codable	colours	Comtian	conjure
cloacal	coddler	coloury	Comtism	conkers
clobber	codeine	coltish	Comtist	connate
clocker	codfish	combine	concave	connect
clogged	codices	combout	conceal	conning
clogger	codicil	combust	concede	connive
closely	codling	comedic	conceit	connote
closeup	coeliac	come off	concent	conquer
closure	cocqual	come out	concept	consent
clothes	coexist	cometic	concern	consign

consist	cordage	cosmist	cowhand	crenate
console	cordate	cossack	cowheel	crested
consort	cordial	costard	cowherd	crevice
consult	cordite	costate	cowhide	cribbed
consume	cordoba	costean	cowlick	cribble
contact	corella	costing	cowling	cricket
contain	corkage	costive	cowpoke	cricoid
contemn	corking	costrel	cowshed	crimine
contend	cornage	costume	cowslip	crimper
content	corncob	coterie	coxcomb	crimple
contest	corneal	cotidal	coyness	crimson
context	cornett	cottage	cozener	cringer
contort	cornfed	cottier	crabbed	cringle
contour	cornice	cottony	cracked	crinite
control	cornily	Coueism	cracker	crinkle
contuse	Cornish	couldst	crackle	crinkly
convect	cornist	couloir	crackly	crinoid
convene	cornual	coulomb	crackup	criollo
convent	cornuto	coulter	cragged	cripple
convert	corolla	council	crammed	crisper
convict	coronae	counsel	crammer	crisply
convoke	coronal	counter	crampet	cristae
cookery	coronas	country	crampit	croaker
cooking	coroner	coupler	crampon	crochet
cookout	coronet	couplet	cranage	crocket
coolant	corpora	courage	cranial	Croesus
coolish	correct	courier	cranium	crofter
cool off	corrida	courlan	crankle	crooked
copepod	corrode	courser	crappie	crooner
copilot	corrody	courtly	crassly	cropped
copious	corrupt	couthie	craunch	cropper
coppery	corsage	couture	craving	croquet
coppice	corsair	couvade	crawler	crosier
copular	corslet	couvert	crazily	crossly
copycat	cortege	coverup	creamer	crouton
copyist	cortile	cowbane	creator	crowbar
coquito	corvina	cowbell	credent	crowdie
coracle	corvine	cowbird	creedal	crowned
coranto	corydon	cowfish	creeper	crowner
corbeil	cosmism	cowhage	cremate	crozier

crucial	cullion	curtana	Dadaism	deadeye
crucian	culotte	curtsey	Dadaist	dead men
crucify	culprit	curvate	dallier	deadpan
crudely	cultism	cushion	damming	deafaid
crudity	cultist	cuspate	damnify	dealing
cruelly	culture	custard	damning	deanery
cruelty	culvert	custody	damosel	deathly
cruiser	cumquat	customs	damozel	debacle
cruller	cumshaw	cutaway	dampish	debater
crumble	cumulus	cutback	dandify	debauch
crumbly	cuneate	cuticle	Danelaw	debouch
crumpet	cunette	cutlass	dangler	Debrett
crumple	cunning	cutlery	danseur	debrief
crunchy	cupcake	cutline	Dantean	decadal
crupper	cupmoss	cutrate	dapsone	decagon
crusade	cupping	cutting	darbies	decanal
crusado	cuprite	cutworm	dariole	decapod
crusher	cuprous	cuvette	darkish	decease
crustal	cupsful	cyanide	darling	deceive
crusted	cupular	cyanine	darning	decency
crybaby	curable	cyclist	dashiki	decibel
cryogen	curacao	cycloid	dashing	decided
cryptal	curacoa	cyclone	dashpot	decider
cryptic	curator	cyclops	dastard	decidua
crystal	curcuma	cymbalo	dasyure	decimal
cry wolf	cureall	cynical	datable	decking
csardas	curette	cypress	datival	declaim
ctenoid	curiosa	Cyprian	dauphin	declare
cubbing	curious	Cypriot	dawdler	declass
cubhood	curling	cypsela	dawning	decline
cubical	currach	cystine	daybook	decoder
cubicle	curragh	cystoid	daylong	decorum
cubital	currant	czardas	dayroom	decrier
cuckold	current	czardom	daystar	decrypt
cudbear	currier	czarina	daytime	decuple
cudweed	currish	czarism	day trip	deep end
cuirass	cursive	czarist	daywork	deepfry
cuisine	cursory	dabbing	dazedly	deepsea
cuittle	curtail	dabbler	dazzier	default
culices	curtain	dacoity	deadend	defence

defiant	densely	devalue	dignify	discant
deficit	density	develop	dignity	discard
defiler	dentate	deviant	digraph	discern
definer	dentine	deviate	digress	discerp
deflect	dentist	devilry	dilated	discoid
defocus	denture	devious	dilator	discord
deforce	deodand	devisal	dilemma	discuss
defraud	deodara	devisee	diluent	disdain
defrock	deplane	deviser	dilutee	disease
defrost	deplete	devisor	diluter	diseuse
defunct	deplore	devolve	dilutor	disfame
degauss	deplume	devoted	dimeric	disgust
degrade	deposal	devotee	dimeter	dishorn
dehisce	deposit	dewclaw	dimmest	disjoin
deicide	deprave	dewdrop	dimming	dislike
deictic	depress	dewfall	dimmish	dislimn
deiform	deprive	dewpond	dimness	dismast
deistic	derange	dextral	dinette	dismiss
delaine	derider	dextran	dingily	disobey
delator	derrick	dextrin	dingoes	dispark
delayer	dervish	diabase	dinning	dispart
delight	descant	diabolo	diocese	display
Delilah	descend	diagram	diopter	disport
delimit	descent	dialect	dioptre	dispose
deliver	deserve	dialled	diorama	dispute
delouse	despair	dialyse	diorism	disrank
Delphic	despise	diamond	diorite	disrate
deltaic	despite	diarchy	dioxide	disrobe
deltoid	despoil	diarise	diploid	disroot
deluder	despond	diarist	diploma	disrupt
demerit	dessert	dibbing	dipolar	dissave
demesne	destine	dickens	dipping	disseat
demigod	destiny	dictate	diptera	dissect
demirep	destroy	diction	diptych	dissent
demoded	deterge	diddler	direful	distaff
demonic	detinue	diehard	dirtily	distain
demotic	detract	dietary	disable	distant
demount	detrain	diffuse	disavow	distend
denarii	detrude	digging	disband	distent
denizen	deutzia	digital	disbark	distich

distill	dollish	draftee	drosera	dulcify
distort	dolphin	drafter	droshky	dullard
disturb	doltish	dragged	drought	dullish
ditcher	domical	draggle	drouthy	dulness
dithery	dominie	dragnet	droving	dumpish
dittany	donator	dragoon	drubbed	dunbird
diurnal	Don Juan	drainer	drudger	dungeon
diverge	donning	drapery	drugged	Dunkirk
diverse	donnish	drastic	drugget	dunnage
divider	doodler	dratted	druidic	dunning
diviner	doomful	draught	drumlin	dunnock
divisor	doorman	drawbar	drummed	duodena
divorce	doormat	drawing	drummer	duopoly
divulge	doorway	drawler	drunken	dupable
dizzard	Dorking	drayage	dry cell	durable
dizzily	dormant	drayman	dry dock	durably
djibbah	dormice	dreamed	dry eyed	duramen
docetic	dornick	dreamer	dry land	durance
dockage	dortour	dredger	dryness	duskily
dockise	dossier	dresser	drysalt	dustbin
doddard	dotting	dribble	dryshod	dustily
doddery	doubler	driblet	dualise	dustman
dodgems	doubles	dried up	dualism	dustpan
dodgery	doublet	drifter	dualist	duteous
doeskin	doubter	driller	duality	dutiful
dogbane	doucely	drinker	dubbing	duumvir
dogdays	douceur	drink up	dubiety	dwarves
dogfish	doughty	drip dry	dubious	dweller
doggery	dovecot	dripped	ducally	dwindle
dogging	dovekie	drive in	duchess	dyarchy
doggish	dowager	driving	ducking	dyewood
doggone	dowdily	drizzle	duckpin	dynamic
dogrose	downbow	drizzly	ductile	dynasty
dogshow	doyenne	drogher	ducting	eagerly
dogskin	dozenth	dromond	dudgeon	earache
dogstar	drabber	droplet	due east	eardrop
dogtrot	drabbet	drop off	duelled	eardrum
dogvane	drabble	dropout	dueller	earflap
dogwood	drabler	dropped	due west	earhole
doleful	drachma	dropper	dukedom	earldom

earlobe	effendi	elusory	empress	engross
earlock	effulge	elution	emptier	enhance
earmark	egality	eluvial	emptily	enlarge
earmuff	egg cosy	eluvium	emption	enliven
earnest	egg flip	elysian	emulate	ennoble
earplug	egghead	Elysium	emulous	enounce
earring	egotise	elytron	enactor	enplane
earshot	egotism	elytrum	enamour	enprint
earthen	egotist	Elzevir	enation	enquire
earthly	ego trip	emanate	enchain	enquiry
easeful	eidetic	embargo	enchant	enslave
eastern	einkorn	embassy	enchase	ensnare
easting	eirenic	emblaze	enclasp	ensnarl
eatable	ekistic	embolic	enclave	entasis
ebb tide	elastic	embolus	enclose	entente
ebonise	elation	embosom	encoder	enteral
ebonite	elderly	embowed	encomia	enteric
eccrine	Eleatic	embowel	Encraty	enteron
ecdyses	elector	embower	encrust	enthral
ecdysis	electro	embrace	endemic	enthuse
echelon	elegant	embroil	endless	entitle
echidna	elegiac	embrown	endlong	entotic
echinus	elegise	embryon	endmost	entozoa
echoism	elegist	emerald	endogen	entrain
eclipse	element	emeriti	endorse	entrant
eclogue	elenchi	emersed	endways	entreat
ecology	elevate	eminent	endwise	entropy
economy	elevens	emirate	enemata	entrust
ecstasy	elfbolt	emitted	energid	entwine
ectopic	elfland	emitter	enfeoff	entwist
edacity	elflock	emotion	enfiled	envelop
edaphic	elision	emotive	enforce	envenom
edictal	elitism	empanel	enframe	envious
edifice	elitist	empathy	engaged	environ
edition	ellipse	emperor	English	enwound
educate	elm tree	empiric	engorge	enzymic
eductor	Elohism	emplace	engraft	eparchy
eelpout	Elohist	emplane	engrail	epaulet
eelworm	elusion	emporia	engrain	epergne
effects	elusive	empower	engrave	ephedra

epicene	erotism	evacuee	expiate	fabliau
epicure	errancy	evangel	explain	fabular
epidote	erratic	evanish	explant	faceoff
epigeal	erratum	evasion	explode	faceted
epigean	erudite	evasive	exploit	faction
epigone	escapee	evening	explore	factory
epigram	escaper	evictor	exposal	factual
epilate	escheat	evident	exposed	facture
episode	escolar	evolute	exposer	faculae
epistle	escribe	ewe lamb	exposit	faculty
epitaph	esotery	ewe neck	expound	faddish
epitaxy	esparto	exactly	express	faddism
epithem	espouse	exactor	expulse	faddist
epithet	esquire	examine	expunge	fadedly
epitome	essayer	example	exscind	fadeout
epizoic	essence	exarate	externe	fagging
epochal	essoyne	excerpt	extinct	fagotto
eponymy	estrade	excited	extract	faience
epoxide	estreat	exciter	extreme	failing
epsilon	etaerio	exciton	extrude	failure
equable	etamine	excitor	exudate	faintly
equably	etching	exclaim	exurban	fairing
equally	eternal	exclave	exurbia	fairish
equator	etesian	exclude	exuviae	fairway
equerry	ethanol	excrete	exuvial	Falange
equinal	etheric	excurse	eyeball	falcate
equinox	ethical	excusal	eyebath	fallacy
erasure	ethiops	execute	eyebolt	fallguy
erectly	ethmoid	exedrae	eyebrow	falling
erector	Etonian	exegete	eyedrop	falloff
erelong	euclase	exempla	eyehole	fallout
eremite	eucrite	exergue	eyelash	falsely
erepsin	eugenic	exhaust	eyeless	falsies
eristic	euglena	exhibit	eyelike	falsify
erlking	eulogia	exhumer	eyeshot	falsity
ermined	eupepsy	exigent	eyesore	famulus
erodent	euphony	exogamy	eyespot	fanatic
erosion	Euratom	exotica	eyewash	fancier
erosive	eustasy	expanse	eyewink	fancily
erotica	eutexia	expense	Faberge	fanclub

fanfare	faucial	fetidly	filbert	fitment
fanfold	faunist	fetlock	filemot	fitness
fanmail	fauvism	fetters	filiate	fittest
fanning	fauvist	feudist	filibeg	fitting
fantail	fearful	fewness	filings	fixable
fantasm	feaster	feyness	filling	fixedly
fantast	feather	fiancee	filmdom	fixings
fantasy	feature	fibbing	filmset	fixture
faraday	febrile	fibroid	finagle	flaccid
faradic	fedayee	fibroin	finally	flag day
faraway	federal	fibroma	finance	flagged
farceur	feeding	fibrous	finback	flagman
farcing	feedlot	fibster	finding	flaming
Far East	feeling	fibulae	fine leg	flaneur
fargone	feigner	fibular	finesse	flanker
farming	felonry	fibulas	finical	flannel
farmost	felsite	fictile	finicky	flapped
Faroese	felspar	fiction	finings	flapper
farrago	felting	fictive	finning	flareup
farrier	felucca	fiddler	Finnish	flasher
farruca	felwort	fideism	fir cone	flatcap
farther	feminal	fideist	firearm	flatcar
fascial	femoral	fidgets	firebox	flatlet
fascine	fencing	fidgety	firebug	flatout
Fascism	fenfire	fiefdom	firedog	flatten
Fascist	fenland	fielder	firefly	flatter
fashion	ferment	fierily	fireman	flattop
fastday	fermion	fifteen	firstly	flaught
fast one	fermium	fifthly	fir tree	flaunty
fatally	fernery	fifties	fishery	flavine
fateful	fernowl	figging	fisheye	flavour
fathead	ferrate	fighter	fishily	fleabag
fatigue	ferrety	fig leaf	fishing	fleapit
fatling	ferrite	figment	fishnet	flecker
fatness	ferrous	fig tree	fishway	fleeced
fattest	ferrule	figural	fissile	fleecer
fatting	fertile	figured	fission	fleeing
fattish	fervour	figwort	fissure	fleetly
fatuity	festive	filaria	fistful	Fleming
fatuous	festoon	filasse	fistula	Flemish

fleshed	fluting	foolery	forgoer	frameup
flesher	flutist	foolish	forgone	frankly
fleshly	flutter	footage	for good	frantic
fletton	fluvial	footboy	for hire	frapped
fleuret	fluxion	footing	forkful	fratery
fleuron	flyable	footman	fork out	fraught
flexile	flyaway	footpad	forlorn	frazzle
flexion	flyback	footrot	for luck	freaked
flexure	flybane	footsie	formant	freckle
flicker	flybelt	footway	formaté	freckly
flighty	flyblow	fopling	formula	freebie
flipped	flyboat	foppery	forsake	freedom
flipper	flybook	foppish	for sale	freeman
flitted	flyhalf	forager	forsook	freesia
flitter	flyleaf	foramen	forties	freeway
flivver	flyover	forayer	fortify	freezer
floater	flypast	forbade	Fortran	freight
floccus	flyting	forbear	fortune	Frenchy
flogged	flytrap	forbore	forward	frenula
floorer	fobbing	forceps	forwent	frescos
floosie	focused	fordone	forworn	freshen
floozie	fogbank	forearm	fossick	fresher
flopped	foggage	foreign	fouette	freshet
floreat	foggily	foreleg	foulard	freshly
florist	fogging	foreman	foumart	fretful
floruit	foghorn	forepaw	founder	fretsaw
flotage	foglamp	foreran	foundry	fretted
flotsam	fogydom	forerun	foveate	friable
flounce	fogyish	foresaw	foveola	friarly
flowage	fogyism	foresay	fowling	fribble
flowery	folding	foresee	foxhole	frigate
flubbed	foldout	foretop	foxhunt	frijole
fluence	foliage	forever	foxtail	fripper
fluency	foliate	forfeit	foxtrot	friseur
fluidal	foliole	forfend	fracted	Frisian
fluidic	foliose	for free	fraenum	frisker
fluidly	folkway	forgave	fragile	frisson
flummox	follies	forgery	frailly	fritted
flunkey	fondant	forging	frailty	fritter
fluster	fondler	forgive	Fraktur	frizzle

frizzly	furcate	Galahad	garpike	geneses
frogeye	fur coat	galanga	gascoal	genesis
frogged	furcula	galatea	gaseous	genetic
frogman	furioso	galeate	gasfire	genette
fronded	furious	galenic	gas leak	Genevan
frontal	furlong	galilee	gas mark	genista
front on	furmety	galipot	gas ring	genitor
frosted	furmity	gallant	gassing	genizah
froward	furnace	gallate	gastric	genning
frowsty	furnish	galleon	gateaux	Genoese
fructed	furrier	gallery	gateleg	genteel
fruited	furring	gallfly	gateway	gentian
fruiter	furrowy	galling	gathers	gentile
frustum	further	galliot	gatling	genuine
fuchsia	furtive	gallium	gaudery	geodesy
fuddler	fuscous	gallnut	gaudily	geogony
Fuehrer	fusible	galloon	Gaulish	geoidal
fuelled	fussily	gallows	gauntly	geology
fueller	fusspot	galumph	gauntry	Geordie
fugally	fustian	gambade	gavotte	georgic
fugging	fustily	gambado	gawkily	germane
fuguist	futhark	gambier	gayness	gestalt
fulcrum	futhorc	gambler	gazelle	gestapo
fulgent	futhork	gamboge	gazette	gestate
fullage	futtock	gambrel	gearbox	gesture
fullout	fuzzily	gamebag	gearing	get a job
fulmine	gabbing	gametic	geckoes	getaway
fulness	gabbler	ganglia	geebung	get even
fulsome	gabelle	gangrel	Gehenna	get over
fulvous	gabfest	gangway	gelatin	getting
fumbler	gabnash	gantlet	gelding	get well
funeral	gadding	garbage	gelidly	gharial
funfair	gadgety	garbler	gelling	ghastly
fungoid	gadroon	garboil	gemmate	gherkin
fungous	gadwall	gardant	gemmery	ghettos
funicle	gagging	garfish	gemming	ghillie
funnies	gagster	garland	gemmule	ghostly
funnily	gahnite	garment	gemsbok	giantry
funning	gainful	garnish	general	gibbous
furbish	gainsay	garotte	generic	giblets

giddily	glisten	godless	goulash	grating
gigging	glister	godlike	gourami	graunch
giggler	glitter	godling	gourmet	gravely
gilbert	globoid	godsend	goutfly	gravure
gilding	globose	godship	grabbed	grazier
gillnet	globule	godward	grabber	grazing
giltcup	glorify	go for it	grabble	greaser
gimbals	glossal	goggler	gracile	greaten
gimmick	Glossic	goggles	grackle	greatly
gingery	glottal	goitred	gradate	greaves
gingham	glottis	goldbug	gradely	Grecian
gingili	glozing	golfbag	gradine	grecise
ginning	glucose	golfing	gradual	Grecism
ginseng	glummer	goliard	grafter	greenly
giraffe	gluteal	Goliath	grained	greisen
girasol	gluteus	gombeen	grainer	gremlin
girdler	glutted	gomeral	gramary	grenade
girlish	glutton	gomeril	grammar	greyhen
gittern	glycine	gonadal	grampus	greyish
give out	glyphic	gondola	granary	greylag
gizzard	glyptal	gonidia	grandad	gribble
glacial	glyptic	goodbye	grandam	griddle
glacier	gnarled	goodday	grandee	griffin
gladded	gnathic	goodish	grandly	griffon
gladden	gnocchi	good job	grandma	grifter
gladder	gnomish	goodman	grandpa	grilled
glad eye	gnostic	gooiest	granger	griller
glaikit	go ahead	Gordian	granita	grimace
glamour	goat god	gorilla	granite	grimmer
glaring	goatish	gorsedd	grannie	grinder
glassen	gobbler	goshawk	grantee	grinned
glasses	Gobelin	gosling	granter	gripped
glazier	go below	gossipy	grantor	gripper
glazing	go by air	gossoon	granule	griskin
gleaner	goddamn	got a job	grapery	gristle
gleeful	goddess	got away	graphic	gristly
gleeman	godetia	got even	grapnel	gritted
glenoid	godevil	go to bed	grapple	grizzle
glimmer	godhead	go to sea	grasper	grizzly
glimpse	godhood	gouache	gratify	Grobian

grocery	Guignol	hacking	handoff	hashish
grogram	guilder	hackler	handout	hassock
Grolier	guisard	hackney	handsaw	hastate
grommet	gullery	hacksaw	handsel	hastily
groover	gumboil	haddock	handset	hatable
grossly	gumboot	hafnium	hands up	hatband
grottos	gumdrop	hagfish	hangdog	hatcher
grouchy	gumming	Haggada	hanging	hatchet
grouper	gummite	haggard	hangman	hateful
groupie	gumshoe	haggish	hangout	hatless
grouser	gum tree	haggler	Hansard	hatting
growler	gunboat	hagweed	hanuman	hauberk
grown up	gunfire	haircut	hapence	haughty
grubbed	gunlock	hairnet	hapenny	haulage
grubber	gunnera	hairpin	hapless	haulier
gruffly	gunnery	Halakah	haploid	haunted
grumble	gunning	halberd	haporth	haunter
grumbly	gunplay	halbert	happily	hautboy
grummet	gunroom	halcyon	happing	hauteur
grunion	gunship	halfway	harbour	have a go
grunter	gunshot	halfwit	hardhit	have fun
gruntle	gunwale	halibut	hardpan	havenot
grutten	gurnard	hallway	hardset	hawkish
gruyere	gushing	halogen	hardtop	haycock
gryphon	gustily	halting	hard won	hayfork
grysbok	gutless	halvers	harelip	hayloft
G string	gutsily	halyard	haricot	hayrick
guanaco	guttate	Hamburg	harijan	hayseed
guanine	gutting	Hamitic	harmala	haywire
guarana	guy rope	ham it up	harmful	headily
guarani	guzzler	hamming	harmony	heading
guarded	gwyniad	hammock	harness	headman
guardee	gymnast	hamster	harpist	head off
gubbins	gymslip	hamulus	harpoon	headpin
gudgeon	gypping	handbag	harrier	headset
Guelfic	habitat	handcar	harshen	headway
guerdon	habitue	handful	harshly	healthy
guereza	hachure	handgun	harslet	hearing
guesser	hackbut	handily	harvest	hearken
guichet	hackery	handler	hasbeen	hearsay

hearted	heretic	hip roof	Homerid	however
hearten	heritor	hipster	home win	howling
heathen	herniae	hirable	hominid	huanaco
heather	hernial	hircine	homonym	hueless
heating	hernias	hirsute	honesty	huffish
heavily	heroics	hirudin	honeyed	hugeous
Hebraic	heroine	histone	honours	hugging
heckler	heroise	history	hoodlum	hulking
hectare	heroism	hit back	hooklet	humanly
hedonic	heronry	hitcher	hopbind	humbles
heedful	herring	hitting	hopeful	humbuzz
heeltap	herself	Hittite	hophead	humdrum
heftily	hessian	hoarsen	hoplite	humeral
heighho	hetaera	hoatzin	hopping	humerus
heinous	hetaira	Hobbian	hopsack	humidly
heiress	hexadic	Hobbism	horizon	humidor
helical	hexagon	Hobbist	hormone	humming
helices	hexapod	hobbler	hornmad	hummock
helicon	heyduck	hobnail	horrent	humoral
hellbox	hiccupy	hockday	horrify	hundred
hellcat	hickory	hocused	horsily	hunkers
Hellene	hidalga	hoecake	hosanna	Hunnish
hellion	hidalgo	hoedown	hosiery	hunting
hellish	hideous	hogback	hospice	hurdler
helluva	hideout	hogfish	hostage	hurdles
helotry	higgler	hoggery	hostess	hurling
helpful	highboy	hogging	hostile	hurried
helping	highhat	hoggish	hostler	hurtful
hemiola	highman	hogwash	hotfoot	husband
hemline	highway	hogweed	hothead	hushaby
hemlock	hilding	holdall	hot line	huskily
hemming	hillman	holding	hot milk	husking
henbane	hillock	hold off	hotness	Hussite
hencoop	hilltop	holiday	hot seat	hustler
hennery	himself	holland	hotshot	hutment
henpeck	hindgut	holmium	hottest	hutting
heparin	hipbath	holm oak	hottish	hyaline
hepatic	hipbone	holster	housing	hydrant
heptane	hipness	homburg	howbeit	hydrate
herbage	hipping	Homeric	how come	hydrous

hygeian	ill fame	improve	indwelt	innards
hygiene	illicit	impulse	ineptly	innerve
hymenia	illness	in a daze	inertia	innings
hymnary	ill used	in aid of	inertly	in no way
hymnist	ill will	in a mess	inexact	inocula
hymnody	ill wind	inanely	infancy	in order
hyperon	imagery	inanity	infanta	inphase
hypnoid	imagine	inaptly	infante	inquest
hypoxia	imagism	in a rush	infarct	inquire
hypoxic	imagist	in a spin	infauna	inquiry
iceberg	imbiber	in a word	inferno	insecty
iceboat	imbower	inboard	infidel	inshore
icecold	imbrute	inbreed	infield	in short
ice cube	imitate	in brief	inflame	insider
icefall	immense	inbuilt	inflate	insight
icefloe	immerge	incense	inflect	insigne
icefoot	immerse	incipit	inflict	insipid
icepack	immoral	incised	in focus	insofar
icerink	impaint	incisor	infract	inspect
iceshow	impanel	inciter	ingenue	inspire
ichabod	impasse	incline	ingesta	install
iciness	impaste	inclose	ingoing	instant
icteric	impasto	include	ingraft	instate
icterus	impeach	incomer	ingrain	instead
ideally	impearl	incrust	ingrate	insular
identic	imperil	incubus	ingress	insulin
idiotic	impetus	incudes	ingroup	insured
idlesse	impiety	incurve	ingrown	insurer
idolise	impinge	incused	inhabit	inswing
idyllic	impious	indepth	inhaler	integer
igneous	implant	indexer	inherit	intense
igniter	implead	indices	inhibit	interim
ignoble	implete	inditer	inhouse	interne
ignobly	implode	indoors	inhuman	intoner
ignorer	implore	indorse	initial	in touch
ikebana	imposer	indraft	injurer	intrant
ileitis	impound	indrawn	inkhorn	intreat
ilkaday	impress	inducer	inkling	introit
illbred	imprest	indulge	inkwell	intrude
illegal	imprint	indwell	inlayer	intrust

intwine	issuant	jealous	Judaism	kenning
inutile	isthmus	jejunum	Judaist	kentish
invader	itacism	jellaba	judoist	keratin
invalid	Italian	jellied	jugging	kermess
inveigh	Italiot	jerkily	juggins	kerogen
inverse	iterant	jetting	juggler	kerygma
invitee	iterate	jewelry	jugular	kestrel
inviter	ivories	jewfish	juicily	ketchup
invoice	jabbing	Jezebel	jujitsu	keyhole
involve	jacamar	jibbing	jukebox	keyless
inwards	jacinth	jibboom	jumbuck	keynote
inweave	jackass	jibdoor	jumpjet	keyring
inwoven	jackdaw	jigging	jumpoff	keyword
Iranian	jackpot	jimjams	juncoes	khaddar
irately	jacktar	jingler	Jungian	khamsin
irideal	Jacobin	jitters	juniper	khanate
iridise	jacobus	jittery	Jupiter	khedive
iridium	jaconet	jobbery	jurally	kibbutz
Irishry	jadedly	jobbing	juryman	kickoff
irksome	jadeite	jocular	jussive	kidding
ironing	jaggery	jogging	justice	kiddish
ironist	Jainism	jogtrot	justify	kidskin
iron ore	jaloppy	joinder	jutting	killick
ischial	jamming	joinery	kabbala	killing
ischium	jam tart	joining	Kaddish	killjoy
Ishmael	Janeite	jointer	kainite	kilobar
Islamic	jangler	jointly	kalends	kiloton
Ismaili	janitor	jollify	Kalmuck	kinchin
isobath	jannock	jollity	kampong	kindler
isochor	January	jonquil	Kannada	kindred
isogamy	japonic	jotting	Kantian	kinesis
isogeny	jargoon	journal	Karaite	kinetic
isogram	jarring	journey	karakul	kinfolk
isohyet	jasmine	jouster	karting	kingcup
isolate	javelin	joyance	kathode	kingdom
isonomy	jawbone	joyless	katydid	kinglet
isotope	jaybird	joyride	keelson	kingpin
isotopy	jaywalk	jubilee	keeping	kinship
isotron	jazzily	Judaean	keep mum	kinsman
Israeli	jazzman	Judaise	keep out	Kirghiz

kissing	laconic	Laotian	lay flat	leisure
kitchen	lacquer	lapilli	lazaret	lemmata
kitschy	lactate	lapping	leading	lemming
klipdas	lacteal	Laputan	leadoff	lending
knacker	lactose	lapwing	leafage	lengthy
knapped	lacunae	larceny	leafbud	lenient
knapper	lacunal	lardoon	leaflet	lentigo
knavery	lacunar	largely	leaguer	lentoid
knavish	lacunas	largess	leakage	leonine
kneader	ladanum	largish	leaning	leopard
kneecap	ladybug	lasagna	learned	leotard
kneeler	ladykin	lasagne	learner	leprosy
kneepan	laggard	lashing	leather	leprous
kneesup	lagging	lash out	lechery	lesbian
knitted	laicise	lassoes	lectern	letdown
knitter	laicism	lasting	lection	let fall
knobbed	lairage	latakia	lecture	let slip
knobble	lakelet	latchet	lee side	letters
knobbly	Lallans	latency	leeward	letting
knocker	Lamaism	lateral	leftism	Lettish
knockon	Lamaist	latexes	leftist	lettuce
knotted	lambast	lathery	left out	leucine
knotter	lambent	lathing	legally	leucoma
knowall	lambert	latices	legatee	levator
knowhow	lambkin	latrine	legator	levelly
knowing	laminae	lattice	legbail	leveret
knuckle	laminar	Latvian	legging	lexical
knurled	lamming	laugher	leghorn	lexicon
kolkhoz	lampion	launder	legible	liaison
Koranic	lampoon	laundry	legibly	Liassic
koumiss	lamprey	laurels	legiron	liberal
kremlin	lancers	lavolta	legless	liberty
Krishna	landing	lawhand	legpull	library
krypton	languet	lawless	legrest	librate
kumquat	languid	lawlist	legroom	licence
Kurdish	languor	lawlord	legshow	license
kyanite	laniary	lawsuit	leg side	licitly
labella	lanolin	laxness	leg spin	licking
labiate	lantern	layered	legwork	lidless
lacking	lanyard	layette	leister	lieabed

lie back	lissome	longbow	L plates	lyrical
lie down	listing	longday	lubbard	macabre
lifeful	literal	longhop	lucarne	macadam
liftoff	lithely	longing	lucency	macaque
lighted	lithium	longish	lucerne	machair
lighten	litotes	lookout	lucidly	machete
lighter	littery	looksee	Lucifer	machine
lightly	liturgy	loosely	luckily	macrame
lignify	livable	lopping	Luddite	macrami
lignite	live oak	lording	luggage	maculae
likable	llanero	lorette	lugging	macular
lilting	loading	lorgnon	lughole	maddest
limbate	loaning	loricae	lugsail	madding
limbeck	loather	lorimer	lugworm	Madeira
lime pit	loathly	loriner	lullaby	madness
liminal	lobbing	losable	lumbago	madonna
limited	lobelia	lottery	lumenal	madrona
limiter	lobster	lotting	luminal	madrono
linctus	lobular	loudish	lumpily	madwort
lineage	lobworm	lounger	lumpish	maestri
lineate	locally	lousily	lump sum	maestro
lineman	locater	loutish	lunatic	maffick
lineout	lockage	louvred	luncher	mafiosi
lingual	lockjaw	lovable	lunette	mafioso
linkage	locknut	lovably	lunular	magenta
linkboy	lockout	love all	lupulin	maggoty
linkman	locular	loverly	lurcher	magical
Linnean	loculus	lowborn	lurdane	magmata
linocut	lodging	lowbred	luridly	magnate
linsang	loftily	lowbrow	lustful	magneto
linseed	logbook	lowdown	lustily	magnify
lioncel	log fire	lowland	lustral	mahaleb
lioness	logging	lowlily	lustrum	mahatma
lionise	logical	lowness	luteous	Mahdism
lipless	logline	lowrise	lychnis	Mahdist
lipping	logwood	low road	lychowl	mah jong
lipread	Lollard	low tide	lycopod	mahonia
liquate	Lombard	loyally	lyddite	mahound
liquefy	lomenta	loyalty	lying in	mahseer
liqueur	long ago	lozenge	lyingly	maidish

maidism	mandrel	marbled	masters	Mechlin
mailbag	mandril	marbles	mastery	meconic
mailbox	mangily	marcher	mastich	meddler
mailing	mangoes	marconi	mastiff	mediacy
maillot	mangold	margent	mastoid	mediant
mailman	manhole	marimba	matador	mediate
mailvan	manhood	mariner	matchet	medical
maintop	manhour	marital	matelot	medulla
majesty	manhunt	markhor	matinal	medusae
make off	manihot	marking	matinee	medusan
make out	manikin	marline	matrass	medusas
makings	manilla	marlite	mattery	meerkat
malacia	manille	marmite	matting	meeting
malaise	maniple	marplot	mattins	megaron
malaria	manitou	marquee	mattock	megaton
Malayan	manjack	marquis	mattoid	meiosis
malefic	mankind	Marrano	matzoth	meiotic
malines	manless	married	maudlin	Meissen
mallard	manlike	marring	maunder	melange
malleus	manmade	marrowy	mauther	melanic
malmsey	manners	Marsala	mawkish	melanin
maltase	manning	marshal	mawworm	melilot
Maltese	mannish	martial	maxilla	melisma
malting	mannite	Martian	maximal	melodic
maltose	mannose	martini	maximum	melting
mamelon	mansard	martlet	maxwell	memento
mamilla	mansion	martyry	mayoral	memoirs
mammary	mansize	Marxian	maypole	mending
mammate	manteau	Marxism	Maytime	menfolk
mammock	mantlet	marybud	mayweed	menisci
mammoth	mantram	mascara	mazurka	menorah
manacle	mantrap	mashtub	mazzard	menthol
manager	man week	Masonic	meadowy	mention
manakin	Manx cat	masonry	mealies	mercery
manatee	Manxman	Masorah	meander	merchet
manchet	man year	masquer	meaning	mercury
mandala	mapping	massage	measles	mermaid
mandate	marabou	masseur	measure	merrily
mandola	Maratha	massive	meatfly	meseems
mandora	Marathi	mastaba	meatman	mesonic

message	milksop	misdone	mobbish	moodily
messiah	milldam	miserly	mob rule	mooneye
Messias	million	misfire	mobster	moonlit
messily	milreis	misgave	mockery	moonset
mess tin	mimesis	misgive	modally	moorage
mestiza	mimetic	mishear	modesty	moorhen
mestizo	mimical	Mishnah	modicum	mooring
metazoa	mimicry	misknow	modiste	Moorish
methane	mimulus	mislaid	modular	moorlog
metonym	minaret	mislead	modulus	mopping
metopic	mincing	mislike	mofette	moraine
metrics	mindful	mismate	moidore	morally
metrist	mineral	misname	moisten	morassy
mettled	minever	misplay	moither	mordant
Mexican	miniate	misread	mollify	mordent
mezuzah	minibus	misrule	mollusc	moreish
miasmal	minicab	missend	molossi	morello
miasmic	minicar	missent	momenta	Moresco
micelle	minikin	missile	monacal	Morisco
microbe	minimal	missing	monadic	morning
midland	minimum	mission	monarch	morocco
midline	minimus	missish	mondial	moronic
midmost	miniver	missive	moneyed	morphia
midriff	minorca	misstep	moneyer	mortice
midship	minster	mistake	mongrel	mortify
midweek	mintage	mistful	moniker	mortise
Midwest	minuend	mistily	monitor	Moselle
midwife	minutes	mistime	monkery	mottled
midyear	minutia	misting	monkish	mouflon
mightst	Miocene	mistook	monocle	moulder
migrant	miracle	mistral	monocot	mounter
migrate	mirador	mitoses	monodic	Mountie
mildewy	mirkily	mitosis	monomer	mourner
mileage	miscall	mitotic	monsoon	mousaka
milfoil	miscast	mitzvah	monster	mousing
miliary	miscopy	mixedly	montage	mouther
militia	misdate	mixed up	montane	movable
milking	misdeal	mixture	montero	mowburn
milkleg	misdeed	Moabite	monthly	mow down
milkman	misdeem	mobbing	moocher	mozetta

mudbath	muttony	narrate	nephric	nightly
muddily	muzzily	narrows	Neptune	nigrify
muddler	muzzler	narthex	neritic	Nilotic
mudfish	myalgia	narwhal	nervate	nimiety
mudflat	myalgic	nasally	nervine	ninepin
mudlark	myalism	nascent	nervous	niobium
mudpack	mycelia	nastily	nervure	nippers
muezzin	mycoses	nattily	nest egg	nippily
muffler	mycosis	natural	nesting	nipping
mugging	mycotic	naughty	netball	nirvana
muggins	myeloid	nauplii	netfish	nitrate
mugwort	myeloma	nautics	net gain	nitride
mugwump	myiasis	nautili	netlike	nitrify
mulatto	mylodon	navarin	netsuke	nitrile
mullein	mynheer	Naziism	netting	nitrite
mullion	myogram	nearest	network	nitrous
mullock	myology	nebbish	neurine	Noachic
mumbler	myomata	nebulae	neuroma	nobbler
mummery	mystery	nebular	neurone	no claim
mummify	mystify	nebulas	neuston	noctuid
mumming	mythise	necklet	neutral	noctule
mumpish	mythist	necktie	neutron	nocturn
mundane	myxomas	necrose	newborn	nocuous
mundify	nabbing	nectary	newcome	nodally
munting	nacelle	needful	new deal	nodated
muntjac	nacrous	needler	newlaid	nodding
muntjak	nagging	neglect	new leaf	nodical
muriate	Nahuatl	neglige	new moon	no doubt
murkily	naiades	Negress	newmown	nodular
murrain	nailery	Negrito	newness	no entry
murther	naively	negroid	newsman	nogging
muscled	naivete	neither	new wave	noisily
musette	naivety	nemesia	new year	noisome
musical	nakedly	nemesis	nibbler	nomadic
muskrat	namable	Neogaea	niblick	nomarch
mustang	nameday	neolith	niceish	nombril
mustard	nankeen	neology	nictate	nominal
mutable	naphtha	neonate	niggard	nominee
mutably	napless	neoteny	niggler	nonagon
mutagen	napping	Neozoic	nightie	noniron

nonplus	numbles	obovate	offhand	onetime
nonskid	numeral	obscene	officer	ongoing
nonslip	numeric	obscure	offload	on guard
nonstop	nummary	observe	offpeak	on leave
nonsuch	nunatak	obtrude	offside	on offer
nonsuit	nunhood	obverse	oghamic	onshore
nonuser	nunnery	obviate	ogreish	onstage
noonday	nunnish	obvious	oilbath	on the go
nooning	nunship	ocarina	oilbird	on toast
norland	nuptial	occiput	oilcake	on trial
norther	nursery	occlude	oildrum	onwards
norward	nursing	oceanic	oil lamp	onymous
nosebag	nurture	ocellar	oilseed	oolitic
nosegay	nutcase	ocellus	oilskin	oomiack
noserag	nutgall	octagon	oilwell	oophyte
nostril	nutlike	octaval	old gold	oosperm
nostrum	nutpine	octette	old hand	oospore
notable	nutting	October	oldster	opacity
notably	nymphal	octopod	oldtime	opaline
notched	nymphet	octopus	olefine	open air
notedly	oakfern	octuple	O levels	open end
notelet	oakgall	oculate	olivary	opening
notepad	oakling	oculist	olivine	open sea
nothing	oak tree	odalisk	oloroso	operand
notitia	oakwood	oddball	Olympic	operate
noumena	oarfish	oddment	omentum	operose
nourish	oarless	oddness	omicron	ophitic
novella	oarlock	odontic	ominous	opinion
novelle	oarsman	odorant	omitted	opossum
novelty	oarweed	odorous	omneity	oppidan
nowhere	oatcake	odoured	omnibus	opposer
noxious	oatmeal	odyssey	omnific	oppress
nuclear	obelise	oedipal	onanism	opsonic
nucleic	obelisk	oersted	one eyed	opsonin
nuclein	obesity	oestral	oneiric	optical
nucleon	obitual	oestrum	oneness	optimal
nucleus	obligee	oestrus	onerous	optimum
nuclide	obligor	offbeat	oneself	opulent
nullify	oblique	off duty	oneshot	opuntia
nullity	obloquy	offence	one step	opuscle

oration	ouabain	outtalk	ovicide	palaver
oratory	ourself	outturn	oviduct	pale ale
oratrix	outback	outvote	oviform	palette
orbital	outcast	outward	ovoidal	palfrey
orchard	outcome	outwear	ovulate	palings
orderer	outcrop	outwent	own goal	pallium
orderly	outdone	outwore	oxalate	palmary
ordinal	outdoor	outwork	oxfence	palmate
orectic	outface	outworn	oxidant	palmist
oregano	outfall	ovarian	oxidate	palmoil
organic	outflow	ovation	oxidise	palmyra
organon	outfoot	overact	Oxonian	palpate
organum	outgone	overage	oxyacid	palsied
organza	outgrew	overall	oxytone	paludal
orifice	outgrow	overarm	ozonise	pampean
origami	outhaul	overate	pabulum	pampero
orogeny	outland	overawe	pachisi	panacea
orology	outlast	overbid	pacific	panache
orotund	outlier	overbuy	package	pancake
Orphean	outline	overdid	packice	Pandean
Orphism	outlive	overdue	packing	pandect
orphrey	outlook	overeat	packman	pandora
ortolan	outmost	overfed	padding	pandore
osculum	outpace	overfly	paddler	panicky
osmosis	outplay	overlap	paddock	panicle
osmotic	outport	overlay	padlock	Panjabi
osmunda	outpost	overlie	padrone	pannage
osselet	outrage	overman	padroni	pannier
osseous	outrank	overpay	paeonic	panning
osseter	outride	overran	pageant	panocha
ossicle	outrode	overrun	pageboy	panoply
ossific	outrush	oversaw	paginal	panther
ossuary	outsell	oversea	Pahlavi	panties
osteoid	outshot	oversee	pailful	pantile
ostiary	outside	overset	painful	papadam
ostiole	outsize	oversew	painter	papally
ostrich	outsold	overtax	paisley	paperer
otolith	outsole	overtly	pajamas	Paphian
otology	outstay	overtop	paladin	papilla
ottoman	outtake	overuse	palatal	papoose

pappose	passant	peckish	peptide	pessary
paprika	passing	peddler	peptise	petasus
papulae	passion	pedicab	peptone	petiole
papular	passive	pedicel	percale	petrify
papyrus	passkey	pedicle	percent	Petrine
parable	pastern	pedlary	percept	petrous
parader	pasteup	peerage	percher	pet shop
paradox	pastime	peeress	percine	pettily
paragon	pasture	peevish	percoid	petting
parapet	patagia	Pegasus	percuss	pettish
parasol	patella	pegging	perdure	petunia
parboil	patency	pelagic	perfect	pfennig
pardner	pathway	pelican	perfidy	phaeton
parerga	patient	pelisse	perform	phalanx
paresis	patrial	peltate	perfume	phallic
paretic	patriot	pelting	perfuse	phallus
parfait	patroon	pemican	pergola	phantom
parkway	pattern	penally	perhaps	pharaoh
parlour	patting	penalty	peridot	pharynx
parlous	paucity	penance	perigee	phasmid
parodic	Pauline	pendant	perique	phellem
parolee	paunchy	pendent	periwig	philter
paronym	paviour	pending	perjure	philtre
parotid	payable	penguin	perjury	phlegmy
parquet	paydesk	pen name	perkily	phoenix
parsley	payload	pennant	perlite	phonate
parsnip	payment	pennate	Permian	phoneme
partake	pay rise	pennies	permute	phonics
partial	payroll	pennine	perpend	phonily
parting	paysage	pensile	perpent	photism
partita	peacock	pension	perplex	phrasal
partite	peafowl	pensive	Persian	phratry
partlet	pearled	pentane	persist	phrenic
partner	pearler	pentode	persona	phrensy
partook	peasant	pentose	pertain	physics
parvenu	peascod	peonage	perturb	piaffer
paschal	pea soup	peppery	perusal	pianism
passade	peat bog	pep pill	peruser	pianist
passado	peccant	pepping	pervade	piastre
passage	peccary	peptalk	pervert	pibroch

picador	pillowy	piscary	plastid	plugged
piccolo	pillule	piscina	platane	plugger
piceous	pilsner	piscine	plateau	plumage
pickaxe	pilular	pismire	platina	plumate
pickeer	pimento	pissoir	plating	plumber
pickled	pimping	pistole	platoon	plumbic
picotee	pinball	pitapat	platted	plumbob
picquet	pincers	pitched	platter	plumery
picrate	pincher	pitcher	plaudit	plummet
Pictish	pinetum	piteous	play act	plumose
picture	pinfire	pitfall	playboy	plumper
piddock	pinfish	pithead	playful	plumply
pidgeon	pinfold	pithhat	playing	plumule
piebald	pinguid	pithily	playlet	plunder
pieeyed	pinhead	pitiful	playoff	plunger
pierrot	pin high	pit pony	playpen	plunker
pietism	pinhole	pitprop	pleader	plusage
pietist	pinkeye	pit stop	pleased	plushly
piffler	pink gin	pitting	plectra	pluvial
piggery	pinking	pivotal	pledgee	plywood
pigging	pinkish	pivoter	pledger	poacher
piggish	pinnace	placard	pledget	pochard
pigiron	pinnate	placate	pledgor	podagra
piglead	pinning	placebo	plenary	podding
pigling	pinnule	placket	plenish	podesta
pigment	pintado	placoid	pleurae	poetess
pigs ear	pintail	plaided	pleural	poetics
pigskin	pintuck	plainly	pleuron	poetise
pigtail	pinworm	planish	pliable	pofaced
pigwash	pioneer	planned	pliably	poinder
pigweed	piously	planner	pliancy	pointed
pikelet	pipeful	plantar	plicate	pointer
pikeman	piperic	planter	plodded	polacca
pileate	pipette	planula	plodder	polacre
pilgrim	pipping	planxty	plopped	poleaxe
pillage	piquant	plasmic	plosion	polecat
pillbox	piragua	plasmid	plosive	polemic
pillion	piranha	plasmin	plotted	polenta
pillock	piratic	plaster	plotter	politic
pillory	pirogue	plastic	plucker	pollack

pollard	portray	praiser	press up	produce
pollock	poseuse	Prakrit	presume	product
pollute	possess	praline	pretend	profane
poloist	postage	prancer	pretest	profess
polygon	postbag	prattle	pretext	proffer
polymer	postbox	pravity	pretzel	profile
polynia	postboy	preachy	prevail	profuse
polynya	posteen	prebend	prevent	progeny
polypod	postern	precast	preview	program
polypus	postfix	precede	previse	project
pomatum	posting	precept	priapic	prolate
pomfret	postman	precise	pricker	prolong
pompano	posture	precook	pricket	promise
pompous	postwar	predate	prickle	promote
pondage	potamic	predial	prickly	pronate
poniard	potbank	predict	primacy	pronely
pontage	potence	predoom	primage	pronged
pontiff	potency	preempt	primary	pronoun
pontify	pothead	preface	primate	propane
pontoon	potheen	prefect	primely	prophet
poofter	potherb	preform	primero	propjet
poohbah	pothole	preheat	priming	propone
poorish	pothook	prelacy	primmed	propose
popadum	potluck	prelate	primula	propped
popcorn	potshot	prelect	printer	prorate
popeyed	pottage	prelims	prithee	prosaic
popover	pottery	prelude	privacy	prosify
poppied	potting	premier	private	prosily
popping	pouched	premise	privily	prosody
pop shop	poulard	premiss	privity	prosper
popular	poulter	premium	probate	protean
porcine	poultry	prepack	probity	protect
porifer	poundal	prepaid	problem	protege
pork pie	pounder	prepare	proceed	proteid
porrect	poussin	preplan	process	protein
portage	pouting	presage	proctor	protend
portend	poverty	present	procure	protest
portent	powdery	preside	prodded	proteus
portico	praetor	presoak	prodder	protist
portion	prairie	presser	prodigy	protium

proudly	punctum	pyrites	quillet	ragwort
proverb	pungent	pyritic	quilter	railcar
provide	Punjabi	pyrosis	quinary	railing
proviso	punning	pyrrhic	quinate	railman
provoke	punster	Pythian	quinine	railway
provost	puparia	pyxides	quinone	raiment
prowess	pupilar	pyxidia	quintal	rainbow
prowler	pupping	quadrat	quintet	Rajpoot
proximo	puritan	quadric	quintic	rakeoff
prudent	purlieu	quaffer	quipped	rallier
prudery	purloin	quahaug	quitted	Ramadan
prudish	purport	qualify	quitter	rambler
pruning	purpose	quality	quivery	ramekin
prurigo	purpura	quantic	quixote	ramming
prussic	purpure	quantum	quizzed	rampage
psalter	pursuer	quarrel	quizzer	rampant
psychic	pursuit	quartan	quizzes	rampart
ptyalin	purview	quarter	quondam	rampion
puberal	pushful	quartet	rabbity	ramsons
puberty	pushing	quartic	rabbler	ran away
publish	pushrod	quassia	rabidly	rancher
puccoon	pustule	quavery	raccoon	rancour
puckery	putamen	quayage	racemic	ranking
puckish	putdown	Quechua	rackety	ransack
pudding	putlock	queenly	racquet	rape oil
puddler	put oven	queerly	radiant	raphide
pudency	putrefy	queller	radiate	rapidly
puerile	putting	querist	radical	rapping
puffery	puzzler	quester	radices	rapport
pugging	pyaemia	questor	radicle	rapture
puggish	pycnite	quetsch	radulae	rarebit
puggree	pygmean	quetzal	radular	raschel
pugmill	pygmoid	queuing	raffish	rasping
pugnose	pyjamas	quibble	ragbolt	ratable
Pullman	pyloric	quicken	ragdoll	ratafia
pullout	pylorus	quickie	raggedy	ratatat
pulsate	pyramid	quickly	ragging	ratchet
pumpkin	pyretic	quieten	ragtime	rations
	pyrexia	quietly	ragweed	ratlike
	pyrexic	quietus	ragworm	ratling

rat race	recency	referee	reliant	request
ratteen	recital	refined	relieve	requiem
rattery	reciter	refiner	relievo	require
ratting	reclaim	reflate	relight	requite
rattler	reclame	reflect	relique	reredos
rattrap	recline	refloat	remains	rescale
raucous	recluse	refocus	remarry	rescind
raunchy	recount	refract	remnant	rescuer
ravager	recover	refrain	remodel	reseaux
ravelin	recruit	refresh	remorse	reserve
ravined	rectify	refugee	remould	reshape
ravings	rectory	refusal	remount	residua
ravioli	rectrix	refuser	removal	residue
raw deal	recurve	refutal	removed	resolve
rawhide	recycle	refuter	remover	resound
rawness	redcoat	regalia	reneger	respect
rayless	red deer	regally	renegue	respell
reacher	reddest	regatta	renewal	respelt
reactor	reddish	regency	renewer	respire
readily	red flag	regimen	rentier	respite
reading	redhead	reginal	reorder	respond
readout	redlegs	regnant	repaint	respray
reagent	redneck	regorge	repaper	restart
real ale	redness	regrant	repiner	restate
realgar	redoubt	regrate	repique	restful
realign	redound	regress	replace	restiff
realise	redpoll	regrets	replant	restive
realism	redraft	regroup	replete	restock
realist	redress	regular	replica	restore
reality	redskin	regulus	replier	restyle
reallot	red tape	reheard	reposal	resurge
realtor	reducer	rehouse	reposit	retable
rebirth	red wine	reissue	repress	retaken
reboant	redwing	rejoice	reprint	rethink
rebound	redwood	relapse	reprise	retiary
rebuild	reeding	related	reproof	reticle
rebuilt	reelect	relater	reprove	retinae
rebuker	reenact	relator	reptile	retinal
receipt	reenter	relayed	repulse	retinas
receive	reentry	release	reputed	retinol

retinue	rhiancy	ripplet	Romansh	roundup
retired	rhizoid	riptide	romaunt	rousing
retouch	rhizome	risible	Rommany	rouster
retrace	rhodium	risotto	rondeau	routine
retract	rhombic	rissole	rondure	rowboat
retrain	rhombus	rivalry	rontgen	rowdily
retread	rhubarb	rivered	roofing	rowlock
retreat	rhymist	riveter	rooftop	royally
retrial	ribband	riviera	rooinek	royalty
retsina	ribbing	riviere	rookery	royster
rettery	ribston	rivulet	roomful	rubadub
retting	ribwork	roadbed	rooster	rubbers
returns	ribwort	roadhog	rootage	rubbery
reunion	rickets	roadman	rootlet	rubbing
reunite	rickety	roadway	ropable	rubbish
revalue	ricksha	roaring	ropeway	rubdown
revelry	ricotta	roaster	rorqual	rubella
revenge	ridable	robbery	roseate	rubeola
revenue	ridding	robbing	rosebay	rubicon
reverie	riddler	rock eel	rosebud	rubious
reverse	ridging	rockery	rosecut	ruching
reversi	riffler	rockier	rosehip	ruction
reviler	rifling	rockily	rosella	ruddily
revisal	rigging	rocking	roseola	ruddock
reviser	righten	rocklet	rosered	ruffian
revisit	righter	rockoil	rosette	ruffler
revival	rightly	rocktar	rostral	ruinate
reviver	rigidly	rodding	rostrum	ruinous
revivor	rilievo	rodlike	rotator	rum baba
revolve	rimming	rodsman	rotifer	rumbler
revving	ringent	roebuck	rotting	rummage
rewound	ringing	roedeer	rotunda	rumness
rewrite	ringlet	roguery	roughen	rumshop
rewrote	ring off	roguish	roughly	runaway
reynard	riotous	roister	roulade	rundown
rhabdom	ripcord	rollick	rouleau	runless
Rhaetic	ripieni	rolling	rounded	running
rhamnus	ripieno	rollmop	roundel	run wild
rhatany	riposte	rolltop	rounder	rupture
rhenium	ripping	Romanic	roundly	rurally

russety	saltern	sarcasm	sawwort	schnook
Russian	salting	sarcode	saxhorn	scholar
Russify	saltire	sarcoid	saxtuba	scholia
rustily	saltish	sarcoma	sayable	sciarid
rustler	saltpan	sarcous	scabbed	sciatic
ruthful	saluter	sardine	scabble	science
rutting	salvage	sardius	scabies	scirrhi
ruttish	salvoes	sarking	scalder	scissel
Sabaism	sambuca	sashimi	scaldic	scissor
Sabaoth	samisen	satanic	scalene	scoffer
Sabbath	samovar	satchel	scallop	scolder
saccade	Samoyed	satiate	scalper	scollop
saccate	sampler	satiety	scamper	scomber
saccule	samurai	satinet	scandal	scooper
sacculi	sanctum	satiric	scanned	scooter
sackbut	Sanctus	satisfy	scanner	scopula
sackful	sandbag	satrapy	scantly	scoring
sacking	sandbar	satsuma	scapple	scorner
sacring	sandbed	satyral	scapula	Scorpio
sacrist	sandbox	satyric	scarfed	Scotism
saddest	sandboy	satyrid	scarify	Scotist
saddish	sanders	saucily	scarlet	scotoma
saddler	sandfly	saunter	scarper	Scottie
sad eyed	sandlot	saurian	scarred	scourer
sadness	sandman	sauroid	scarves	scourge
saffron	sandpit	sausage	scatted	scouter
sagging	sangria	savable	scatter	scraggy
saguaro	sanicle	savanna	scauper	scranny
sailing	santour	saveall	scenery	scraper
sainted	sapajou	saveloy	scented	scrapie
saintly	saphead	savings	scepsis	scrappy
Saktism	sapient	saviour	sceptic	scratch
salable	sapless	savoury	sceptre	scrawly
salient	sapling	sawbill	schappe	scrawny
Salique	sapphic	sawbuck	schemer	screech
sallowy	sapping	sawdust	scherzi	screeve
salpinx	saprobe	sawfish	scherzo	screwed
salsify	sapsago	sawgate	schlepp	screwer
saltant	sapwood	sawmill	schlock	scribal
saltbox	Saracen	sawnoff	schmuck	scriber

scrieve	seaside	seminar	session	shastra
scrimpy	sea slug	semiped	sestina	shatter
scrooge	seating	Semitic	setback	Shavian
scrouge	seawall	senarii	setdown	shaving
scrubby	seaward	senator	set sail	shearer
scruffy	seaweed	senatus	setting	sheathe
scrumpy	seawhip	sendoff	settler	sheaves
scrunch	seawolf	senecio	settlor	shebang
scruple	seceder	senhora	setwall	she bear
scudded	seclude	senores	seventh	shebeen
scuffle	secondi	sensory	seventy	shedder
sculler	secondo	sensual	several	sheerly
sculpin	secrecy	Senussi	sexfoil	shellac
scumble	secrete	seppuku	sexless	shelled
scummed	sectary	septate	Sextans	sheller
scunner	sectile	septime	sextant	shelter
scupper	section	sequela	sextile	sheltie
scurril	secular	sequent	sferics	shelved
scutage	securer	sequoia	sfumato	shelves
scutate	sedilia	Serbian	shackle	Shemite
scutter	seducer	serfage	shadily	sherbet
scuttle	seeable	serfdom	shading	sheriff
seabass	seedbed	seriate	shadoof	shifter
seabear	seedily	sericin	shadowy	shikari
seabird	seedlip	seriema	shake up	shilpit
sea blue	seeming	seringa	shakily	shimmer
seaboot	seepage	serious	shallop	shindig
seafish	segment	serpent	shallot	shingle
seafood	seismal	serpigo	shallow	shingly
seafowl	seismic	serpula	shamble	shinned
seagull	seizing	serrate	shammed	shinpad
seakale	seizure	serried	shammer	shiplap
sea lane	selenic	servant	shampoo	shipman
sealant	selfish	servery	shanked	shipped
sea legs	sellout	Servian	shapely	shippen
sealery	seltzer	service	sharpen	shipper
sea pink	selvage	servile	sharper	shippon
seaport	sematic	serving	sharply	shipway
searoom	semilog	Servite	shaslik	shirker
seasick	seminal	sessile	shaster	shittim

shivers	shyness	simplex	skidded	slasher
shivery	shyster	simular	skid lid	slather
shocker	siamang	sincere	skidpan	slating
shoeing	Siamese	singlet	skiffle	slatted
shoofly	sibling	sinkage	skijump	slavery
shooter	sibship	sinless	skilful	slavish
shopboy	sick bay	sinning	skilift	Slavism
shopman	sickbed	sinsyne	skilled	sledded
shopped	sickish	sinuate	skillet	sleeken
shopper	sick pay	sinuous	skimmed	sleekit
shoring	sidecar	sipping	skimmer	sleekly
shorten	sideway	sirloin	skimmia	sleeper
shortie	siemens	sirocco	skinful	sleeved
shortly	sierran	Sistine	skinned	sleight
shotgun	sighted	sistrum	skinner	slender
shotten	sightly	sit down	skipped	slicker
shouter	sigmate	sit fast	skipper	slickly
showbiz	sigmoid	sitting	skippet	slidden
showery	signary	situate	skirted	slimily
showily	signify	Sivaism	skirter	slimmer
showing	signior	Sivaite	skitter	slinger
showman	signora	sixaine	skittle	slinker
showoff	signore	sixfold	skulker	slipped
shrieve	signori	sixteen	sky blue	slipper
shrilly	signory	sixthly	skyborn	slipway
shrinal	Sikhism	sixties	skyhigh	slither
shrivel	silence	Sixtine	skyjack	slobber
shriven	silenus	sizable	skylark	sloegin
shrubby	silesia	sizably	skyline	slogged
shucker	silicic	sizzler	skysail	slogger
shudder	silicon	sjambok	skyward	slopped
shuffle	siliqua	skaldic	slabbed	sloshed
shunned	silique	skating	slabber	slotted
shunner	silkily	skeeter	slacken	slouchy
shunter	sillily	skegger	slacker	sloughy
shuteye	silvern	skellum	slackly	Slovene
shutout	silvery	skelter	slagged	slowish
shutter	similar	skepsis	slander	slubbed
shuttle	simitar	sketchy	slantly	slubber
shylock	simpler	skiable	slapped	slugged

slugger	sniggle	solatia	sotting	specify
slumber	snipped	soldier	sottish	speckle
slummed	snipper	solicit	soubise	spectra
slummer	snippet	solidly	souffle	spectre
slurred	snooker	soliped	soulful	specula
slyness	snooper	soloist	sounder	speeder
smacker	snoozer	Solomon	soundly	speed up
smaragd	snoozle	soluble	soupcon	speller
smarten	snorkel	solvate	sourish	spelter
smartly	snorter	solvent	soursop	spencer
smasher	snouted	somatic	soutane	spender
smash up	snowcap	someday	souther	sphenic
smatter	snowily	somehow	sowback	spheral
smeller	snowman	someone	soybean	spicate
smelter	snubbed	someway	sozzled	spicery
smidgen	snubber	somitic	spacial	spicily
smidgin	snuffer	sonance	spacing	spicula
smitten	snuffle	sonancy	spangle	spicule
smokily	snuggle	songful	spangly	spidery
smoking	soakage	sonless	spaniel	spieler
smoochy	soaking	sonship	Spanish	spignel
smother	so and so	soonish	spanker	spikily
smuggle	soapbox	soother	spanned	spiller
smutted	soapily	soothly	spanner	spinach
snaffle	soaring	sootily	sparely	spindle
snagged	sobbing	sophism	sparger	spindly
snakily	soberly	sophist	sparing	spindry
snapped	socager	soppily	sparkle	spinner
snapper	soccage	sopping	sparred	spinney
snarler	society	soprani	sparrow	spinoff
snarlup	sockeye	soprano	Spartan	spinose
snatchy	sofabed	sorbent	spastic	spinous
sneaker	softish	Sorbian	spathic	spinule
sneerer	soggily	sorcery	spatial	spirits
sneezer	soignee	sordini	spatter	spitted
snicker	soilure	sordino	spatula	spitter
sniffer	sojourn	sorghum	spawner	spittle
sniffle	sokeman	sororal	speaker	splashy
snifter	solanum	sorosis	special	spleeny
snigger	solaria	sorrily	species	splenic

splicer	squalor	stapler	stepson	stopgap
splodge	squamae	starchy	sterile	stop off
splotch	squarer	stardom	sternal	stopped
splurge	squashy	starkly	sterned	stopper
spodium	squatty	starlet	sternly	stopple
spoiler	squeaky	starlit	sternum	storage
spondee	squeeze	starred	steroid	storied
spondyl	squelch	starter	stetson	stouten
sponger	squiffy	startle	stetted	stoutly
sponson	squinch	statant	steward	stovies
sponsor	squinny	stately	stewpan	stowage
spoofer	squirmy	statice	stewpot	straits
spooney	squishy	statics	sthenic	strange
spoorer	squitch	station	stibine	stratum
sporran	stabbed	statism	sticker	stratus
sporter	stabber	statist	stickit	strayer
sporule	stabile	statued	stickle	streaky
spotted	stabler	stature	stickup	stretch
spotter	stables	statute	stiffen	stretta
spousal	stacker	staunch	stiffly	stretto
spouter	staddle	stealer	stifler	strewth
sprawly	stadium	stealth	stilted	striate
sprayer	stagger	steamer	Stilton	strider
spriggy	stagily	stearic	stimuli	stridor
springy	staging	stearin	stinger	strigil
spryest	staidly	steekit	stinker	striker
spumous	stainer	steepen	stipend	stringy
spurner	staithe	steeple	stipple	striped
spurred	stalely	steeply	stipule	striven
spurrey	stalked	steerer	stirpes	strophe
spurtle	stalker	stellar	stirred	stroppy
sputnik	stamina	stemmed	stirrer	strudel
sputter	stammel	stemple	stirrup	strumae
spyhole	stammer	stemson	St Leger	stubbed
spy ring	stamper	stenchy	stocker	stubble
squabby	standby	stencil	stoical	stubbly
squaddy	stander	stentor	stomach	stuccos
squails	standin	stepney	stomata	stuckup
squalid	stand up	stepped	stonily	studded
squally	stannic	stepper	stonker	student

studied	subside	sunbeam	surreal	swinery
stuffer	subsidy	sunbear	surtout	swinger
stumble	subsist	sunbird	survive	swingle
stummed	subsoil	sunburn	suspect	swinish
stumper	subsume	sundeck	suspend	swither
stump up	subtend	sundial	suspire	Switzer
stunned	subtile	sundisc	sustain	swizzle
stunner	suburbs	sundown	sutural	swobbed
stunted	subvert	sunfish	sutured	swollen
stupefy	subzero	sunlamp	swabbed	swopped
stutter	succade	sunless	swabber	swopper
stygian	succeed	sunnily	swaddle	swotted
stylise	success	sunning	swagged	syconia
stylish	succory	Sunnite	swagger	sycosis
stylist	succour	sunrise	swagman	syenite
stylite	succuba	sunroof	Swahili	syllabi
styloid	succubi	sunspot	swallow	sylphid
styptic	succumb	sunstar	swanker	sylvine
styrene	sucking	sunsuit	swanned	sylvite
suasion	suckler	suntrap	swapped	symptom
suasive	sucrose	sunward	swapper	synapse
suavely	suction	sunwise	swarded	syncope
suavity	sudaria	supping	swarmer	synergy
subacid	suffice	support	swarthy	synesis
subaqua	Suffolk	suppose	swasher	synodal
subbing	suffuse	supreme	swatted	synodic
subdean	suggest	supremo	swatter	synonym
subdual	suicide	surbase	swearer	synovia
subduct	suiting	surcoat	sweater	syringa
subdued	sulcate	surface	Swedish	syringe
subedit	sulkily	surfeit	sweeper	syrphid
suberic	sullage	surfing	sweeten	systole
suberin	sulphur	surfman	sweetie	tabanid
subfusc	sultana	surgeon	sweetly	tabaret
subhead	summary	surgery	swelter	tabasco
subject	summery	surlily	swiftly	tabbing
subjoin	summing	surmise	swigged	tabetic
sublate	summons	surname	swiller	tabinet
sublime	sumpter	surpass	swimmer	tableau
subplot	sunbath	surplus	swindle	tabloid

taborer	tanbark	tattily	tempera	tessera
tabular	tandoor	tatting	tempest	testacy
tachism	tangelo	tattler	Templar	testate
tachist	tangent	taunter	templet	test ban
tacitly	tanghin	taurine	tempter	test bed
tacking	tangram	taxable	tempura	test fly
tackler	tankage	taxfree	tenable	testify
tactful	tankard	taxicab	tenably	testily
tactics	tankcar	taxiing	tenancy	testoon
tactile	tankful	taximan	tendril	testudo
taction	tannage	taxless	tenfold	tetanic
tadpole	tannate	taxying	tenoner	tetanus
taeniae	tannery	teacake	tenpins	tetrode
taffeta	tanning	teacher	tensely	textile
Tagalog	tannish	teach in	tensile	textual
tagetes	tanooze	tea cosy	tension	texture
tagging	tantara	tea gown	tensity	thalami
tail end	tantivy	tealeaf	tensive	thallic
tailing	tantric	tearful	tenthly	thallus
tail off	tantrum	teargas	tentpeg	thanage
takeoff	tanyard	tearing	tenuity	thankee
takings	taperer	tearoom	tenuous	thanker
talipes	tapioca	tea rose	tepidly	theatre
talipot	tapping	tea shop	tequila	the east
talking	taproom	teatime	terbium	themata
tallage	taproot	tea tray	tergite	the news
tallboy	tapsman	technic	termini	theorem
tallish	tapster	tectrix	termite	therapy
tallith	tarbush	tedding	ternary	thereat
tallowy	tardily	tedious	ternate	thereby
tallyho	tarnish	teeming	terpene	therein
taloned	tarrier	teenage	terrace	thereof
tamable	tarring	tee shot	terrain	thereon
tamarin	tartare	tegmina	terrene	thereto
tambour	tartish	tektite	terrier	theriac
Tammany	tartlet	teleost	terrify	thermal
tamping	Tartufe	telling	terrine	thermic
tampion	tastily	tell off	tersely	theurgy
tanager	tatters	telpher	tertial	the west
tanagra	tattery	Telstar	tertian	thiamin

thicken	tidally	tithing	tophole	tourist
thicket	tiddler	titlark	topiary	tourney
thickly	tiddley	titling	topical	towards
thieves	tideway	titmice	topknot	towboat
thimble	tidings	Titoism	topless	towered
thinker	tieback	Titoist	topmast	towhead
thinned	tiebeam	titrate	topmost	towline
thinner	tiercel	tittupy	toponym	towmond
thirdly	tiercet	titular	topping	towmont
thirsty	tiffany	toaster	topsail	townish
thistle	tighten	tobacco	topside	townlet
thistly	tightly	toccata	topsoil	towpath
thither	tigress	toddler	top spin	towrope
Thomism	tigrish	toeclip	torchon	toy shop
Thomist	tilbury	toehold	torment	tracery
thorite	tillage	toeless	tormina	trachea
thorium	timbale	toenail	tornado	tracker
thorned	timbrel	toggery	torpedo	tractor
thought	time lag	toilful	torpids	tradein
thready	timeous	tollbar	torrefy	trading
thrifty	timidly	tollman	torrent	traduce
thriven	timothy	toluene	torsion	traffic
throaty	timpani	tombola	tortile	tragedy
thrombi	timpano	tombolo	tortrix	trailer
through	tinamou	tomenta	torture	trainee
thrower	tindery	tomfool	torulae	trainer
throw in	tin foil	tompion	Toryism	traipse
thudded	tingler	tonally	tosspot	traitor
thuggee	tinhorn	tone row	totally	traject
thulium	tinnily	tonight	totemic	tramcar
thummim	tinning	tonnage	tottery	trammel
thumper	tin tack	tonneau	totting	trample
thunder	tinware	tonsure	touched	tramway
thymine	tipcart	tontine	toucher	tranche
thyroid	tipping	toolbox	touch up	transit
thyrsus	tippler	tooling	toughen	transom
thyself	tipsify	toothed	toughly	tranter
Tibetan	tipsily	tootsie	touraco	trapeze
ticking	tipster	topcoat	touring	trapped
tickler	titanic	topfull	tourism	trapper

travail	trigamy	tropics	tumbler	twiddly
travois	trigger	tropism	tumbrel	twigged
trawler	trilith	trotted	tumbril	twilled
trayful	trimmed	trotter	tumidly	twinkle
treacle	trimmer	trouble	tumular	twinkly
treacly	trinary	trounce	tumulus	twinned
treader	trindle	trouper	tunable	twin set
treadle	trinity	trouser	tunably	twister
treason	trinket	truancy	tundish	twitchy
treater	trinkum	trucial	tuneful	twitted
treetop	triolet	trucker	tunicle	twitter
trefoil	tripery	truckle	tunning	two feet
trekked	triplet	trudgen	turbary	twofold
trekker	triplex	truffle	turbine	twoness
trellis	tripody	trumeau	turfman	twosome
tremble	tripoli	trumpet	turf out	two step
trembly	tripped	truncal	Turkish	twotime
tremolo	tripper	trundle	turmoil	two tone
trenail	trippet	trusser	turnery	tympani
trepang	tripple	trustee	turning	tympany
tressed	trireme	truster	turnipy	Tynwald
tressel	trisect	try it on	turnkey	typebar
trestle	trishaw	trypsin	turnout	typeset
triable	trismus	trysail	turpeth	typhoid
triacid	tritely	tsardom	tushery	typhoon
triadic	tritium	tsarina	tussive	typhous
tribade	tritone	tsarism	tussock	typical
triblet	triumph	tsarist	tussore	typonym
tribune	trivial	Tsquare	tutelar	tyranny
tribute	trivium	tsunami	tutenag	tzigane
triceps	trochal	tuatara	tutting	tzigany
tricker	trochee	tubbing	twaddle	ukelele
trickle	trochus	tubbish	twaddly	ukulele
tricksy	trodden	tubular	twangle	ulcered
tricorn	troller	tuckbox	tweeter	ululant
trident	trolley	Tuesday	tweezer	ululate
triduan	trollop	tugboat	twelfth	umbones
triduum	trommel	tugging	twelves	umbrage
trifler	trooper	tuition	twibill	Umbrian
triform	trophic	tulchan	twiddle	umpteen

unaptly	ungodly	unroost	upsurge	vacuous
unarmed	unguard	unsaved	upsweep	vagally
unasked	unguent	unscrew	upswept	vagrant
unaware	ungulae	unsexed	upswing	vaguely
unbated	unhandy	unshell	upthrew	vaguish
unblest	unhappy	unsight	upthrow	Vaishya
unblock	unheard	unsnarl	uptight	valance
unbosom	unhinge	unsound	up to now	valence
unbound	unhitch	unstick	uptrend	valency
unbowed	unhoped	unstuck	upwards	valeric
unboxed	unhorse	unswear	uraemia	valiant
unbrace	unhouse	unswore	Uralian	validly
unbuild	unicity	unsworn	uralite	vallate
unbuilt	unicorn	unteach	uranide	valonia
uncanny	unideal	unthink	uranism	valuate
unchain	unifier	untried	uranium	valvate
uncinus	uniform	untruly	uranous	valvula
uncivil	unitive	untruss	urethan	valvule
unclasp	unjoint	untruth	urethra	vamoose
unclean	unkempt	untuned	urgency	vampire
uncloak	unknown	untwine	urinary	vampish
unclose	unladen	untwist	urology	vanadic
uncouth	unlatch	untying	useless	Vandyke
uncover	unlearn	unusual	usually	vanessa
uncross	unleash	unweave	usurper	vanilla
uncrown	unlined	unwound	utensil	vantage
unction	unloose	unwoven	uterine	vanward
underdo	unlucky	upbraid	utilise	vapidly
undergo	unmanly	upfield	utility	vapours
undoing	unmeant	upgrade	utopian	vapoury
undress	unmixed	upheave	utopism	vaquero
undying	unmoral	up north	utopist	variant
unearth	unmoved	upraise	utricle	variate
unequal	unnerve	upright	utterer	varices
unfaith	unpaged	upriser	utterly	variety
unfitly	unquiet	upsides	uxorial	variola
unfrock	unquote	upsilon	vacancy	variole
unfroze	unravel	upstage	vaccine	various
unfunny	unready	upstair	vacuity	varment
unfussy	unright	upstart	vacuole	varmint

varnish	veriest	villein	vocalic	walkout
varsity	verismo	villose	vocally	walkway
vascula	vermeil	villous	voguish	wallaby
vastity	vermian	vinasse	voivode	walleye
Vatican	vernier	vincula	volante	walling
vatting	verruca	vinegar	volcano	Walloon
Vaudois	versant	vintage	voltage	wall rue
vaulted	versify	vintner	voltaic	waltzer
vaulter	versine	violate	voluble	wanness
vaunter	version	violent	volubly	wannish
Vedanta	vertigo	violist	volumed	wanting
Veddoid	vervain	violone	voluted	waratah
vedette	vesicae	virelay	volutin	warbler
vegetal	vesical	virgate	votable	warfare
vehicle	vesicle	virgule	vouchee	war game
veiling	vespers	virtual	voucher	warhead
veining	vespine	visaged	vowelly	warison
veinlet	vestige	viscera	voyager	warlike
velamen	vestral	viscose	vulgate	warlock
velaria	vesture	viscous	vulpine	warlord
veliger	veteran	visible	vulture	warmish
velours	vetiver	visibly	wadable	warning
veloute	vetting	visitor	wadding	warpath
velvety	vexedly	visored	waddler	warrant
venally	vexilla	vistaed	waftage	warring
venatic	viaduct	vitally	wafture	warrior
venerer	viatica	vitamin	wagerer	warship
venison	vibrant	vitelli	waggery	warthog
ventage	vibrate	vitiate	wagging	wartime
ventail	vibrato	vitrify	waggish	washing
ventral	viceroy	vitrine	wagoner	washout
venture	vicinal	vitriol	wagtail	washpot
venturi	vicious	vittate	Wahabee	washtub
veranda	victory	vittles	wailful	waspish
verbena	victual	vitular	waisted	wassail
verbose	vidette	vivaria	waister	wastage
verdant	viduity	vividly	waiting	wastrel
verdict	viewing	vivific	wakeful	watcher
verdure	vilayet	vixenly	wakener	watered
verglas	village	vocable	walking	waterer

wattage	welcome	whimper	willing	woodman
Watteau	welfare	whimsey	willowy	wool fat
wattled	wellies	whinger	windage	woolled
wattles	well off	whipped	windbag	woollen
wavelet	wellset	whipper	windily	wool oil
waverer	welsher	whippet	winding	woolsey
waxbill	wencher	whipsaw	windrow	woomera
waxtree	Wendish	whirler	Windsor	woozily
waxwing	wergild	whirred	winesap	wordage
waxwork	werwolf	whisker	winglet	wordily
waybill	West end	whiskey	wingnut	wording
waylaid	western	whisper	winkers	workbag
wayless	westing	whistle	winning	workbox
waymark	wetback	whitely	winnock	workday
wayside	wetness	whither	win over	working
wayward	wettest	whiting	winsome	workman
wayworn	wetting	whitish	wintery	workout
weakish	wettish	whitlow	wireman	workshy
wealden	whacker	Whitsun	wiretap	worldly
wealthy	whaling	whittle	wise guy	wornout
wearily	whangee	whizkid	wishful	worrier
wearing	wharves	whizzed	wishing	worship
weasand	whatnot	whoever	wistful	worsted
weather	wheaten	whoopee	withers	wottest
webbing	wheedle	whooper	without	wouldbe
webfoot	wheeled	whorish	witless	wouldst
webster	wheeler	whorled	witling	wrangle
webworm	whereas	whoseso	witloof	wrapped
wedding	whereat	wickiup	witness	wrapper
wedging	whereby	widgeon	wittily	wreathe
wedlock	wherein	widowed	witting	wreathy
weekday	whereof	widower	wizened	wrecker
weekend	whereon	wielder	wobbler	wrestle
weevily	whereto	wigging	wolfcub	wriggle
weigher	whether	wiggler	wolfdog	wriggly
weighin	whetted	wigless	wolfish	wringer
weighty	whetter	wildcat	wolfram	wrinkle
weirdie	wheyish	wilding	wolvish	wrinkly
weirdly	whicker	wildish	womanly	writeup
welcher	whiffle	willies	woodcut	writhen

writing	yardarm	Yorkist	zillion	Zoilism
written	yardman	younger	zincify	Zoilist
wrongly	yashmak	yttrium	zincing	zonated
wrought	yatagan	yulelog	zincite	zoogeny
wrybill	ycleped	zapping	zincked	zooidal
wryneck	yeggman	zaptieh	Zingari	zoology
wryness	yellowy	zealous	Zingaro	zoonomy
wych elm	yenning	zebrine	zinkify	zootaxy
xanthic	yestern	zebroid	zinking	zootomy
xiphoid	yew tree	zedoary	Zionism	zygosis
Yahvist	Yiddish	zemstvo	Zionist	zygotic
Yahwist	yielder	zeolite	zip code	zymogen
yapping	yipping	zestful	zipping	zymosis
yardage	yoghurt	zetetic	zithern	zymotic
yardang	yolksac	ziganka	zoarium	zymurgy

8 letter words

aardvark	absentee	aciculae	addendum	aegrotat
aardwolf	absently	acicular	addition	aeration
aasvogel	absinthe	aciculas	additive	aerially
abacuses	absolute	acidfast	adducent	aeriform
abattoir	absolver	acidhead	adductor	aerodyne
Abbaside	absorber	acidosis	adenitis	aerofoil
abbatial	abstract	acid rain	adenoids	aerogram
Abderite	abstrict	aconitic	adequacy	aerolite
abdicate	abstruse	aconitum	adequate	aerolith
abducens	absurdly	acoustic	adherent	aerology
abducent	abundant	acquaint	adhesion	aeronaut
abductor	abutilon	acre foot	adhesive	aeronomy
abelmosk	abutment	acre inch	adiantum	aerostat
aberrant	abuttals	acridine	adjacent	aesthete
abetment	abutting	acridity	adjuster	aestival
abetting	academia	acrimony	adjustor	affected
abeyance	academic	acrolein	adjutage	affecter
abeyancy	acanthus	acrolith	adjutant	afferent
abhorred	acarpous	acrostic	adjuvant	affiance
abhorrer	Accadian	acrotism	Adlerian	affinity
abidance	accentor	acrylate	adlibbed	affirmer
abjectly	accepter	actiniae	admitted	afflatus
ablation	acceptor	actinian	admonish	affluent
ablative	accident	actinias	adoption	afforest
ablution	accolade	actinide	adoptive	affright
abnegate	accoutre	actinism	adorable	affusion
abnormal	accredit	actinium	adorably	aflutter
abomasum	accuracy	activate	adroitly	agar agar
abomasus	accurate	actively	adularia	agedness
aborally	accursed	activism	adulator	agential
abortion	accustom	activist	adultery	aggrieve
abortive	acentric	activity	advanced	agiotage
above all	acerbate	actually	advisory	agitator
abradant	acerbity	actuator	advocaat	agitprop
abrasion	acervate	acturial	advocacy	aglimmer
abrasive	acescent	aculeate	advocate	aglitter
abridger	achenial	Adamical	advowson	agnation
abrogate	achiever	adamitic	adynamia	agnostic
abruptly	achiness	adaption	adynamic	agonised
abscissa	achingly	adaptive	aegirine	agraphia

agrarian	alehouse	all the go	ammonify	anaphora
agrement	aleurone	allusion	ammonite	anarchic
agrestic	alewives	allusive	ammonium	anathema
agrimony	al fresco	alluvial	amnesiac	anatomic
agrology	algicide	alluvion	amniotic	ancestor
agronomy	algidity	alluvium	amoebean	ancestry
aguishly	alginate	almagest	amoeboid	anchoret
aigrette	algology	almanack	amorally	andesine
aiguille	Algonkin	almighty	amoretti	andesite
airborne	algorism	alogical	amoretto	androgen
airbrake	alguazil	alopecia	amortise	anecdote
airbrush	alienage	alphabet	amperage	anechoic
aircraft	alienate	alpinism	amphibia	aneurism
Airedale	alienism	alpinist	amphipod	aneurysm
airfield	alienist	Alsatian	amphorae	angelica
airframe	alizarin	although	amphoras	Anglican
airiness	alkahest	altitude	ampullae	angstrom
airliner	alkalies	altruism	amputate	anhedral
airscrew	alkalify	altruist	amusedly	aniconic
airshaft	alkaline	alumroot	amygdala	animally
airspace	alkaloid	alveolar	anabases	animator
airspeed	all at sea	alveolus	anabasis	anisette
airstrip	all clear	amaranth	anabatic	ankerite
airtight	allegory	amazedly	anabolic	ankylose
airwoman	alleluia	ambiance	anaconda	annalist
Akkadian	allergen	ambience	anaerobe	annotate
a la carte	allergic	ambition	anaglyph	announce
alacrity	alleyway	ambivert	anagogic	annually
alarmist	alliance	ambrosia	analcime	annulate
albacore	all night	ambulant	analcite	annulled
Albanian	allocate	ambulate	analecta	anorexia
albinism	allodial	ambusher	analects	anorexic
alburnum	allodium	amenable	analogic	anorthic
alcahest	allogamy	amenably	analogue	anserine
alchemic	allopath	American	analyser	answerer
aldehyde	allotted	amethyst	analyses	anteater
alderman	allottee	amiantus	analysis	antecede
Alderney	all right	amicable	analytic	antedate
aleatory	all round	amicably	anapaest	antefixa
alebench	allspice	ammonaic	anaphase	antelope

antennae	apiarian	arachnid	armourer	assembly
antennal	apiarist	Aramaean	armyworm	assenter
antennas	apically	Arapahoe	aromatic	assentor
antepost	aplastic	arbalest	arpeggio	assertor
anterior	apocrine	arbalist	arquebus	assessor
anteroom	apodosis	arbitral	arranger	assiento
anthelia	apogamic	arboreal	arrantly	assignat
anthemia	apograph	arboreta	arrestee	assignee
antheral	apologia	arborist	arrester	assignor
anthesis	apologue	Arcadian	arrestor	assonant
anthozoa	apomixis	archaean	arrogant	assonate
antibody	apoplexy	archaise	arrogate	assorted
antidote	apostasy	archaism	arsenate	assuming
antihero	apostate	archaist	arsenide	Assyrian
antilogy	apothegm	archduke	arsonist	astatine
antimask	appalled	archival	arsonous	asterisk
antimony	appanage	archives	artefact	asterism
antinode	apparent	archness	arterial	asteroid
antinomy	appendix	Arcturus	artesian	asthenia
antiphon	appetent	arcuated	artfully	asthenic
antipode	appetite	ardently	articled	astonied
antipole	applause	areolate	artifact	astonish
antipope	apple pie	argentic	artifice	astragal
antisera	applique	argonaut	artistic	astutely
antitype	apposite	arguable	artistry	at a pinch
antlered	appraise	arguably	asbestic	ataraxia
antrorse	approach	argufier	asbestos	ataraxic
anyplace	approval	argument	ascender	atheling
anything	apres ski	Arianism	ascidian	Athenian
anywhere	apterous	arillate	ascidium	atheroma
aoristic	aptitude	aristate	ascocarp	athletic
aperient	aquacade	Armagnac	aseptate	Atlantic
aperitif	aqualung	armament	asperges	Atlantis
aperture	aquanaut	armature	asperity	at length
aphasiac	aquarist	armchair	asphodel	atomiser
aphelion	aquarium	Armenian	asphyxia	at random
aphicide	aquatint	arm in arm	aspirant	atremble
aphorise	aqueduct	Arminian	aspirate	atrocity
aphorism	aquiline	armorial	assassin	atropine
aphorist	araceous	armoured	assemble	attender

attested	autotype	backfire	balladry	barbican
attester	autumnal	backhand	ballcock	barbital
attestor	autunite	backlash	balletic	bareback
atticism	averment	backless	ballista	barefoot
attitude	averring	backlist	ballonet	bareness
attorney	aversely	backmost	ballroom	bargeman
attrited	aversive	backpack	ballyhoo	baritone
atwitter	aviarist	backrest	ballyrag	barkless
atypical	aviation	backroom	Balmoral	barnacle
aubretia	aviatrix	backseat	balsamic	barndoor
audacity	avidness	backside	baluster	barnyard
audience	avifauna	backspin	bambinos	baronage
audition	avionics	backstay	banality	baroness
auditive	avowable	backstud	banausic	baronial
auditory	avowedly	backveld	bandanna	barouche
Augustan	avulsion	backward	bandeaux	barracks
augustly	aweather	backwash	banderol	barrator
aurelian	axiality	backyard	banditry	barratry
auricula	axillary	Baconian	banditti	barrenly
auriform	axiology	bacteria	bandsman	barrette
aurorean	axletree	Bactrian	bangtail	barterer
auspices	Ayrshire	bad blood	banister	bartizan
autacoid	babirusa	bad habit	banjoist	barytone
autarchy	babouche	badinage	bankable	basaltic
autarkic	babushka	badlands	bankbill	baseball
autistic	babyhood	bad patch	bankbook	baseborn
autobahn	baccarat	bad penny	banknote	baseless
autocade	bacchant	bagpiper	bankroll	baseline
autocrat	bachelor	baguette	bankrupt	basement
auto da fe	bacillar	bailable	bannered	baseness
autodyne	bacillus	bailment	banneret	basicity
autogamy	backache	bailsman	bannerol	basidial
autogiro	back away	bakshish	banterer	basidium
autogyro	backbite	balanced	bantling	basilica
autolyse	backbone	balancer	banxring	basilisk
automata	backchat	baldhead	barathea	basinful
automate	backcomb	baldness	barbaric	basketry
autonomy	backdate	Balinese	barbecue	bassinet
autosome	backdoor	balkline	barberry	basswood
autotomy	backdrop	balladic	barbette	bastardy

bastille	bedstead	benignly	biconvex	birdcall
Batavian	bedstraw	Benjamin	bicuspid	birdlime
bateleur	bedtable	bentwood	biddable	birdseed
bath chap	beebread	benzoate	biennial	birdseye
bathetic	beechnut	benzylic	biennium	birthday
bathotic	bee eater	bequeath	bifacial	bisector
bathrobe	beefcake	berberis	bifocals	bisexual
bathroom	beefwood	berceuse	bigamist	bistable
battalia	beeswing	bereaved	bigamous	bistoury
battleax	beetling	bergamot	big match	bit by bit
baudrons	beetroot	beriberi	bignonia	bitchily
bauxitic	befallen	Bermudas	big wheel	bitingly
Bavarian	befogged	besigner	bilabial	bitterly
bayadere	befriend	beslaver	bilberry	bivalent
bayberry	befuddle	besmirch	billfold	biweekly
bdellium	begetter	besotted	billhead	biyearly
beadroll	beggarly	besought	billhook	blabbing
beadsman	beginner	bespoken	billiard	blackboy
beadwork	begirded	bestiary	billyboy	blackcap
beagling	begotten	bestowal	billycan	black eye
beamends	begrudge	bestrewn	bilobate	blackfly
beanpole	beguiler	bestride	bimanual	blacking
bearable	behemoth	bestrode	bimbashi	blackish
bearably	beholden	betacism	binaural	blackleg
bearings	beholder	betatron	bindweed	blackout
bearskin	bejabers	Bethesda	binnacle	black tie
be a sport	belabour	betrayal	binomial	blacktop
beatific	believer	betrayer	bioassay	bladdery
beautify	belittle	bevelled	biocidal	blahblah
bebopper	bellbird	beveller	biogenic	blamable
becalmed	bell buoy	beverage	biograph	blamably
bechamel	bellcote	bewigged	biometry	blameful
bechance	bellpull	bewilder	biomorph	blandish
becoming	bellpush	bezonian	bionomic	blankety
bedabble	bellwort	biannual	bioplasm	blastoff
bedazzle	bellyful	biassing	bioplast	blastula
bedeguar	beltless	biathlon	bioscope	blatancy
bedimmed	benedick	bibation	biparous	blazoner
bedmaker	benedict	biblical	birdbath	blazonry
bedplate	benefice	bibulous	birdcage	bleacher

bleakish	bluefish	boneless	bouncily	brazenry
blearily	blue moon	bonemeal	bouncing	braziery
bleeding	blueness	boneyard	boundary	breakage
Blenheim	bluenose	bonhomie	bourgeon	breaking
blesbuck	blueweed	boniface	boutique	breakout
blessing	blurrily	boniness	bouzouki	breasted
blighter	blurring	bonspiel	bowfront	breather
blimpish	blushful	bontebok	bowsprit	breeches
blindage	blustery	bookcase	boxpleat	breeding
blinding	boarding	bookends	boyishly	breezily
blinkers	boastful	bookland	bracelet	bregmata
blinking	boatbill	booklice	brachial	brethren
blissful	boatdeck	booklore	brachium	breveted
blistery	boathook	bookmark	brackish	breviary
blithely	boatload	bookpost	bracteal	brewster
blizzard	boatrace	bookrest	bractlet	Briarean
blockade	bobbinet	bookwork	Bradshaw	bribable
blockage	bobbypin	bookworm	braggart	brickbat
blockish	bobolink	bootjack	bragging	brick red
blondish	bobwheel	bootlace	braiding	briefing
bloodily	bobwhite	bootlast	brainish	brighten
blood red	bodement	bootless	brainpan	brightly
bloomers	bodiless	boot tree	brakeman	brimfull
bloomery	Bodleian	boracite	brake van	brimless
blooming	bodyshop	Bordeaux	brancard	brimming
blossomy	bodywork	bordello	branched	brindled
blotting	Boeotian	borderer	brancher	bring off
blowball	bogeyman	borecole	branchia	bring out
blowfish	bohemian	borehole	brandied	briskish
blowhard	boldface	boringly	brandish	brisling
blowhole	boldness	borrower	brand new	britches
blowlamp	bollworm	bosseyed	brassage	britzska
blowpipe	bolthole	botanise	brassard	broacher
blubbery	boltrope	botanist	brassart	broadish
bludgeon	bombsite	botflies	brass hat	broadway
bluebell	bondmaid	botryoid	brassica	brocaded
bluebird	bondmans	bottomry	brassily	brocatel
blue chip	bondsman	botulism	brattice	broccoli
bluecoat	bonefish	bouffant	brattish	brochure
blue eyed	bonehead	bouillon	brazenly	broidery

brokenly
bromelia
bromidic
bronchia
bronchus
broodily
brookite
brooklet
brougham
brouhaha
browband
browbeat
browning
brownish
brunette
brush off
brutally
bryology
bryozoan
bubaline
buckaroo
buckbean
buckhorn
buckling
buckshee
buckshot
buckskin
Buddhism
Buddhist
buddleia
budgeree
buhlwork
building
bulkhead
bullcalf
bulldoze
bulletin
bullfrog
bullhead
bullhorn

bullocky
bullring
bullseye
bullyboy
bully off
bullyrag
bummaree
buncombe
bundling
bunfight
bungalow
bunghole
bunkered
buntline
buoyancy
Burberry
burglary
burgonet
burletta
burnouse
burnt out
burrower
bursitis
bushbaby
bushbuck
bushfire
bushveld
business
bustling
busybody
busyness
butchery
buttoner
buttress
butylene
butyrate
buzzword
by chance
by rights
Byronism

bystreet
by the way
cabalism
cabalist
caballed
cabinboy
cableway
cabochon
caboodle
cabotage
cabriole
cabstand
cachalot
cachepot
cachexia
cachucha
cacology
cacomixl
cactuses
cadastre
cadenced
caducean
caduceus
caducity
caducous
caesious
caesural
caffeine
cagebird
cageling
caginess
cajolery
cakewalk
calabash
caladium
calamary
calamine
calamint
calamite
calamity

calcanea
calcaria
calcific
calcitic
calcspar
calctuff
calculus
calendar
calender
calfskin
calidity
califate
calipash
calipers
callable
callgirl
calliope
calliper
calmness
calthrop
calvados
calyptra
Cambrian
cameleer
camellia
camisole
camomile
campagna
campaign
campfire
camphene
camphine
campsite
camshaft
Canadian
canaille
canalise
canaster
cancrine
cancroid

candidly
canister
cannabin
cannabis
cannibal
cannikin
cannonry
cannulae
cannular
cannulas
canoeing
canoeist
canoness
canonise
canonist
canon law
canoodle
canthari
canticle
cantonal
cantoris
canzonet
capacity
capeline
capellet
capeskin
capitate
capitula
caponise
caprifig
capriole
capsicum
capstone
capsular
captious
capuchin
capybara
carabine
caracara
caracole

carapace	casement	cattleya	cerebral	Chartist
carbolic	casework	caudally	cerebrum	chasseur
carbonic	cashbook	caudated	cerement	chastely
carbonyl	cash down	caudexes	ceremony	chastise
carboxyl	cashmere	caudices	cernuous	chastity
carburet	cassette	caudillo	cerulean	chasuble
carcajou	castaway	cauldron	cerusite	chateaux
carcanet	cast down	causally	cervelat	chattily
cardamom	castiron	causerie	cervical	chatting
cardamum	castrate	causeway	cervices	chaunter
card game	castrati	cautious	cesspool	chauntry
cardigan	castrato	cavalier	cetacean	cheapish
cardinal	casually	cavatina	chaconne	checkers
carefree	casualty	caverned	chainsaw	checkout
careless	catacomb	cavesson	chairman	cheekily
careworn	catalase	cavicorn	chalazae	cheerful
carillon	cataloes	cavilled	Chaldaic	cheerily
carinate	catalyse	caviller	Chaldean	cheering
carnally	catalyst	celeriac	chaldron	Chellean
carnauba	catamite	celerity	chalkpit	chemical
carnival	catapult	celibacy	chambers	chemurgy
Carolean	catchall	celibate	chambray	chenille
Caroline	catchfly	cellarer	champers	chequers
carolled	catching	cellaret	champion	Cherokee
carotene	catechol	cellular	chancery	cherubic
carousal	category	cemetery	chandler	cherubim
carousel	catenary	cenotaph	chapatti	chessman
carouser	catenate	Cenozoic	chapbook	chestnut
carriage	cateress	centaury	chapelry	Cheyenne
carriole	catering	centring	chaperon	chiasmus
carryall	cathedra	centrism	chapiter	chiastic
carryout	catheter	centrist	chaplain	chickpea
cartload	cathexes	centroid	chapping	chiefdom
cartouch	cathexis	centuple	charcoal	childbed
caruncle	cathodal	cephalic	charisma	childish
caryatid	cathodic	ceramics	charlady	children
Casanova	catholic	ceramist	charlock	chiliasm
cascabel	cationic	cerastes	charming	chiliast
casebook	catsfoot	ceratoid	charring	chimaera
casemate	catstail	cercaria	Chartism	chimeric

Chinaman	chummily	clamming	cliquism	coauthor
chinchin	chumming	clanging	cloddish	cobaltic
chinless	chupatti	clangour	clodpole	cobblers
chipmuck	chupatty	clannish	clodpoll	cobwebby
chipmunk	churchly	clanship	clogging	coccyges
chipping	churinga	clansman	cloister	cochleae
chirpily	churlish	clapping	clopclop	cochlear
chirrupy	churning	claptrap	close set	cockatoo
chitchat	chutzpah	claqueur	closeted	cockboat
chivalry	ciborium	clarence	cloth cap	cockcrow
chlorate	cicatrix	clarinet	clothier	cockerel
chloride	cicerone	classics	clothing	cockeyed
chlorine	ciceroni	classify	clotting	cockloft
chlorite	cicisbei	clavicle	cloudily	cockshut
chlorous	cicisbeo	clawback	cloudlet	cocksure
choicely	ci devant	claymore	clownery	cocktail
choirboy	ciliated	cleancut	clownish	codifier
choleric	cinchona	cleaning	clubbing	codpiece
chondrus	cincture	cleanser	clubfoot	codriver
chopchop	cineaste	clearcut	clubhaul	coelomic
chopping	cinerary	clearing	clubland	coenobia
chopsuey	cingulum	clear out	clueless	coenzyme
choragic	cinnabar	clearway	clumsily	coercion
choragus	cinnamic	cleavage	clupeoid	coercive
chorally	cinnamon	cleavers	clustery	cofactor
chordate	Circaean	clematis	clypeate	cogently
choregic	circuity	clemency	coachdog	cogitate
choregus	circular	clerical	coachman	cognomen
choriamb	cirriped	clerihew	coaction	cognosce
chorioid	cislunar	clerkdom	coactive	cognovit
chowchow	citation	clerkess	coagulum	cogwheel
chow mein	citified	cleverly	coaldust	coherent
christen	cityfied	climatic	coalesce	cohesion
christie	civilian	clincher	coalfish	cohesive
Christly	civilise	clinical	coalhole	coiffeur
chromate	civility	clinking	coalmine	coiffure
chromite	cladding	clipclop	coalsack	coincide
chromium	claimant	clippers	coarsely	coistrel
chthonic	clambake	clipping	coatrack	cokernut
chugging	clammily	cliquish	coatroom	colander

cold feet	commuter	congress	convenor	corniced
coldness	compiler	conidial	converge	corniche
coleseed	complain	conidium	converse	cornicle
coleslaw	compleat	coniform	convexly	cornific
colewort	complete	conjoint	conveyer	cornpone
coliform	complice	conjugal	conveyor	coronach
coliseum	complier	conjunct	convince	coronary
collagen	compline	conjurer	convolve	coronoid
collapse	composed	conjuror	convulse	corporal
collared	composer	conniver	cookbook	corridor
collator	compound	conoidal	coolabah	corrival
colleger	compress	conquest	cool down	corselet
colliery	comprise	conserve	cool head	corseted
collogue	computer	consider	coolibah	corsetry
colloquy	conation	consoler	coolness	cortical
collyria	conative	consomme	coonskin	cortices
colonial	concasse	conspire	cooption	corundum
colonise	conceder	constant	cooptive	corvette
colonist	conceive	construe	coplanar	Corybant
colophon	concerti	consular	copperas	coryphee
colossal	concerto	consumer	copulate	cosecant
colossus	concetti	contagia	copybook	cosiness
coloured	concetto	contango	copy edit	cosmetic
colubrid	conchate	contempt	copyhold	cosmical
columnal	conchoid	contents	coquetry	costmary
columnar	conclave	contessa	coquette	cost plus
columned	conclude	continua	coracoid	cost push
comatose	concrete	continue	cordless	costumer
combings	condense	continuo	cordovan	cotenant
comeback	conferee	contline	corduroy	cothurni
comedian	confetti	contorno	cordwain	cotillon
comedist	confider	contract	cordwood	cotquean
comedown	confiner	contrail	corelate	Cotswold
cometary	confines	contrary	corkwing	cottager
commando	conflate	contrast	corkwood	cottagey
commence	conflict	contrate	cornball	couchant
commerce	confound	contrite	corneous	couching
commoner	confrere	contrive	cornetcy	couldest
commonly	confront	conurbia	cornetti	coulisse
communal	congener	convener	cornetto	coumarin

countess	crashing	crofting	culpable	cutwater
coupling	crashpad	cromlech	culpably	cyanogen
courante	cratches	cropping	cultivar	cyanoses
coursing	cravenly	crossbar	cultural	cyanosis
courtesy	crawfish	crossbow	cultured	cyanotic
courtier	crayfish	crosscut	culverin	cyclamen
couscous	creakily	crossing	Cumbrian	cycleway
cousinly	creamery	crosslet	cumbrous	cyclical
covalent	creatine	crossply	cumulate	cyclonic
covenant	creation	crosstie	cumulous	cyclopes
coverage	creative	crossway	cupboard	cyclosis
coverall	creatrix	crotched	cupelled	cylinder
covering	creature	crotchet	cup final	cynicism
coverlet	credence	croupier	cupidity	cynosure
covertly	credenza	croupous	cup of tea	Cypriots
covetous	credible	crowbill	cupreous	cypselae
cowardly	credibly	crowfoot	cupulate	Cyrenaic
cowberry	credited	cruciate	curarine	Cyrillic
cowgrass	creditor	crucible	curarise	cysteine
coworker	creeping	crucifer	curassow	cystitis
coxalgia	crenated	crucifix	curative	cytidine
coxswain	crenelle	crueller	cureless	cytology
cozenage	creosote	crumhorn	curlicue	cytosine
crabbing	crepitus	crummock	currency	czaritza
crackers	crescent	crusader	curricle	dabchick
cracking	crescive	crustily	cursedly	dactylar
crackjaw	cretonne	cruzeiro	curtains	dactylic
cracknet	crevasse	cryogeny	curtness	daemonic
crackpot	cribbage	cryolite	curveted	daffodil
cradling	cribbing	cryostat	cushiony	daftness
craftily	criminal	cryotron	Cushitic	daimonic
cragsman	cristate	cubature	cuspidor	daintily
cramfull	criteria	cubiform	cussedly	daiquiri
cramming	critical	cuboidal	cussword	dairying
cramoisy	critique	cucumber	customer	dairyman
cranefly	croakily	cucurbit	cut a dash	dalesman
craniate	Croatian	cul de sac	cuteness	dalmatic
crankily	croceate	culicine	cut loose	damnable
crankpin	crockery	culinary	cutprice	damnably
crannied	crocoite	culottes	cutpurse	dampness

dancette	debonair	deferrer	demonism	destrier
dancetty	debugged	defiance	demotion	destruct
dandruff	debutant	defilade	demurely	detached
dandyish	decadent	definite	demurred	detailed
dandyism	decagram	deflower	demurrer	detainee
danegeld	decanter	deforest	denarius	detainer
dankness	deceased	deformed	denature	detector
danseuse	decedent	defrayal	denazify	deterred
daringly	deceiver	deftness	dendrite	deterrer
darkling	December	degrease	dendroid	dethrone
darkness	decemvir	deionise	deniable	detonate
darkroom	decennia	dejected	denounce	detoxify
darksome	decently	delation	dentated	detrital
dastardy	decigram	delegacy	denticle	detritus
dateless	decimate	delegate	departed	deucedly
dateline	decipher	deletion	depicter	deuteron
daughter	decision	delicacy	depictor	deviance
daybreak	decisive	delicate	depilate	deviancy
daydream	deckhand	delirium	deponent	deviator
daylight	declarer	delivery	deportee	deviling
deadbeat	declasse	Delphian	depraved	devilish
deadener	declutch	delusion	deprival	devilism
deadfall	decolour	delusive	deprived	devilkin
deadhead	decorate	delusory	deputise	devilled
deadline	decorous	demagogy	deration	deviltry
deadlock	decouple	demander	derelict	Devonian
deadness	decrease	demarche	derision	devotion
deadwood	decrepit	demented	derisive	devourer
deaerate	decretal	dementia	derisory	devoutly
deafmute	dedicate	demerara	derivate	dewberry
deafness	deemster	demersal	derogate	dewiness
dealfish	deeplaid	demijohn	derriere	dewpoint
deanship	deepness	demiurge	describe	dewy eyed
dearness	deerskin	demobbed	deserter	dextrine
deathbed	defector	democrat	designer	dextrose
deathcap	defender	demolish	desirous	dextrous
deathray	deferral	demoness	desolate	diabasic
debagged	deferent	demoniac	despatch	diabetes
debarred	deferral	demonian	despiser	diabetic
debility	deferred	demonise	despotic	diabolic

diaconal	diffract	directly	displode	dividual
diagnose	diffuser	director	displume	divinely
diagonal	digamist	dirigism	disposal	divinise
diagraph	digamous	disabuse	disposer	divinity
diallage	digester	disagree	disprize	division
dialling	diggings	disallow	disproof	divisive
dialogic	digitate	disarray	disprove	divorcee
dialogue	digitise	disaster	disquiet	djellaba
dialyser	dihedral	disbench	disseise	Docetism
dialyses	dihybrid	disbound	disserve	Docetist
dialysis	dilatant	disburse	dissever	docilely
dialytic	dilation	disciple	dissolve	docility
diamante	dilative	disclaim	dissuade	dockland
diameter	dilatory	disclose	distally	dockside
dianthus	diligent	discount	distance	dockyard
diapause	dilution	discover	distaste	doctoral
diaphone	diluvial	discreet	distinct	doctrine
diarchal	diluvian	discrete	distract	document
diarchic	diluvium	discrown	distrain	doddered
diarrhea	dimerism	diseased	distrait	dodderer
diaspora	dimerous	disendow	distress	dogberry
diaspore	diminish	disfrock	district	dogeared
diastase	dimmable	disgorge	distrust	dogfaced
diastema	diner out	disgrace	disunion	dogfight
diastole	dingdong	disguise	disunite	doggedly
diatomic	dinosaur	dishevel	disunity	doggerel
diatonic	diocesan	disinter	disusage	doggy bag
diatribe	dioecism	disjoint	disvalue	doghouse
dichroic	diopside	disjunct	ditheism	dogmatic
dicrotic	dioptase	dislodge	ditheist	dogooder
dictator	dioptric	disloyal	ditherer	dogsbody
dicyclic	dioramic	dismally	dittybag	dogshore
didactic	dioritic	dismount	dittybox	dogtired
didapper	diphenyl	disorder	diuresis	dogtooth
didymium	diploidy	dispatch	diuretic	dogwatch
dieldrin	diplomat	dispense	divagate	dogwhelk
diereses	diplopia	disperse	divalent	doldrums
dieresis	dipstick	dispirit	divebomb	dolerite
diestock	dipteral	displace	dividend	dolesome
dietetic	dipteran	displant	dividivi	dolomite

doloroso	dovetail	dreadful	drunkard	dustless
dolorous	dowdyish	dreamful	drupelet	dustlike
domestic	dowelled	dreamily	dry clean	dustshot
domicile	downbeat	dreaming	dry nurse	Dutchman
dominant	downcast	drearily	drypoint	dutiable
dominate	downcome	drencher	drystone	dutyfree
domineer	downfall	dressage	duchesse	dutypaid
dominion	downhaul	dressing	duckbill	dwarfish
dominoes	downhill	dribbler	duckhawk	dwarfism
donation	downland	dribblet	duckling	dwelling
Donatism	downmost	driftage	duckpond	dybbukim
Donatist	downpipe	drift ice	duckweed	dyestuff
donative	downpour	driftway	ductless	dynamics
donatory	downtime	drilling	duelling	dynamism
doomsday	downtown	drinking	duellist	dynamist
doomsman	downturn	dripfeed	due north	dynamite
doomster	downward	dripping	due south	dynastic
doorbell	downwind	drivable	duettist	dynatron
doorcase	doxology	driveway	dulciana	dysgenic
doorknob	doziness	drollery	dulcimer	dyslexia
doornail	drabbler	drophead	Dulcinea	dyslexic
doorpost	drabness	dropkick	dullness	dyspnoea
doorsill	drachmas	dropleaf	dumbbell	dystopia
doorstep	draconic	dropping	dumbhead	eagle owl
doorstop	dragging	dropshot	dumbness	earmuffs
dooryard	dragline	dropwort	dumbshow	earnings
dopiness	dragoman	droughty	dumfound	earphone
dormancy	dragomen	drownded	dumpling	earpiece
dormouse	dragonet	drowsily	dungaree	earthnut
dorsally	dragsman	drubbing	dungcart	easement
dotingly	dragster	drudgery	dunghill	easiness
dotterel	drainage	drugging	duodenal	easterly
douanier	dramatic	druggist	duodenum	eastmost
doubloon	drammock	druidess	duologue	eastward
doubtful	dramshop	druidism	durables	east wind
doughboy	draughts	drumfire	duration	ebriated
doughnut	draughty	drumhead	durative	echinate
doumpalm	drawable	drumming	dustbowl	echinoid
dourness	drawback	drummock	dustcart	echogram
dovecote	drawtube	drumroll	dustcoat	echoless

eclectic	ejection	emceeing	encroach	enshroud
ecliptic	ejective	emendate	encumber	ensiform
eclosion	ekistics	emergent	encyclic	ensigncy
ecologic	elatedly	emeritus	endamage	ensilage
economic	El Dorado	emersion	endanger	enslaver
ecstatic	eldritch	emetical	endemism	ensphere
ectoderm	election	emigrant	endermic	enswathe
edacious	elective	emigrate	endocarp	entailer
edentate	electret	eminence	endoderm	entangle
edgeless	electric	eminency	endogamy	entellus
edgeways	electron	emissary	endogeny	enterate
edgewise	electrum	emission	endorsee	enthalpy
edginess	elegance	emissive	endorser	enthrall
editress	elegancy	emitting	endpaper	enthrone
educable	elenchus	Emmental	energise	entirely
educated	elephant	empathic	enervate	entirety
educator	elevated	empeople	enfeeble	entoderm
educible	elevator	emphasis	enfetter	entoptic
eduction	eleventh	emphatic	enfilade	entracte
eelgrass	elflocks	employee	enforcer	entrails
eeriness	eligible	employer	enforest	entrance
effector	eligibly	empoison	engaging	entreaty
efferent	elkhound	emporium	engender	entrench
efficacy	ellipses	empurple	engineer	entrepot
effluent	ellipsis	empyreal	enginery	entresol
effluvia	elliptic	empyrean	engirdle	enuresis
effusion	elongate	emulator	engramme	enuretic
effusive	eloquent	emulgent	engraver	envelope
eftsoons	emaciate	emulsify	enkindle	enviable
egestion	embalmer	emulsion	enlarger	enviably
egestive	embattle	emulsive	enormity	environs
eggplant	embedded	emulsoid	enormous	envisage
eggshell	embezzle	enaction	enquirer	envision
eggtimer	embitter	enactive	enricher	enzootic
egoistic	emblazon	encaenia	enrolled	eohippus
egomania	embolden	enceinte	ensample	eolithic
Egyptian	embolism	encipher	ensconce	ephemera
eighteen	embosser	encircle	ensemble	Ephesian
eighthly	embracer	enclothe	ensheath	ephorate
eighties	embussed	encomion	enshrine	epically

epicotyl	erodible	eternise	eutectic	execrate
epicycle	erogenic	eternity	eutrophy	executor
epidemic	erotical	ethereal	evacuant	exegesis
epidural	errantly	etherial	evacuate	exegetic
epifauna	errantry	etherise	evadable	exemplar
epigeous	eruption	etherism	evaluate	exemplum
epigraph	eruptive	etherist	evanesce	exequies
epilepsy	escalade	ethicism	evection	exercise
epilogue	escalate	ethicist	evenfall	exertion
epinasty	escallop	Ethiopic	evenness	exhalant
epiphany	escalope	ethnarch	evensong	exhorter
epiphyte	escapade	ethnical	eventful	exigence
episcope	escapism	ethology	eventide	exigency
episodal	escapist	ethylene	eventual	exigible
episodic	escargot	etiolate	evermore	exiguity
epistler	escarole	Etrurian	eversion	exiguous
epistyle	eschalot	Etruscan	everyday	existent
epitasis	eschewal	eucalypt	everyman	ex libris
epyllion	esculent	eucritic	everyone	exocrine
equalise	Eskimoan	eugenics	everyway	exogamic
equality	esoteric	eugenism	eviction	exorcise
equalled	espalier	eugenist	evidence	exorcism
equation	especial	eulogise	evildoer	exorcist
equinity	espousal	eulogist	evilness	exordial
equipage	espouser	eulogium	evincive	exordium
equipped	espresso	euonymus	evitable	exospore
equitant	Esquimau	eupatrid	evulsion	exoteric
equities	essayist	eupepsia	exacting	expander
equivoke	Essenism	eupeptic	exaction	expedite
erasable	essonite	euphonic	examinee	expelled
Erastian	esterify	euphoria	examiner	expellee
erectile	estimate	euphoric	exanthem	expertly
erection	Estonian	euphrasy	excavate	expiable
eremitic	estopped	euphuism	excelled	expiator
erethism	estoppel	euphuist	exchange	expirant
erewhile	estovers	Eurasian	excision	explicit
ergogram	estrange	Eurocrat	excitant	exploder
ergotise	estuaril	European	exciting	explorer
ergotism	esurient	europium	excluder	exponent
erigeron	etcetera	eustatic	excursus	exporter

exposure	faineant	farthing	federate	fibrosis
exserted	faintish	fascicle	feeblish	fibrotic
extender	fair deal	fasciola	feedback	fiddling
extensor	fairlead	fasciole	feedhead	fidelity
exterior	fairness	Fascista	feedpipe	fiducial
external	fairyism	Fascisti	feedtank	fiendish
extolled	faithful	fastback	feldspar	fiercely
extrados	falcated	fastener	felicity	fiftieth
extremes	falconer	fast food	felinity	fiftyish
extrorse	falconet	fast line	fellable	fighting
exultant	falconry	fastness	fellahin	fight shy
exuviate	falderal	fast talk	fellness	figurant
eyeglass	fallback	fatalism	fellowly	figurine
eyeliner	fallfish	fatalist	felsitic	filagree
eyepiece	fallible	fatality	feminine	filament
eyerhyme	fallibly	fatherly	feminise	filariae
eyeshade	falsetto	fatigues	feminism	filarial
eyesight	familial	fatstock	feminist	filature
eyestalk	familiar	fattener	feminity	filefish
eyetooth	famously	faubourg	fenberry	filially
eyewater	fanciful	faultily	fencible	filiform
fabliaux	fancyman	faunally	fenestra	filigree
fabulist	fan dance	Faustian	feretory	Filipina
fabulous	fandango	fauteuil	fernshaw	Filipino
faceache	fanfaron	favonian	ferocity	filmgoer
facecard	fangless	favoured	ferreter	filmstar
faceless	fanlight	favourer	ferriage	filthily
facelift	fantasia	fearless	ferritic	filtrate
facepack	faradaic	fearsome	ferryman	fimbriae
facetiae	faradism	feasible	fervency	finalise
facially	farcical	feasibly	fervidly	finalism
facilely	farewell	feastday	festally	finalist
facility	farflung	feathery	festival	finality
factious	farinose	featured	fetching	finedraw
factotum	farmhand	features	feticide	fineness
fadeaway	farmland	febrific	feudally	finespun
fadeless	farmyard	February	feverfew	fingered
fagoting	farouche	feckless	feverish	finisher
failsafe	farriery	feculent	feverous	finitely
fain deal	farthest	fedayeen	fibrilla	finitude

firearms	fistular	fleabane	flounder	fondling
fireback	fitfully	fleabite	flourish	fondness
fireball	fivefold	fleawort	flowered	fontanel
firebird	fivestar	flection	flowerer	foodless
fireboat	fixation	fleeting	floweret	foolscap
firebomb	fixative	fleshfly	flubbing	football
firebrat	flagella	fleshpot	fluellin	footbath
fireclay	flagging	fletcher	fluently	footfall
firedamp	flagpole	flexible	fluepipe	footgear
fire eyed	flagrant	flexibly	fluidics	foothill
firehose	flagship	flexuose	fluidify	foothold
firelock	flambeau	flexuous	fluidise	footless
fire opal	flamenco	flexural	fluidity	footling
fireplug	flamingo	flickery	flummery	footmark
fireship	flapjack	flimflam	fluoride	footmuff
fireside	flapping	flimsily	fluorine	footnote
firetrap	flashgun	flincher	fluorite	footpace
fireweed	flashily	flinders	fluttery	footpath
firewood	flashing	flintily	flyblown	footpost
firework	flatboat	flipflap	flypaper	footrace
firmness	flatfeet	flipflop	flywheel	footrest
firstaid	flatfish	flippant	foamless	footrope
fiscally	flatfoot	flipping	focalise	footrule
fishable	flathead	flipside	focusing	footslog
fishball	flatiron	flitting	focussed	footsore
fishbone	flatling	floatage	foetidly	footstep
fishbowl	flatmate	floating	fogbound	footwear
fishcake	flatness	floccose	foldaway	footwork
fishfarm	flatrace	floccule	foldboat	foramina
fishglue	flat spin	flocculi	folderol	forborne
fishhawk	flattery	flogging	foliaged	forcedly
fishhook	flattest	floodlit	folklore	forcefed
fishless	flattish	floodway	folkmoot	forceful
fishmeal	flatware	flooring	folksong	forcible
fishpond	flatways	floppily	folktale	forcibly
fishtail	flatwise	flopping	follicle	fordable
fishwife	flatworm	florally	follower	fordoing
fissiped	flautist	floridly	follow on	forebear
fistical	flawless	florigen	follow up	forebode
fistulae	flaxseed	flotilla	fomenter	forecast

foredeck	foreword	fourthly	fretwork	frumpish
foredoom	foreyard	fowlpest	Freudian	frustule
fore edge	forgiven	foxglove	friction	frutices
forefeel	forgoing	foxhound	friendly	fuchsine
forefelt	for keeps	foxiness	Friesian	fuelling
forefoot	forklift	foxshark	frighten	fugacity
foregoer	formalin	frabjous	frigidly	fugitive
foregone	formally	fraction	frijoles	fugleman
forehand	formless	fracture	frillies	fullback
forehead	formroom	fraenula	fringing	full moon
foreknew	formulae	fragment	frippery	fullness
foreknow	formulas	fragrant	frisette	full of go
forelady	formwork	framesaw	friskily	fullpage
foreland	fornices	francium	fritting	fullsize
forelock	forrader	Frankish	frocking	fulltime
foremast	forsaken	franklin	frogfish	fumarole
foremost	forsooth	frapping	frogging	fumigant
forename	forspeak	Fraulein	frogspit	fumigate
forenoon	forspent	freakish	frondage	fumitory
forensic	forswear	freakout	frondent	function
forepart	forswore	freeborn	frondeur	funebral
forepast	forsworn	freedman	frondose	funerary
forepeak	fortieth	freefall	frontage	funereal
foreplay	fortress	freehand	frontier	fungible
foresaid	fortuity	freehold	frontlet	funkhole
foresail	fortyish	freeload	frostily	funnyman
foreseen	forwards	freeness	frosting	furbelow
foreshow	forzando	freesoil	frothily	furcated
foreside	fosterer	freewill	frottage	furculae
foreskin	foulness	freezeup	froufrou	furcular
forestal	founding	freezing	fructify	furfural
forestay	fountain	frenetic	fructose	furfuran
forested	fourball	frenulum	frugally	furlough
forester	foureyes	frenzied	fruitage	furriery
forestry	fourfold	frequent	fruitbat	furthest
foretell	fourleaf	frescoes	fruitery	furuncle
foretime	fourpart	fresh air	fruitfly	fuselage
foretold	foursome	freshman	fruitful	fusiform
forewarn	fourstar	freshrun	fruition	fusileer
forewent	fourteen	fretting	frumenty	fusilier

futilely	gangling	gazogene	gestagen	glassily
futility	ganglion	gazpacho	gestural	glassine
futurism	gangrene	gearcase	get ahead	glaucoma
futurist	gangster	gelatine	get clear	glaucous
futurity	ganister	gelation	get round	glaziery
gabbroic	gantline	gelidity	Ghanaian	gleaning
gabbroid	gantlope	geminate	ghastful	gleesome
gable end	gaolbird	gemstone	ghettoes	glibness
gadabout	gapeworm	gendarme	ghoulish	glissade
gadarene	gapingly	generate	giantess	glittery
gadgetry	garboard	generous	giantism	gloaming
Gadhelic	gardener	genetics	giftbook	globally
gadzooks	gardenia	Genevese	gigantic	globular
gainable	gardyloo	genially	gillaroo	globulin
gainings	garefowl	genitive	gilthead	gloomily
gainless	garganey	geniture	gimcrack	gloriole
gainsaid	gargoyle	genocide	gimmicky	glorious
galactic	garishly	genotype	gin and it	glossary
galangal	garlicky	gentrice	gingerly	glossily
galbanum	garotter	geodesic	gingival	glossina
galeated	garreted	geodetic	gin rummy	glowworm
Galenism	garrison	geognosy	gin sling	gloxinia
galenite	garrotte	geologic	gipsydom	glucagon
Galilean	gaselier	geomancy	gipsyism	glummest
galleass	gasfired	geometer	girasole	glumness
galliard	gashouse	geometry	girlhood	glutting
Gallican	gaslight	geophagy	giveaway	gluttony
gallipot	gas meter	geophone	glabella	glycerin
galloper	gasolene	geophyte	glabrous	glycerol
Galloway	gasolier	geoponic	glaciate	glyceryl
galluses	gasoline	Georgian	gladdest	glycogen
gall wasp	gastight	geotaxis	gladding	glyconic
galvanic	gastrula	geraniol	gladhand	glyptics
gamebird	gasworks	geranium	gladioli	gnathite
gamecock	gatefold	gerbille	gladness	gneissic
gameness	gatepost	Germanic	gladsome	gnomonic
gamesome	gatherer	germcell	glancing	goadster
gamester	Gaullism	germfree	glanders	goalkick
gaminess	Gaullist	germinal	glandule	goalline
gangland	gauntlet	gerontic	glassful	goalpost

goatfish	gormless	gratuity	groschen	gusseted
goatherd	gossamer	gravamen	grottoes	guttural
goatling	gossiper	gravelly	grounder	gymkhana
goatmoth	gossipry	graviton	grouping	gymnasia
goatskin	gossypol	grayling	grouting	gynandry
Gobelins	got drunk	greasily	growling	gynocrat
godawful	go to seed	great tit	grubbily	gynoecia
godchild	gourmand	greedily	grubbing	gypseous
Godspeed	goutweed	greegree	grudging	gypsydom
godwards	goutwort	greenery	gruesome	gypsyism
gogetter	governor	greenfly	grumbler	gyration
Goidelic	gownsman	greening	grumpily	gyratory
going out	Graafian	greenish	gruntled	gyrostat
goings on	grabbing	greenlet	guacharo	habanera
goitrous	grabbler	greeting	guaranty	habitant
Golconda	graceful	greyfish	guardant	habitual
gold dust	gracious	greyness	guardian	habitude
goldenly	gradient	gridiron	Guelphic	hacienda
goldfish	graduand	grievous	guerilla	hadronic
goldfoil	graduate	grillage	guernsey	haematic
goldleaf	Graecise	grimacer	guidable	haematin
goldmine	Graecism	grimmest	guidance	Haggadah
goldrush	graffiti	grimness	guide dog	hairgrip
golfclub	graffito	grimoire	guideway	hairless
golliwog	graining	grindery	guileful	hairlike
gonfalon	gralloch	grinning	guiltily	hairline
gonidial	gramarye	gripping	Gujarati	hairworm
gonidium	gram atom	gripsack	gulfweed	Halachah
goodness	gramercy	Griselda	gullable	halation
good news	grandame	griseous	gullible	haleness
good time	granddad	grisette	gulosity	halfback
good turn	grandeur	grisgris	gummosis	halfbeak
goodwife	grandson	grissini	gumption	halfboot
goodwill	granitic	gritting	gunfight	halfbred
goodyear	granular	grizzled	gunflint	halflife
goofball	grapheme	groggily	gunlayer	halfmast
goosegog	graphics	grogshop	gunmetal	halfmoon
go places	graphite	gromwell	gunpoint	halfnote
gorgeous	grasping	groogroo	gunsmith	halfpint
gorgonia	grateful	grosbeak	gunstock	halfsole

halfterm	harakiri	havildar	heavenly	henchman
halftime	harangue	havocked	hebdomad	henequen
halftone	harasser	Hawaiian	hebetate	hen party
haliotis	hardback	hawfinch	hebetude	hen roost
halliard	hardbake	hawkeyed	hebraise	hepatica
hallmark	hardcase	hawklike	Hebraism	hepatise
hallowed	hardcore	hawkmoth	Hebraist	heptagon
halteres	hardener	hawkweed	hecatomb	heraldic
handball	hardhack	hawthorn	hedgehog	heraldry
handbell	hardhead	hayfield	hedgehop	herbaria
handbill	hardline	haymaker	hedgepig	herbless
handbook	hard luck	haystack	hedgerow	Hercules
handcart	hardness	hazelnut	hedonics	herdbook
handclap	hardship	haziness	hedonism	herdsman
handcuff	hardtack	headache	hedonist	herdwick
handfast	hard time	headachy	heedless	hereaway
handgrip	hardware	headband	heelball	heredity
handheld	hardwood	headfast	heelless	Hereford
handhold	hard work	headgear	Hegelian	hereunto
handicap	harebell	headlamp	hegemony	hereupon
handless	hari kari	headland	heighten	herewith
handline	harlotry	headless	heirless	heritage
handling	harmless	headline	heirloom	hermetic
handlist	harmonic	headlock	heirship	heroical
handloom	harp seal	headlong	heliacal	herpetic
handmade	harridan	headmost	helicoid	Hertzian
handmaid	harrumph	headnote	heliosis	hesitant
handmill	hasheesh	headrace	heliport	hesitate
handpick	hastener	headrest	Helladic	Hesperus
handrail	hastings	headroom	hellbent	hetaerae
handsewn	hatchery	headsail	Hellenic	hetairai
hands off	hatching	headsman	hellfire	hexagram
handsome	hatchway	headwind	hellhole	hexapody
handwork	hateable	headword	helmeted	hexylene
handyman	hatstand	headwork	helminth	hibernal
hangable	haulyard	hear hear	helmsman	hibiscus
hangeron	haunting	heartily	helotism	hiccough
hangnail	hausfrau	heatedly	helpless	hickwall
hangover	have a nap	heathery	helpmate	hideaway
haploidy	havelock	heathhen	helpmeet	hidrosis

hidrotic	histogen	homogamy	hospital	humuncle
hidyhole	historic	homogeny	hostelry	hungrily
hielaman	hitherto	homology	hot cakes	huntress
hierarch	hoarding	homonymy	hotchpot	huntsman
hieratic	hoarsely	homuncle	hotelier	hurtless
highball	hobbitry	honestly	hothouse	hushhush
highborn	hobbyist	honeybee	hotplate	hustings
highbred	hocusing	honeydew	hotpress	hyacinth
highbrow	hocussed	honeypot	hot stuff	hydatoid
higher up	Hogmanay	honorary	hot toddy	hydranth
highjack	hogsback	honourer	hot water	hydrogen
high jump	hogshead	hoodwink	hourlong	hydromel
highland	holdback	hoofbeat	houseboy	hydropic
high life	holdfast	hookworm	housedog	hydropsy
highlows	holdover	hooligan	housefly	hydroxyl
highmost	holidays	hoosegow	houseful	hygienic
highness	holiness	hopeless	houseman	hymenial
highrise	holistic	Horatian	housetop	hymenium
high road	hollands	hormonal	hoverfly	hymnbook
hightail	hollowly	hornbeam	howitzer	hyoscine
hightest	Holocene	hornbill	hows that	hypnoses
high tide	hologram	hornbook	huckster	hypnosis
high time	holozoic	hornfels	hugeness	hypnotic
hijacker	holstein	hornless	huggable	hypobole
hilarity	homebody	hornpipe	Huguenot	hypogeal
hillfort	homebred	hornrims	hulahula	hypogean
hillocky	homebrew	horntail	humanely	hypogene
hillside	homefelt	hornworm	humanise	hypogyny
himation	homeland	hornwort	humanism	hypothec
hinderer	homeless	horologe	humanist	hysteria
hindlegs	homelike	horology	humanity	hysteric
hindmost	homemade	horrible	humanoid	Ibsenism
hinduise	homesick	horribly	humidify	iceblink
Hinduism	homespun	horridly	humidity	icebound
hipflask	home town	horrific	humility	ice cream
hipsters	homeward	horsebox	hummocky	icefield
hireable	homework	horsecar	humorist	iceplant
hireling	homicide	horsefly	humorous	iceskate
hirrient	hominoid	horseman	humoured	ice water
Hispanic	homodont	hosepipe	humpback	ice yacht

idealess	immanent	in a flash	inexpert	innately
idealise	immature	inasmuch	infamise	innocent
idealism	immersed	in camera	infamous	innovate
idealist	imminent	inceptor	infantry	innuendo
ideality	immingle	inchmeal	infector	inoculum
ideation	immobile	inchoate	inferior	in person
identify	immodest	inchworm	infernal	in pocket
identity	immolate	incident	inferred	inquirer
ideogram	immortal	incision	infilter	insanely
ideology	immunise	incisive	infinite	insanity
idiolect	immunity	incitant	infinity	inscient
idiotism	impacted	incivism	infirmly	inscribe
idleness	imparity	included	inflamer	inscroll
idocrase	impelled	incoming	inflated	insecure
idolater	impeller	increase	inflator	inserted
idolatry	imperial	increate	inflatus	insignia
idoliser	imperium	incubate	inflexed	insolate
idyllist	impetigo	incurred	inflight	insolent
ignition	impishly	indagate	influent	insomnia
ignitron	impledge	indebted	informal	insomuch
ignominy	implicit	indecent	informed	insphere
ignorant	impolder	Indiaman	informer	inspired
illation	impolicy	indicant	infrared	inspirer
illative	impolite	indicate	infringe	inspirit
ill fated	imponent	indicium	infusion	instable
illiquid	importer	indigene	ingather	instance
ill timed	imposing	indigent	ingrowth	instancy
ill treat	impostor	indirect	inguinal	instinct
illumine	impotent	indocile	inhalant	instruct
illusage	imprimis	indolent	inherent	insulant
illusion	imprison	inductee	inhesion	insulate
illusive	improper	inductor	inhumane	insulter
illusory	improver	indulger	inimical	insurant
Illyrian	impudent	indurate	iniquity	intaglio
ilmenite	impugner	industry	initiate	intarsia
imaginal	impunity	inedible	injector	integral
imagines	impurely	inedited	inkiness	intended
imbecile	impurity	inequity	inkstand	intently
imitable	inaction	inerrant	inlander	interact
imitator	inactive	inertial	in league	interbed

intercom	investor	isomeric	Jehovist	judgment
intercut	inviable	isometry	jejunely	judicial
interest	inviting	isomorph	jeopardy	jugglery
interior	invocate	isophote	jeremiad	Jugoslav
intermit	involute	isopleth	Jeremiah	jugulate
intermix	inwardly	isoprene	jeroboam	julienne
internal	iodinate	isoptera	jerrican	jumpedup
internee	iodoform	isospory	jerrycan	jumpseat
Interpol	iotacism	isostasy	jesuitic	jumpsuit
interred	irenical	isothere	jesuitry	junction
interrex	irenicon	isotherm	jetblack	juncture
intersex	Irishism	isotonic	jetplane	junkshop
intertie	Irishman	isotopic	jettison	junkyard
interval	ironbark	isotropy	jewelled	Jurassic
interwar	ironclad	issuable	jeweller	juristic
in the air	iron duke	issuance	jiggered	just a sec
in the bag	irongray	isthmian	jingoish	justness
in the way	irongrey	Italiote	jingoism	juvenile
inthrall	ironical	iterance	jingoist	Kaffiyeh
intimacy	ironside	ivory nut	jipijapa	kailyard
intimate	ironware	jabberer	jiujitsu	kakemono
intimism	iron will	jackaroo	jobation	kalaazar
intitule	ironwood	jackboot	jocosely	kamikaze
intonate	ironwork	jackeroo	jocosity	Kanarese
intrados	Iroquois	jackstay	jocundly	kangaroo
intrench	irrigate	Jacobean	jodhpurs	Kashmiri
intrepid	irritant	Jacobite	joinable	katakana
intrigue	irritate	jacquard	jointure	kedgeree
intromit	ischemia	jaggedly	jokingly	keelhaul
introrse	ischemic	jailbird	jolthead	keelless
intruder	Islamise	jalousie	Jonathan	keenness
inundate	Islamism	jamboree	jongleur	keepsake
inurbane	Islamite	janizary	jovially	keeshond
invasion	islander	Japanese	joyfully	kefuffle
invasive	isocracy	japanned	joyously	keratose
invected	isogloss	japonica	joystick	kerchief
inveigle	isogonal	jaundice	jubilant	kerosene
inventor	isogonic	jauntily	jubilate	kerosine
inverted	isolable	Javanese	Judaical	keyboard
inverter	isolator	jealousy	Judaiser	keystone

khedival	knitting	ladyfern	lanneret	lavender
Khmerian	knitwear	ladyhood	lanthorn	laverock
khuskhus	knocking	ladylike	lapboard	lavishly
kibitzer	knock off	ladylove	lapelled	lawcourt
kickback	knockout	ladyship	lapicide	lawfully
kickshaw	knothole	laically	lapidary	lawgiver
kidglove	knotting	lakeland	lapidate	lawmaker
killdeer	knotwork	lallygag	lapidify	lawyerly
kilogram	knowable	lamasery	larboard	laxative
kilowatt	Kohinoor	lambaste	larcener	layabout
kindless	kohlrabi	lambency	largesse	layshaft
kindling	kolinsky	lamblike	larkspur	laystall
kindness	Komsomol	lambskin	larrikin	laywoman
kinesics	korfball	lamellae	larynges	Lazarist
kinetics	kreutzer	lamellar	larynxes	laziness
kingbird	kromesky	lameness	lashings	lazulite
kingbolt	krumhorn	lamented	latchkey	lazurite
kingcrab	kurtosis	laminate	lateness	leadenly
kingfish	kyphosis	lamp post	latently	leadless
kinghood	kyphotic	lancelet	laterite	leadsman
kinglike	labdanum	land army	Latinate	leadwork
kingship	labelled	land crab	latinise	leafless
kingsize	labellum	landfall	Latinism	leaflike
kinkajou	labially	landform	Latinist	leanness
kinsfolk	lability	landgirl	latinity	leapfrog
kissable	labourer	landlady	latitant	leap year
kisscurl	labrador	landless	latitude	learning
klephtic	laburnum	landline	latterly	leathern
klondike	lacerate	landlord	latticed	leathery
klystron	lacewing	landmark	laudable	leave out
knackery	lacework	landmass	laudably	leavings
knapping	lackaday	land mine	laudanum	lecithin
knapsack	laconian	land rail	laudator	lecturer
knapweed	lacrimal	landslip	laughing	leeboard
kneedeep	lacrosse	landsman	laughter	left flat
kneehigh	lacrymal	langlauf	launcher	lefthand
kneehole	lacunary	Langshan	laureate	leftover
kneejerk	lacunate	language	lava lava	leftward
knickers	lacunose	languish	lavation	left wing
knightly	ladybird	lankness	lavatory	legalese

legalise	levirate	lignitic	littling	lodgment
legalism	levitate	ligulate	littoral	lodicule
legalist	levulose	likeable	liturgic	logician
legality	lewdness	likewise	liveable	logistic
legatine	lewisite	limbless	liveborn	logogram
legation	libation	lime kiln	livelily	logotype
legbreak	libatory	limerick	livelong	loiterer
legendry	libeccio	lime twig	live rail	Lollardy
legerity	libelled	limewash	liveried	lollipop
leggings	libellee	limitary	liverish	lollypop
leg guard	libeller	limonite	livewire	lomentum
legioned	liberate	limpidly	lividity	Londoner
leisured	libretti	limpness	lixivium	loneness
lemonade	libretto	linchpin	loadline	lonesome
lemon tea	licensed	lineally	loadstar	longboat
lemurine	licensee	linearly	loanable	longeron
lemuroid	licenser	linesman	loanword	longeval
lengthen	lichened	lingerer	loathful	longhair
lenience	lichenin	lingerie	loathing	longhand
leniency	lichgate	linguist	lobation	longhorn
Leninism	licorice	liniment	lobbyist	long jump
Leninist	liegeman	Linnaean	lobeline	longness
Leninite	lifebelt	linoleum	loblolly	long odds
lenitive	lifeboat	linstock	lobotomy	longship
lensless	lifebuoy	lintseed	lobulate	long shot
lenticel	lifeless	lipogram	localise	longsome
lenticle	lifelike	lipomata	localism	longstop
lepidote	lifeline	lipsalve	locality	longterm
leporine	lifelong	lipstick	locative	longtime
lethally	lifesize	liquidly	lockable	longueur
lethargy	lifetime	liripoop	lockfast	longwall
let me see	lifework	listener	lockknit	longwave
lettered	liftable	listless	lockstep	longways
leucitic	ligament	literacy	locofoco	longwise
levanter	ligation	literary	locomote	looker on
levelled	ligature	literate	loculate	look over
leveller	light ale	literati	locution	loonybin
leverage	lighting	litharge	locutory	loophole
leviable	lightish	litigant	lodestar	loosebox
levigate	ligneous	litigate	lodgings	loosener

lopeared	luminary	maculate	majolica	mangabey
lopgrass	luminist	madapple	majority	manganic
lopsided	luminous	made it up	makebate	mangonel
lordless	lumpfish	madhouse	makefast	mangrove
lordling	lunarian	madrigal	make it up	maniacal
lordosis	lunation	madwoman	makimono	Manichee
lordotic	luncheon	Maecenas	Malagasy	manicure
Lord's day	lungfish	maenadic	malamute	manifest
lordship	lungwort	maestoso	malapert	manifold
loricate	lunulate	magazine	malaprop	maniform
lorikeet	luscious	magdalen	malarial	mannered
lothario	lushness	magician	malarian	mannerly
loudness	lustrate	magister	malarkey	mannikin
louvered	lustrine	magmatic	maledict	mannitol
lovebird	lustring	magnesia	maleforn	man of war
loveknot	lustrous	magnetic	malemute	manorial
loveless	lutanist	magneton	maleness	manpower
lovelily	lutecium	magnific	maligner	mansized
lovelock	lutenist	magnolia	malignly	mantelet
lovelorn	lutetium	maharaja	malinger	mantilla
lovenest	Lutheran	maharani	malodour	mantissa
loveseat	luxation	mah jongg	maltreat	mantling
lovesick	lychgate	mahogany	maltster	manually
lovesome	lykewake	Mahratta	malvasia	manubria
lovesong	lymphoid	Mahratti	Mameluke	manurial
lovingly	lymphoma	maidenly	mamillae	maquette
lowering	lynchpin	maidhood	mamillar	marabout
lowgrade	lynxeyed	maieutic	manciple	marasmic
lowlevel	lyophile	mailable	Mandaean	marasmus
lowlying	lyrebird	mailboat	mandamus	marathon
loyalist	lyricism	mailcart	mandarin	marauder
lubberly	lyricist	mainland	mandator	maravedi
lubrical	lysosome	mainline	mandible	marbling
lucidity	lysozyme	mainmast	Mandingo	marchesa
luckless	macaroni	mainsail	mandolin	marchese
luculent	macaroon	mainstay	mandorla	marginal
Lucullan	macerate	maintain	mandrake	margrave
lukewarm	machinaw	mainyard	mandrill	marigold
lumberer	machismo	maiolica	maneater	marinade
luminant	mackerel	majestic	manfully	marinate

maritage	matrices	megalith	meshwork	mightily
maritime	matrixes	megapode	mesially	migraine
marjoram	matronal	megawatt	mesmeric	migrator
markdown	matronly	melamine	mesocarp	mildness
markedly	mattress	melanism	mesoderm	milepost
marketer	maturate	melanite	mesotron	Milesian
marksman	maturely	melinite	Mesozoic	militant
marmoset	maturity	mellowly	mesquite	military
marocain	maverick	melodeon	messmate	militate
maroquin	maxillae	melodise	messuage	milkmaid
marquess	maximise	melodist	metalled	milkweed
marquise	mayapple	membered	metallic	milkwort
marriage	mayoress	membrane	metamere	millhand
marrieds	Mayqueen	mementos	metaphor	milliard
marrying	mazarine	memorise	metazoan	milliary
marshman	Mazdaism	memsahib	metazoon	millibar
martello	mazement	menarche	meteoric	millieme
martenot	maziness	mendable	methanol	milliner
martinet	meagrely	menhaden	methinks	millpond
marzipan	mealtime	menially	methodic	millrace
mascaron	mealworm	meninges	methylic	Miltonic
Masorete	mealybug	meniscus	metonymy	mimester
Masoreth	meanness	menology	metrical	mimicked
massacre	meantime	menstrua	mezereon	mimicker
masseter	measured	mensural	miasmata	minacity
masseuse	meatball	menswear	miasmous	minatory
massicot	meatsafe	mentally	micellar	mince pie
massless	mechanic	mephitic	microbar	mindless
masterly	medalled	mephitis	microbic	minimise
masthead	medallic	merchant	microdot	minister
mastitis	medially	merciful	micrurgy	ministry
mastodon	mediator	mercuric	midbrain	Minoress
matamata	medicate	mergence	middling	Minorite
matchbox	medicine	meridian	midfield	minority
matelote	medieval	meringue	midlands	Minotaur
material	mediocre	meristem	midnight	minstrel
materiel	meditate	meristic	midpoint	mintmark
maternal	medusoid	merosome	midshops	minutely
matgrass	meekness	mescalin	midwives	minutiae
matiness	meetness	Mesdames	mightest	mirepoix

mirthful	mistrial	momently	monotint	morpheme
misalign	mistrust	momentum	monotone	morphine
misapply	misusage	monachal	monotony	mortally
misbegot	miswrite	monadism	monotype	mortgage
miscarry	Mithraic	monandry	monoxide	mortmain
miscegen	mitigant	monarchy	monsieur	mortuary
mischief	mitigate	monastic	monteith	moshavim
miscible	mittened	monaural	monument	mosquito
miscount	mittimus	monaxial	moonbeam	mossback
misdealt	mitzvoth	monazite	mooncalf	mothball
misdoing	mnemonic	mondaine	moonface	motherly
misdoubt	mobilise	monetary	moonfish	motility
miserere	mobility	monetise	moonless	motional
misgiven	mobocrat	moneybag	moonrise	motivate
misguide	moccasin	moneybox	moonsail	motivity
misheard	modalism	Mongolic	moonshee	motorail
mishmash	modalist	monicker	moonshot	motorcar
Mishnaic	modality	monistic	moonwort	motorial
misjudge	modelled	monition	moorcock	motoring
mismatch	modeller	monitive	moorfowl	motorise
misnomer	moderate	monitory	moorings	motorist
misogamy	moderato	monkfish	moorland	motorium
misogyny	modernly	Mon Khmer	mopishly	motorman
misology	modestly	monkhood	moquette	motormen
misplace	modifier	monkseal	morainic	motorway
misprint	modishly	monkship	moralise	mottling
misprise	modulate	monoacid	moralism	moufflon
misprize	Moharram	monocrat	moralist	moulding
misquote	moisture	monocyte	morality	mountain
misshape	molality	monodist	moratory	mounting
missilry	molarity	monogamy	Moravian	mournful
misspell	molasses	monoglot	morbidly	mourning
misspelt	molecule	monogony	morbific	mouse ear
misspend	molehill	monogram	mordancy	moussaka
misspent	moleskin	monogyny	moreover	mouthful
misstate	molester	monolith	moresque	moveable
mistaken	Molinism	monomial	moribund	moveless
misthink	Molinist	monopode	mornings	movement
mistreat	molossus	monopoly	morosely	movingly
mistress	molybdic	monorail	morosity	muchness

mucilage	mutchkin	narceine	nebulous	neuroses
muckluck	muteness	narcissi	neckband	neurosis
muckrake	muticous	narcoses	necklace	neurotic
muckworm	mutilate	narcosis	neckline	neutrino
mucosity	mutineer	narcotic	necropsy	newblown
mucrones	mutinous	narghile	necrosis	new broom
mudguard	mutterer	narrator	necrotic	newcomer
mudstone	mutually	narrowly	nectared	newfound
Muharram	mycelial	nasalise	needfire	newlywed
mulberry	mycelium	nasality	needless	newscast
muleteer	mycology	nascence	needment	newsheet
mulishly	myelinic	nascency	negation	newspeak
mulloway	myelitis	natality	negative	newsreel
multeity	mylonite	natation	negatory	newsroom
multifid	myoblast	nathless	negatron	new world
multiped	myogenic	national	negligee	nextdoor
multiple	myograph	natively	Negrillo	niceness
multiply	myositic	nativism	negroism	nickelic
muniment	myositis	nativist	nematode	nicknack
munition	myosotis	nativity	nematoid	nickname
murderer	myriapod	naturism	nenuphar	nicotian
murmurer	myriopod	naturist	NeoLatin	nicotine
murrelet	myrmidon	nauplius	neomycin	nielloed
murrhine	mystical	nauseant	neonatal	niggling
muscadel	mystique	nauseate	neophyte	nightcap
muscatel	mythical	nauseous	neoplasm	nighthag
muscling	myxomata	nautical	neoprene	nightjar
muscular	nacreous	nautilus	neotenic	nightowl
mushroom	nailfile	navigate	neoteric	nihilism
musicale	nainsook	Nazarene	Nepalese	nihilist
musician	nameable	Nazarite	nepenthe	nihility
musingly	namedrop	Nazirite	nephrite	nimbused
muskdeer	nameless	neaptide	nepotism	ninefold
muskduck	namepart	Nearctic	nescient	ninepins
musketry	namesake	near miss	nestling	nineteen
muskrose	nametape	nearness	neurally	nineties
musktree	nanogram	neatherd	neuritic	nitrogen
musquash	naphthol	neatness	neuritis	Noachian
mustache	napiform	nebulise	neuronal	nobelium
mutation	napoleon	nebulium	neuronic	nobility

nobleman	normalcy	nugatory	obstacle	offprint
noblesse	normally	nuisance	obstruct	offshoot
no chance	Norseman	nullness	obtainer	offshore
no charge	northern	numberer	obtected	offsider
no claims	northing	numbfish	obturate	offstage
nocturne	Northman	numbness	obtusely	oft times
nodalise	noseband	numeracy	obtusity	ohmmeter
nodality	nosecone	numerary	occasion	oilcloth
nodation	nosedive	numerate	occident	oilfield
nodosity	nosepipe	numerous	occluded	oilfired
nodulose	nosering	numinous	occlusal	oiliness
nodulous	nosiness	numskull	occultly	oilstone
no excuse	nosology	nuptials	occupant	ointment
noisette	notarial	nursling	occupier	oiticica
no longer	notation	nurturer	occurred	okeydoke
nomadise	notching	nutarian	ocellate	old flame
nomadism	notebook	nutation	ochreous	oldtimer
no matter	notecase	nutbrown	octarchy	old world
nominate	noteless	nuthatch	octaroon	oleander
nomistic	notional	nuthouse	octoroon	oleaster
nomogram	notornis	nutrient	ocularly	olibanum
nomology	noumenal	nutshell	oddments	oligarch
nonclaim	noumenon	nymphean	odiously	oligomer
nondairy	nouvelle	oafishly	odograph	oliphant
nonesuch	novation	oakapple	odometer	olympiad
nonevent	novelise	oatgrass	odontoid	Olympian
nonhuman	novelist	obduracy	Odyssean	omadhaum
nonjuror	November	obdurate	oeillade	omelette
nonlegal	novercal	obedient	oenology	omission
nonmetal	nowadays	obeisant	oenophil	omitting
nonmoral	nubiform	obituary	oestrone	ommateum
nonparty	nubility	objector	oestrous	omnivore
nonrigid	nubilous	oblation	of course	omophagy
nonsense	nucellus	oblatory	off and on	omoplate
nonstick	nuclease	obligate	offbreak	omphalic
nonunion	nucleate	obliging	offdrive	omphalos
nonusage	nucleole	oblivion	offender	on and off
nonwhite	nucleoli	observer	offering	onceover
noontide	nuclidic	obsidian	off guard	oncidium
noontime	nudeness	obsolete	official	oncology

oncoming	oppugner	oscinine	outshone	overfish
on course	opsimath	osculant	outsider	overflew
one horse	optative	osculate	outsight	overflow
onepiece	optician	Ossianic	outsmart	overfold
onesided	optimise	osteitis	outspend	overfond
onetrack	optimism	ostinato	outspent	overgrew
onlooker	optimist	ostracod	outstare	overgrow
on parole	optional	ostracon	outstrip	overhand
on safari	opulence	ostrakon	out to win	overhang
on strike	opuscule	otiosely	outvalue	overhaul
on the hop	oracular	otiosity	outvying	overhead
on the job	orangery	otoscope	outwards	overhear
on the way	Orangism	outboard	outwatch	overheat
on tiptoe	oratorio	outbound	outweigh	overhung
ontogeny	oratress	outbrave	outworks	overjump
ontology	Orcadian	outbreak	ovalness	overkill
onychite	orchilla	outburst	ovariole	overlaid
oogamous	ordainer	outcaste	ovaritis	overlain
oogonial	ordinand	outclass	ovenbird	overland
oogonium	ordinary	outdated	oven chip	overleaf
oologist	ordinate	outdoors	ovenware	overleap
ooziness	ordnance	outdrawn	overalls	overload
opaquely	organdie	outfield	overarch	overlong
openable	organise	outflank	overbear	overlook
open arms	organism	outgoing	overbook	overlord
opencast	organist	outgrown	overbore	overmuch
open door	orgasmic	outguess	overbusy	overnice
openeyed	orgastic	outHerod	overcall	overpaid
openness	oriental	outhouse	overcame	overpass
openplan	oriented	outlawry	overcast	overpast
openwork	origanum	outlying	overcoat	overplay
operable	original	outmatch	overcome	overplus
operatic	ornament	outmoded	overcrop	overrate
operator	ornately	outpoint	overdone	override
opercula	ornithic	outrange	overdose	overripe
operetta	orogenic	outreach	overdraw	overrode
ophidian	orpiment	outreign	overdrew	overrule
oppilate	orthicon	outright	overfall	oversail
opponent	orthodox	outrival	overfeed	overseas
opposite	orthoepy	outshine	overfill	overseen

overseer	paganism	papalist	paroquet	patronal
oversell	paginate	paper bag	paroxysm	pattypan
oversewn	painless	paperboy	parrotry	patulous
overshoe	paintbox	papillae	Parsiism	pavement
overshot	palatial	papillar	parsonic	pavilion
overside	palatine	papillon	partaken	pawnshop
oversize	paleface	papistic	parterre	payphone
overslip	paleness	papistry	Parthian	paysheet
oversold	palestra	pappadom	partible	peaceful
oversoul	palinode	papulose	particle	peacocky
overstay	palisade	papulous	partisan	peagreen
overstep	palliate	parabola	partizan	peak hour
overtake	pallidly	paradigm	partsong	peardrop
overtask	pallmall	paradise	part time	pearlies
overtime	palmette	paraffin	passable	pearling
overtone	palmetto	paragoge	passably	pearlite
overtook	palm tree	parakeet	passbook	pearmain
overture	palomino	parallax	passerby	peasecod
overturn	palpable	parallel	passible	peccable
overview	palpably	paralyse	Passover	peccancy
overwear	palterer	paramour	passport	pectines
overwind	paludism	paranoia	password	pectoral
overwork	pamperer	paranoid	pastiche	peculate
overworn	pamphlet	paraquat	pastille	peculiar
oviposit	pancreas	parasang	pastoral	pedagogy
owlishly	pandanus	parasite	pastrami	pedalier
oxidiser	pandemic	paravane	pastries	pedalled
oximeter	pandowdy	parcener	pastural	pedantic
oxpecker	panelled	parclose	patagium	pedantry
oxtongue	pangolin	pardoner	patchily	pederast
oxymoron	panicked	parental	patellae	pedestal
oxytocin	panmixia	parergon	patellar	pedicled
ozoniser	pannikin	pargeter	patentee	pedicure
pacifier	panorama	parhelia	patently	pedigree
pacifism	panpipes	parhelic	patentor	pediment
pacifist	pantheon	parietal	paternal	pedipalp
padishah	pantofle	parkland	pathetic	pedology
paduasoy	pantsuit	parlance	pathless	peduncle
paganise	papalise	parlando	pathogen	peekaboo
paganish	papalism	parodist	patience	peelings

peephole	peridote	pharisee	piecrust	piperack
peepshow	perigean	pharmacy	piedmont	piperine
peerless	perilled	phase out	piercing	piquancy
Pegasean	perilous	pheasant	piffling	piscator
pegboard	perilune	phenolic	pigswill	piscinae
peignoir	perineal	phenylic	pilaster	pisiform
Pekinese	perineum	Philomel	pilchard	pisolite
Pelagian	periodic	phlegmon	pileated	pitiable
Pelasgic	periotic	phonemic	pilewort	pitiably
pelerine	peripety	phonetic	pilferer	pitiless
pellagra	periplus	phosgene	piliform	pittance
pellicle	perisher	phosphor	pillager	pitviper
pellmell	perjurer	photogen	pillwort	pivotman
pellucid	perlitic	photopia	pilosity	pixieish
pelorism	permeate	photopic	pilotage	pixiness
pembroke	peroneal	photopsy	pilsener	pizzeria
pemmican	perorate	phrasing	pimiento	placable
penalise	peroxide	phreatic	pinafore	placably
penchant	personae	Phrygian	pinaster	placeman
pendency	personal	phthalic	pincenez	placenta
pendicle	perspire	phthisis	pinchers	placidly
pendular	persuade	phyletic	Pindaric	plagiary
pendulum	pertness	phyllary	pinecone	plaguily
penitent	Peruvian	phyllode	pinewood	plaiding
penknife	perverse	phylloid	pinkness	plaister
penology	pervious	phyllome	pin money	planchet
penstock	petaline	physical	pinnacle	plangent
pentacle	petalled	physicky	pinnated	planking
pentagon	petaloid	physique	pinniped	plankton
pentroof	petalous	piacular	pinnular	planning
penumbra	petiolar	pianiste	pinochle	plantain
peperino	petioled	piassava	pinpoint	planulae
perceive	petition	picaroon	pinprick	planular
perfecto	petronel	pickerel	pintable	plastery
perforce	petrosal	picketer	pintsize	plastics
perfumer	pettifog	pickings	pinwheel	plastron
perianth	petulant	picklock	pipeclay	plateaux
pericarp	phalange	picnicky	pipefish	plateful
pericope	phantasm	pictures	pipeline	platelet
periderm	phantasy	piddling	pip emma	platform

platinic	plumbate	polygyny	posology	practise
platinum	plumbing	polymath	possible	praecipe
platonic	plumbism	polypody	possibly	praedial
platting	plumelet	polypoid	postcard	prandial
platypus	plumpish	polyseme	postcode	prankful
plaudits	plumular	polysemy	postdate	prankish
playable	plurally	polyzoan	postfree	pratique
playback	plussage	polyzoic	posthorn	prattler
play ball	plutonic	polyzoon	postiche	preacher
playbill	pluvious	pomander	postlude	preamble
playbook	pochette	pomology	postmark	precinct
play down	pockmark	ponderer	postmill	precious
playgirl	podagral	pondweed	postobit	preclude
playgoer	podagric	pontifex	postpaid	predator
playmate	podiatry	ponytail	postpone	predella
playroom	poetical	poohpooh	postural	preelect
playsuit	poignant	pool room	posturer	preexist
playtime	pointing	poorness	potassic	pregnant
pleading	poisoner	popinjay	potation	prehuman
pleasant	polarise	popishly	potbelly	prejudge
pleasing	polarity	poppadum	potbound	prelatic
pleasure	polemics	populace	potently	prelease
plebeian	polemise	populate	potholer	premiere
plectrum	polemist	populism	pothouse	premolar
plein air	polestar	populist	potlatch	premorse
pleonasm	polisher	populous	pot of tea	prenatal
plethora	politely	porosity	potplant	prentice
pleurisy	politick	porphyry	potroast	preparer
pliantly	politico	porpoise	potsherd	preprint
plighted	politics	porridge	potstill	presager
plimsoll	polliwog	portable	potstone	prescind
Pliocene	pollster	portfire	potterer	presence
plodding	polluter	porthole	poultice	preserve
plopping	pollywog	porticos	poundage	presidio
plotting	polonium	portiere	pounding	pressbox
plougher	poltroon	portrait	pourable	pressing
pluckily	polygamy	portress	powdered	pressman
plugging	polygene	position	power cut	pressure
plumaged	polygeny	positive	powerful	prestige
plumbago	polyglot	positron	practice	presumer

pretence	prohibit	protonic	pulmonic	purslane
prettify	prolamin	protozoa	pulpiter	pursuant
prettily	prolapse	protract	pulpwood	purulent
previous	prolific	protrude	pulsator	purveyor
priapism	prolixly	provable	pulvilli	pushball
prideful	prologue	provably	pulvinus	pushbike
priedieu	prolonge	provided	pump room	pushcart
priestly	promisee	provider	puncheon	pushover
priggery	promiser	province	punctate	pushpull
priggish	promisor	provisor	punctual	pussycat
priggism	promoter	proximal	puncture	pustular
primally	prompter	prudence	punditry	putative
Primates	promptly	pruinose	pungency	putridly
primeval	promulge	prunella	puniness	pygmaean
primming	pronator	prunelle	punisher	pyogenic
primness	proofing	prunello	punition	pyrenoid
primrose	propense	prurient	punitive	pyrexial
princely	properly	pruritic	punitory	pyridine
princess	property	pruritus	puparial	pyroxene
printing	prophase	Prussian	puparium	pyrrhoea
printout	prophecy	pryingly	pupation	pyrrhous
priorate	prophesy	psalmist	pupilage	pythonic
prioress	proposal	psalmody	pupilary	pyxidium
priority	proposer	psaltery	pupillar	quackery
prismoid	propound	psilosis	puppetry	quackish
prisoner	propping	psychics	puppydog	quadrant
prissily	propylic	psychism	puppydom	quadrate
pristine	prorogue	pteropod	puppyfat	quadriga
probable	prosaism	pubertal	puppyish	quadroon
probably	prosaist	publican	purblind	quaestor
proceeds	prosodic	publicly	purchase	quagmire
proclaim	prospect	puffball	purebred	quaintly
procurer	prostate	puffbird	pureness	Quakerly
prodding	prostyle	puggaree	purfling	qualmish
prodigal	protasis	pugilism	purifier	quandary
producer	protatic	pugilist	puristic	quandong
profaner	protease	pugnosed	purplish	quantify
profiler	protegee	puissant	purpuric	quantise
profound	protista	pullback	purpurin	quantity
progress	protocol	pullover	pursenet	quarrier

quartern	rabidity	ranarium	reappear	redeemer
quarters	racecard	ranchero	rearlamp	redefine
quartile	racegoer	ranchman	rearmice	redeless
quatrain	racemate	randomly	rearmost	redeploy
quayside	racemise	rankness	rearview	redesign
queasily	racemose	ransomer	rearward	red faced
Quechuan	rachides	rapacity	reascend	redirect
queen bee	rachitic	rapecake	reasoner	redistil
queendom	rachitis	rapeseed	reassert	red light
queening	racially	rapidity	reassess	redolent
queenlet	raciness	rapparee	reassign	redouble
queerish	rackrent	raptness	reassure	redshank
quencher	radially	raptures	reawaken	red shift
quenelle	radiance	rarefied	rebelled	redstart
question	radiancy	rareness	rebeller	reed bird
queueing	radiator	rascally	rebellow	reedling
quibbler	radicant	rashness	rebuttal	reedmace
quickset	radicate	rasorial	rebutted	reedpipe
quiddity	radio set	rataplan	rebutter	reedstop
quidnunc	raftsman	rateable	recapped	reed wren
quietism	raggedly	ratguard	receiver	reef knot
quietist	railhead	ratifier	recently	reembark
quietude	raillery	rational	receptor	reemerge
quillpen	railroad	ratsbane	recharge	reemploy
quilting	rainbird	ratstail	recision	reexport
quincunx	raincoat	ravelled	reckless	referent
quintain	raindrop	ravenous	reckoner	referral
quipping	rainfall	ravisher	recommit	referred
quirkily	rainwash	rawboned	reconvey	refinery
quisling	rainwear	reabsorb	recorder	refitted
quitrent	rakehell	reactant	recourse	reflexed
quitting	rakishly	reaction	recovery	refluent
quixotic	rallying	reactive	recreant	reforest
quixotry	rallyist	readable	recreate	reformed
quizzing	rambling	readably	rectoral	reformer
quotable	rambutan	readjust	recurred	regalism
quotient	ramentum	reaffirm	recusant	regality
rabbinic	ramequin	reagency	redactor	regelate
rabbiter	rampancy	realness	redblind	regicide
rabbitry	ranarian	realtime	redbrick	regiment

regional	remittal	rescript	retiring	rhonchal
register	remitted	research	retorted	rhonchus
registry	remittee	resemble	retrench	rhyolite
regolith	remitter	reserved	retrieve	rhythmic
regrater	remotely	resetter	retroact	ribaldry
regrowth	renderer	resettle	retrorse	ribbonry
regulate	renegade	resident	reusable	ribgrass
rehandle	renegado	residual	revanche	ribosome
rehearse	reneguer	residuum	revealer	ricebird
reignite	reniform	resigned	reveille	ricercar
reimpose	renitent	resinate	revelled	richness
reindeer	renounce	resinify	reveller	rickrack
reinless	renovate	resinoid	revenant	rickshaw
reinsert	renowned	resinous	revenger	ricochet
reinsman	rentable	resister	reverend	riddance
reinsure	renumber	resistor	reverent	rideable
reinvest	reoccupy	resolute	reversal	ridgeway
rejecter	reorient	resonant	reverser	ridicule
rejigger	repairer	resonate	reverter	Riesling
rejoicer	repartee	resorcin	revetted	rifeness
rekindle	repealer	resorter	reviewal	riffraff
relation	repeater	respects	reviewer	rifleman
relative	repelled	response	reviling	rigadoon
relaxant	repeller	respring	revision	right arm
releasee	repenter	resprung	revisory	rightful
releaser	repeople	restcure	revivify	rightist
releasor	replacer	restless	revolter	rigidify
relegate	replevin	restorer	revolute	rigidity
relevant	reporter	restrain	revolver	rigorism
reliable	repotted	restrict	rewaking	rigorist
reliably	repousse	resurvey	rewarder	rigorous
reliance	reprieve	retailer	Rhaetian	rimbrake
reliever	reprisal	retainer	rhapsody	rimester
religion	reproach	retarded	rheology	ringbark
relocate	reproval	retarder	rheostat	ringbolt
remanent	republic	retiarii	rhetoric	ringbone
remedial	requital	reticent	rhinitis	ringdove
remember	requiter	reticule	Rhinodon	ring down
reminder	rerecord	retiform	rhizopod	ringmain
remissly	rereward	retinula	rhomboid	ringneck

ringroad	roentgen	Rotarian	ruminant	sagittal
ringside	rogation	rotation	ruminate	sailable
ringtail	rogatory	rotative	rummager	sailboat
ringwall	rollcall	rotatory	rum punch	sailfish
ringworm	roll down	rotenone	runabout	sailless
rinsings	rollneck	rottenly	runagate	sailorly
riparian	roll over	rotundly	run along	sailyard
ripeness	rolypoly	roturier	runcible	sainfoin
ritually	romancer	roughage	run for it	saintdom
rivalled	Romanian	roughdry	runner up	salacity
rivelled	romanise	roughhew	ruralise	salariat
riverain	Romanism	roughish	ruralism	salaried
riverbed	Romanist	rouleaus	ruralist	saleable
riverine	Romansch	rouleaux	rurality	saleroom
riverman	romantic	roulette	rush hour	Salesian
riverway	rondeaux	rounders	rushlike	salesman
roadbook	roodbeam	roundish	rustical	salience
roadless	roodloft	round off	rustless	saliency
roadside	roofless	roundtop	rustable	salinity
roadsign	roofrack	rowdyish	ruthless	salivary
roadster	rooftree	rowdyism	rutilant	salivate
roasting	room mate	royalism	ryegrass	Salopian
roborant	roothold	royalist	sabbatic	saltbush
robustly	rootless	rub along	sabotage	saltless
rocaille	ropeable	rubbishy	saboteur	saltlick
rockbird	ropewalk	rubidium	sackcoat	saltmine
rockcake	ropeyarn	rubrical	sackless	saltness
rockcork	ropiness	rubytail	sackrace	saltwort
rockdove	rosarian	rucksack	sacraria	salutary
rocketry	rosebowl	rudeness	sacredly	salvable
rockfall	rosebush	rudiment	sacristy	salvific
rockfish	roseleaf	ruefully	saddlery	samarium
rockhewn	rosemary	ruggedly	Sadducee	sameness
rocklike	roseolar	rugosely	sadistic	samizdat
rockling	rose pink	rugosity	safeness	Samoyede
rockrose	rosetree	rugulose	saffrony	samphire
rocksalt	rosewood	ruinable	safranin	sampling
rockweed	rosiness	ruleless	sagacity	sanative
rockwood	rostrate	Rumanian	sagamore	sanatory
rockwork	rosulate	Rumansch	sageness	sanctify

sanction	Sassanid	scallion	scirocco	scrofula
sanctity	satanism	scammony	scirrhus	scrounge
sandarac	satanist	scampish	scissors	scrubbed
sandbank	sateless	scandent	scleroma	scrubber
sandbath	satiable	Scandian	sclerose	scrutiny
sandflea	satiably	scandium	sclerous	scudding
sandshoe	satirise	scanning	scolding	scullery
sandwich	satirist	scansion	scombrid	scullion
sandworm	saturant	scanties	scoopful	sculptor
sandwort	saturate	scantily	scoopnet	scumming
sandyish	Saturday	scapulae	scopulae	scurrile
saneness	saturnic	scapular	scopulas	scurvily
sangaree	saucebox	scapulas	scorcher	scutcher
Sangrail	saucepan	scarcely	scornful	scutella
Sangreal	saunders	scarcity	scorpion	seaboard
sanguine	sauropod	scarf pin	scot free	seaborne
sanitary	Sauterne	scarious	scotopic	sea chest
sanitate	savagely	scarless	Scotsman	sea coast
sanitise	savagery	scarring	scottice	seacraft
sannyasi	savannah	scathing	Scottish	seadrome
sanserif	savorous	scattily	scourger	seafarer
Sanskrit	Savoyard	scatting	scouting	sea floor
santonin	sawbones	scavenge	scrabble	sea front
sapgreen	saw edged	scenario	scragend	seagoing
sapidity	sawed off	sceptred	scragged	seagreen
sapience	sawframe	schedule	scramble	sea holly
saponify	sawhorse	schemata	scrammed	seahorse
saponite	sawtooth	scheming	scrannel	sealable
saporous	saxatile	schiller	scraping	sea level
sapphics	Saxondom	schizoid	scrapped	sealskin
sapphire	Saxonism	schmaltz	scrapper	sealyham
sapphism	Saxonist	schnapps	scratchy	seamanly
saraband	sayonara	scholium	scrawler	seamless
sarcenet	scabbard	schooner	screamer	seamount
sardelle	scabious	sciagram	screechy	seamouse
sardonic	scabrous	sciatica	screener	seamster
sardonyx	scaffold	scilicet	screever	sea onion
sargasso	scalable	scimitar	screwtop	seapiece
sarsenet	scalawag	sciolism	scribble	seaplane
sashcord	scalepan	sciolist	scribbly	seapurse

seaquake	seedsman	Semitist	serotine	shamrock
searcher	seedtime	semitone	serranid	shanghai
seascape	segreant	semolina	serrated	shantung
seashell	seicento	semplice	servient	shapable
seashore	seigneur	sempster	servitor	shareout
sea snail	seignior	senarius	sesterce	sharpish
sea snake	seignory	senility	set apart	sharpset
seasonal	seizable	sennight	set right	shashlik
seasoner	seladang	senorita	setscrew	sheading
seatbelt	selcouth	senseful	severely	shealing
seatrout	selectee	sensible	severity	shedding
seawards	selector	sensibly	sewellel	shedevil
seawater	selenate	sensoria	sewerage	sheep dip
secluded	selenide	sensuous	sewer gas	sheepdog
seconder	selenite	sentence	sewer rat	sheepish
secondly	selenium	sentient	sexiness	sheepked
secretin	selfborn	sentinel	sexology	sheep pen
secretly	selfheal	sepaloid	sextette	sheep run
secretor	selfhelp	sepalous	sextuple	sheeting
sectoral	selfhood	separate	sexually	sheikdom
securely	selfless	Sephardi	sforzato	Shekinah
security	selflove	septette	shabbily	shelduck
sedately	selfmade	septfoil	Shabuoth	shellful
sedation	selfmate	septimal	shadbush	shelving
sedative	selfness	septuple	shaddock	Shemitic
sederunt	selfpity	sequence	shadower	shepherd
sediment	selfrule	seraglio	shafting	Sheraton
sedition	selfsame	seraphic	shagbark	sherlock
sedulity	selfsown	seraphim	shaggily	Shetland
sedulous	selfwill	serenade	shagreen	shielder
seedcake	selvedge	serenata	shagroon	shieling
seedcase	semantic	serenely	shakable	shiftily
seedcoat	semester	serenity	shakeout	shift key
seedcorn	semibull	serfhood	Shaktism	shigella
seedfish	semidome	sergeant	shale oil	shikaree
seedleaf	seminary	serially	shalloon	shilling
seedless	seminude	seriatim	shallows	shimmery
seedling	semiotic	serjeant	shambles	shinbone
seedlobe	Semitise	serology	shameful	shingler
seedplot	Semitism	serosity	shamming	shingles

shinning	showroom	sidestep	sinister	skipjack
shipload	shrapnel	side view	sinkable	skipping
shipmate	shredded	sidewalk	sinkhole	skirmish
shipment	shredder	sideward	sinology	skirting
shipping	shrewdly	sideways	sinophil	ski slope
shipworm	shrewish	sidewind	sinusoid	skittish
shipyard	shrieval	sidewise	siphonal	skittles
shirring	shrimper	siftings	siphonet	skullcap
shirting	shrinker	sigmatic	siphonic	skylight
shocking	shrugged	signally	sirenian	skypilot
shoddily	shrunken	signpost	siriasis	skyscape
shoebill	shuddery	silencer	sirvente	skywards
shoehorn	shuffler	silently	sisterly	slabbing
shoelace	shunning	silicate	sitarist	slagging
shoeless	shut down	silicify	sitology	slagheap
shoetree	shutting	silicone	situated	slamming
shofroth	Siberian	silkworm	sitzbath	slangily
shogging	sibilant	sillabub	sixpence	slapbang
shooting	sibilate	Silurian	sixpenny	slapdash
shootout	Sicilian	siluroid	sixtieth	slapjack
shop bell	sickener	silvatic	sizeable	slapping
shopgirl	sickerly	silverly	sizzling	slashing
shopping	sickflag	similise	skeletal	slattern
shoptalk	sicklist	simoniac	skeleton	Slavonic
shopworn	sickness	simonist	skerrick	sleazily
shortage	sickroom	simplify	sketcher	sledding
shortarm	sidearms	simplism	skewback	sleepily
shortcut	sideband	simulant	skewbald	sleeping
shortday	side dish	simulate	skewness	slideway
shortish	side door	Sinaitic	skidding	slightly
shothole	side drum	sinapism	skilless	slimmest
shoulder	sidekick	sinciput	skilling	slimming
shouldst	sideline	sinecure	skim milk	slimmish
show a leg	sidelong	sinfonia	skimming	slimness
showbill	sidereal	sinfully	skimpily	slinkily
showboat	siderite	singable	skindeep	slipcase
showcard	side road	singeing	skin food	slipform
showcase	sideshow	singsong	skinhead	slipknot
showdown	sideslip	singular	skinless	slipover
showgirl	sidesman	sinicise	skinning	slippage

slippery	smallpox	snipsnap	sodalite	solvency
slipping	smaltite	snitcher	sodality	somatism
slipring	smarmily	snobbery	sodomite	sombrely
sliproad	smartish	snobbish	softball	sombrero
slipshod	smashing	snobbism	softboil	sombrous
slipslop	smelling	snogging	softener	somebody
slithery	smeltery	snootily	softhead	sometime
slitting	smithers	snowball	softness	someways
slobbery	smithery	snowbird	softshoe	somewhat
slobbish	smocking	snowboot	softsoap	somnific
slobland	smokable	snowdrop	software	sonatina
sloeeyed	smoothen	snowfall	softwood	songbird
slogging	smoothie	snowlike	soilless	songbook
sloppail	smoothly	snowline	soilpipe	songless
sloppily	smothery	snowshoe	solander	songster
slopping	smoulder	snubbing	solanine	sonobuoy
slopshop	smudgily	snuff box	solarise	sonority
slopwork	smuggler	snuffers	solarism	sonorous
slothful	smugness	snuffler	solarist	soothing
slotting	smuttily	snuffles	solarium	soothsay
sloucher	snackbar	snuggery	solation	sorcerer
slovenly	snagging	snugness	solatium	sordidly
slovenry	snakepit	soakaway	solderer	sorehead
slowdown	snapbrim	soapbark	soldiery	soreness
slowness	snaplink	soapdish	solecism	sorochen
slowpoke	snappily	soapless	solecist	sororate
slowworm	snapping	soaproot	solemnly	sorority
slubbing	snappish	soapsuds	soleness	sorption
slugabed	snapshot	soapwort	solenoid	sorptive
sluggard	snatcher	soberise	solfaist	sorrower
slugging	snazzily	sobriety	solfeggi	sortable
sluggish	sneakily	sobstory	solidary	soterial
slumbery	sneakish	sobstuff	solidify	souchong
slumming	sneeshan	socalled	solidity	soulless
slurring	sniffily	sociable	solitary	soundbow
sluttish	sniffler	sociably	solitude	soundbox
slyboots	sniffles	socially	solleret	sounding
smallage	sniggler	societal	solstice	sourdine
small fry	snippety	Socinian	solution	sourness
smallish	snipping	Socratic	solvable	sourpuss

soutache	specific	splinter	spurling	staggers
southern	specimen	splitter	spurrier	staghorn
southing	specious	splotchy	spurring	stagnant
southpaw	spectral	splutter	spyglass	stagnate
Southron	spectrum	spoilage	squabble	stair rod
souvenir	specular	spoliate	squadron	stairway
sovranty	speculum	spondaic	squaller	stallage
sowbread	speedily	spongily	squamate	stall fed
spacebar	speedway	spookily	squamose	stalling
spaceman	spelling	spookish	squamous	stallion
spacious	spermary	spoonfed	squamule	stalwart
spadeful	sphagnum	spoonful	squander	stampede
spadices	sphenoid	spoonily	squarely	stancher
spadille	spherics	sporadic	squarish	stanchly
spaewife	spheroid	sporozoa	squasher	standard
spalpeen	spherule	sportful	squatted	standing
spandrel	sphingid	sportily	squatter	standish
spandril	spicated	sporting	squawker	standoff
Spaniard	spiccato	sportive	squaw man	stanhope
spanking	spice box	sporular	squeaker	stannary
spanning	spicknel	spotless	squealer	stannate
spanroof	spiffing	spottily	squeedge	stannite
sparable	spikelet	spotting	squeegee	stannous
sparbuoy	spillage	spousage	squeezer	stanzaic
spardeck	spillway	spraints	squelchy	stardust
sparkgap	spinifex	sprawler	squibbed	starfish
sparkish	spinning	spraygun	squidded	stargaze
sparkler	spinster	spreader	squiggle	starkers
sparklet	spiracle	sprigged	squiggly	starless
sparling	spirally	springal	squinter	starlike
sparring	spirited	springer	squireen	starling
sparsely	spiritus	spring up	squirely	starrily
sparsity	spiteful	sprinkle	squirrel	starring
spathose	spitfire	sprinter	squirter	starting
spatting	spitting	sprocket	stabbing	startler
spatular	spittoon	sprucely	stabling	start out
spavined	spivvery	spryness	stablish	starwort
speaking	splasher	spunkily	staccato	statable
spearman	splatter	spur gear	staffage	statedly
speciate	splendid	spurious	staggard	statical

statuary	stickler	stormily	strobile	stylised
statured	stiffish	stoutish	strobili	subacute
staylace	stigmata	stowaway	stroller	subagent
staysail	stilbene	strabism	stromata	subclass
steadily	stilbite	straddle	strongly	suberect
steading	stiletto	straggle	strontia	suberise
stealing	stillage	straggly	strophic	subfloor
stealthy	stimulus	straight	stropped	subframe
steamily	stingily	strained	strucken	subgenus
stearate	stingray	strainer	struggle	subgroup
stearine	stinkard	straiten	strummed	subhuman
steatite	stinking	straitly	strummer	subimago
stedfast	stinkpot	stramash	strumose	subjoint
steenbok	stippler	stranded	strumous	sublease
steening	stipular	stranger	strumpet	sublunar
steepish	stirring	strangle	strutted	submerge
steepled	stitcher	strapoil	strutter	submerse
steerage	stoccado	strapped	stubbing	suborder
steering	stoccata	strapper	stubborn	suborner
steinbok	stockade	strategy	stubnail	suboxide
stellate	stock car	stratify	stuccoes	subphyla
stellify	stockily	stravaig	stud book	subpoena
stellion	stocking	streaked	studding	subprior
stemless	stockish	streaker	stud farm	subserve
stemmata	stockist	streamer	studious	subshrub
stemming	stockman	streeted	studwork	subsolar
stenosed	stockpot	strength	stuffily	subsonic
stenosis	stodgily	stretchy	stuffing	substage
stenotic	stoicism	stricken	stultify	subtitle
stepping	stolidly	strickle	stumbler	subtlety
stepwise	stomachy	strictly	stumming	subtonic
sterigma	stomatal	stridden	stumpily	subtopia
sterling	stomatic	strident	stunning	subtotal
sternite	stonefly	strigose	stunsail	subtract
sternway	stopcock	striking	stuntman	subulate
stetting	stopover	stringed	stupidly	suburban
stibnite	stoppage	stringer	stuprate	suburbia
stickful	stopping	stripped	sturdied	subvocal
stickily	storeman	stripper	sturdily	succinct
stickjaw	storeyed	strobila	sturgeon	succinic

succinum	sunshade	susurrus	syllabic	tabouret
succubae	sunshine	suzerain	syllable	tabulate
succubus	sunshiny	swabbing	syllabub	tachisme
suchlike	sunstone	swagging	syllabus	tachiste
suckling	sunwards	swainish	sylvatic	taciturn
Sudanese	superadd	swanherd	symbiont	tackling
sudarium	superate	swanking	symbolic	tackroom
sudatory	superbly	swanlike	symmetry	tactical
suddenly	superego	swanmark	sympathy	tactless
sufferer	superior	swanneck	symphile	taenioid
suffrage	superman	swannery	symphony	taffrail
suicidal	supernal	swanning	symposia	tagalong
suitable	supertax	swanshot	synapsis	Tahitian
suitably	supinate	swanskin	synaptic	tailback
suitcase	supinely	swansong	synastry	tailcoat
suitings	supplant	swapping	syncline	tailgate
sukiyaki	supplely	swastika	syncopal	tailings
sullenly	supplial	swatting	syncytia	tailless
sulphate	supplier	swayback	syndesis	tailpipe
sulphide	supplies	swearing	syndetic	tailrace
sulphite	supposal	sweeping	syndical	tailspin
sulphone	supposed	sweepnet	syndrome	tainture
sultrily	suppress	sweeting	synergic	take a nap
Sumerian	surcease	sweetish	synergid	takeaway
summerly	surefire	sweet pea	syngamic	take down
summitry	sureness	sweetsop	synonymy	take home
summoner	surfacer	swelling	synopses	taken off
sunbaked	surfboat	swiftlet	synopsis	takeover
sunbathe	surgical	swigging	synoptic	take time
sunblind	suricate	swimming	synovial	takingly
sunburnt	surmisal	swimsuit	syphilis	talapoin
sunburst	surmiser	swindler	syringes	talented
sundance	surplice	swinging	syrinxes	talesman
sunderer	surprise	switchel	systemic	talisman
sundress	surround	swobbing	systolic	tallness
sundried	surroyal	swopping	syzygial	tallyman
sundries	surveyor	swotting	tableaux	Talmudic
sundrops	survival	sybarite	tableful	tamandua
sunlight	survivor	sycamine	tablemat	tamarack
sunproof	suspense	sycamore	tabletop	tamarind

tamarisk	tattooer	telemark	termtime	thematic
tamboura	tautness	telepath	terraced	the north
tameable	tautomer	teleport	terrapin	theocrat
tameless	tautonym	telethon	terraria	theodicy
tameness	taverner	teleview	terrazzo	theogony
Tamilian	tawdrily	televise	terrible	theology
tamperer	taxation	tellable	terribly	theorise
tandoori	taxingly	telltale	terrific	theorist
tangency	taxonomy	telluric	tertiary	therefor
tangible	taxpayer	temerity	tesserae	thereout
tangibly	tea bread	tempered	tesseral	thermion
tangoist	teabreak	temperer	testable	thermite
tanistry	tea caddy	template	testator	thesauri
tannable	tea chest	temporal	testatum	the south
tantalic	teaching	tempting	test tube	thespian
tantalum	teacloth	tenacity	tetanise	thetical
tantalus	tea dance	tenacula	tetchily	theurgic
Tantrism	tea house	tenaille	tetradic	thiamine
tantrist	team mate	tenantry	tetragon	thickety
tapdance	teamster	tendence	tetrapla	thickish
tapedeck	teamwork	tendency	tetrapod	thickset
tapeless	teaparty	tenderly	tetrarch	thievery
tapelike	tearaway	Tenebrae	Teutonic	thievish
tapeline	teardrop	tenement	textbook	thingamy
tapestry	tearduct	tenesmus	texthand	thinking
tapeworm	teaspoon	tenon saw	textuary	thinness
taphouse	tea table	tenorite	textural	thinnest
tapwater	teatowel	tenpence	textured	thinning
tarboosh	technics	tenpenny	thalamic	thinnish
tarlatan	tectonic	tensible	thalamus	thin skin
tarragon	teddy boy	tentacle	thallium	thirlage
tartaric	teenager	tenurial	thalloid	thirster
tartness	teething	teocalli	thallous	thirteen
tartrate	teetotal	tepidity	Thanatos	tholepin
Tartuffe	teetotum	teraphim	thanedom	thoraces
taskwork	telecast	teratoma	thankful	thoracic
tasselly	telecine	terminal	thankyou	thoraxes
tastebud	telefilm	terminer	thatcher	thorough
tasteful	telegony	terminus	thearchy	thoughts
tattered	telegram	termless	theistic	thousand

thraldom	tideless	tithable	tonicity	tovarish
thrasher	tidelock	titivate	toolroom	towardly
thrawart	tidemark	titmouse	toolshed	towelled
threader	tidemill	tittuped	toothful	townhall
threaten	tidewave	tittuppy	toothily	township
threeway	tidiness	toadfish	toothing	townsman
threnode	tiebreak	toadflax	topdress	toxaemia
threnody	tigereye	toadyish	topheavy	toxaemic
thresher	tigerish	toadyism	toplevel	toxicant
thriller	tightwad	to and fro	topliner	toxicity
thriving	tilefish	toboggan	toplofty	trabeate
throated	tillable	tocology	topnotch	tracheae
throbbed	tiltyard	toepiece	topology	tracheal
thrombin	timbered	toeplate	toponymy	tracheid
thrombus	timeball	together	top speed	trachoma
throstle	timebomb	toiletry	topstone	trachyte
throttle	timefuse	toilette	top to toe	trackage
thrummed	timeless	toilsome	torchere	tracking
thruster	timework	toilworn	toreador	trackman
thudding	timeworn	tokenism	toreutic	trackway
thuggery	timidity	tokology	tornadic	traction
thuggism	timorous	tolbooth	toroidal	trade off
thumbpot	timously	tolerant	torpidly	traducer
thumping	tincture	tolerate	torridly	tragical
thundery	tininess	tollcall	tortilla	tragopan
thurible	tinkerer	tolldish	tortious	trailnet
thurifer	tinnitus	tollgate	tortoise	training
Thursday	tinplate	tomahawk	tortuous	tramline
thusness	tinselly	tomalley	torturer	trammels
thwacker	tinsmith	tombless	totalise	trampler
thwarter	tinstone	tomentum	totality	tramroad
thwartly	tintless	tommybar	totalled	tranquil
thyroxin	tipstaff	tommygun	totemism	transact
thyrsoid	tireless	tommyrot	totemist	transect
ticklish	tiresome	tomorrow	totterer	transept
tickseed	titanate	tonality	touchily	transfer
ticktack	titaness	tonedeaf	touching	transfix
ticktock	titanism	toneless	toughish	tranship
tidegate	titanite	tonepoem	touristy	transmit
tideland	titanium	tonguing	tournure	trapball

trapdoor	trichina	troilite	tuckahoe	tutoress
trapezia	trichite	trollopy	tuckshop	tutorial
trappean	trichoid	trombone	tumbling	twaddler
trapping	trichome	trophied	tumidity	tweezers
Trappist	trichord	tropical	tumorous	twelvemo
traprock	trickery	trotting	tuneable	twenties
trashery	trickily	trottoir	tuneless	twiddler
trashily	trickish	troupial	tungsten	twilight
traumata	tricorne	trousers	tungstic	twinborn
traverse	tricycle	troutlet	tunicate	twinkler
travesty	triennia	trouvere	Tunisian	twinling
trawlnet	trifling	truantry	tuppence	twinning
treacher	trifocal	truckage	tuppenny	twinship
treadler	triforia	trucking	Turanian	twitcher
treasure	triglyph	truckler	turbaned	twittery
treasury	trigonal	trueblue	turbidly	twitting
treatise	trigraph	trueborn	turbinal	twoedged
trecento	trilling	truebred	turbofan	twofaced
treefern	trillion	true love	turbojet	twopence
treefrog	trillium	trueness	Turcoman	twopenny
treeless	trilobed	truistic	turgidly	twopiece
treenail	trimaran	trumeaux	Turkoman	twosided
trekking	trimeter	trumpery	turmeric	twotimer
trembler	trimming	truncate	turnable	Tychonic
trembles	trimness	trunnion	turnback	tympanic
trencher	trioxide	trussing	turncoat	tympanum
trendily	triplane	trustful	turncock	typecast
trephine	triploid	trustily	turndown	typeface
trespass	tripodal	truthful	turnings	typehigh
tressure	trippery	tryingly	turnover	typhonic
trevally	tripping	try it out	turnpike	typifier
trialist	triptych	tsarevna	turnskin	typology
triangle	tripwire	tsaritsa	turnsole	tyrannic
triarchy	triskele	tsaritza	turnspit	Tyrolean
Triassic	triumvir	tubeless	turreted	tyrosine
triaxial	triunity	tubercle	turtling	Tyrrhene
tribally	trochaic	tuberose	tussocky	ubiquity
tribasic	trochili	tuberous	tutelage	udometer
tribrach	trochlea	tubiform	tutelary	ugliness
tribunal	trochoid	tubulate	tutorage	uintaite

ulcerate	unclench	unfetter	unlovely	untented
ulcerous	unclinch	unfilial	unmanned	untether
ulterior	unclothe	unfitted	unmarked	unthread
ultimacy	uncoined	unforced	unmeetly	unthrift
ultimata	uncommon	unformed	unmuffle	unthrone
ultimate	uncouple	unfreeze	unmuzzle	untidily
ultraism	uncreate	unfrozen	unopened	untimely
ultraist	unctuous	unfunded	unpaired	untitled
umbonate	underact	ungainly	unpegged	untoward
umbrella	underage	unglazed	unperson	unvalued
umbrette	underarm	ungotten	unpinned	unversed
umpirage	underbid	ungulate	unplaced	unvoiced
umptieth	undercut	unhinged	unreason	unwanted
unabated	underdid	unhoused	unriddle	unwarily
unaneled	underdog	uniaxial	unrigged	unwashed
unawares	underfur	unicycle	unroofed	unweaned
unbacked	underlap	unifilar	unsaddle	unwieldy
unbarred	underlay	unionise	unsealed	unwisdom
unbeaten	underlet	unionism	unseated	unwisely
unbelief	underlie	unionist	unseeded	unwished
unbiased	underlip	unipolar	unseeing	unwonted
unbidden	underpin	uniquely	unseemly	unwordly
unbolted	underrun	unisonal	unsettle	unworthy
unbottle	undersea	unitedly	unshaped	unzipped
unbridle	underset	univalve	unsocial	upheaval
unbroken	undertow	universe	unsought	upholder
unbuckle	underway	univocal	unsprung	up in arms
unburden	undraped	unjustly	unstable	uplander
unburied	undreamt	unkennel	unstably	uplifter
unbutton	undulant	unkindly	unstated	uppercut
uncalled	undulate	unkingly	unsteady	uppishly
uncandid	unearned	unlawful	unstring	uprising
uncapped	uneasily	unleaded	unstrung	uprooter
uncaused	unedited	unlearnt	unstuffy	upsetter
unchancy	unending	unlikely	unsuited	upsprang
unchaste	unerring	unlimber	unsunned	upspring
unchurch	unevenly	unlinked	unswathe	upsprung
uncially	unfading	unlisted	untangle	upstairs
unciform	unfairly	unloader	untapped	upstream
uncinate	unfasten	unloosen	untaught	upstrike

upthrown	validity	Vedantic	veristic	viewable
upthrust	valorise	vegetate	verjuice	viewless
upwardly	valorous	vegetive	vermouth	vigilant
uralitic	valuable	vehement	vernally	vigneron
urbanely	valuably	veilless	vernicle	vignette
urbanise	valuator	velarium	veronica	vigorous
urbanism	valvular	velocity	verrucae	vileness
urbanist	vambrace	velskoen	versicle	vilifier
urbanite	vampiric	venality	vertebra	villadom
urbanity	vanadate	venation	vertexes	villager
urethane	vanadium	vendetta	vertical	villainy
urgently	vanadous	vendible	vertices	vincible
urochord	Vandalic	veneerer	verticil	vinculum
urostyle	vaneless	venerate	vesicant	vinegary
Ursuline	vanguard	venereal	vesicate	vineyard
urticant	vanillin	Venetian	vesperal	vinosity
urticate	vanisher	vengeful	vespiary	vinously
usefully	vanquish	venially	vestiary	vintager
usufruct	vapidity	venomous	vestment	violable
usurious	vaporise	venosity	vesturer	violably
utiliser	vaporous	venously	vesuvian	violator
uvularly	vapourer	ventless	vexation	violence
uvulitis	varactor	venturer	vexillum	viperine
uxorious	variably	Venusian	viameter	viperish
vacantly	variance	veracity	viaticum	viperous
vacation	varicose	verandah	vibrancy	virement
vaccinal	variedly	veratrin	vibrator	virginal
vaccinia	varietal	veratrum	vibrissa	Virginia
vacuolar	variform	verbally	viburnum	viricide
vagabond	variolar	verbatim	vicarage	viridian
vagility	variorum	verbiage	vicarate	viridity
vagrancy	varletry	verboten	vicarial	virilism
vainness	vascular	verdancy	vicinage	virility
valanced	vasculum	verderer	vicinity	virology
valerate	vasiform	verderor	victoria	virtuosa
valerian	vastness	verditer	victress	virtuosi
Valhalla	vaulting	verdured	victuals	virtuoso
valiance	vauntful	verecund	Viennese	virtuous
valiancy	vavasory	vergence	Vietcong	virulent
validate	vavasour	verifier	Vietminh	viscacha

visceral	volition	wallgame	waterish	wellhead
viscidly	volitive	wallknot	waterlog	wellknit
viscount	volplane	walloper	waterloo	well made
Visigoth	voltaism	wallower	waterman	wellnigh
visional	volution	wanderer	waterski	wellread
visitant	volvulus	wanderoo	waterway	Wellsian
visually	vomerine	wantonly	watthour	well to do
vitalise	vomitive	warcloud	waveband	wellworn
vitalism	vomitory	wardance	waveform	Welshman
vitalist	voracity	wardenry	waveless	weregild
vitality	vortexes	wardress	waviness	werewolf
vitellin	vortical	wardrobe	waxberry	Wesleyan
vitellus	vortices	wardroom	waxcloth	westerly
vitiable	votaress	wardship	waxiness	westward
vitiator	votarist	warhorse	waxlight	west wind
vitiligo	voteless	wariness	waxworks	wetlands
vitreous	voussoir	warmness	wayfarer	wetnurse
vituline	vowelise	warpaint	waygoing	wettable
vivacity	vowelled	warplane	weakfish	whacking
vivarium	voyageur	warranty	weakling	whapping
vivifier	vulcanic	warrener	weakness	wharfage
vivisect	vulgarly	wartweed	weanling	whatever
vixenish	waggoner	wartwort	weaponry	whatness
vizarded	wagonage	warweary	wearable	wheatear
vizcacha	wagonlit	war whoop	weariful	wheedler
vocalise	Wahabism	washable	wear well	wheelman
vocalism	Wahabite	washbowl	weaselly	wheezily
vocalist	wainscot	washroom	Wedgwood	whenever
vocality	waitress	wastable	weedless	wherever
vocation	wakeless	wasteful	weeklong	whetting
vocative	wakening	watchdog	weeviled	wheyface
voicebox	waleknot	watchful	weevilly	whidding
voiceful	Walhalla	watchkey	weldable	whiffler
voidable	walkable	watchman	weldment	Whiggery
voidance	walkaway	waterage	welladay	Whiggish
voidness	walkover	waterbed	wellaway	Whiggism
volatile	Walkyrie	waterbus	wellborn	whimbrel
volcanic	wallaroo	water gas	wellbred	whimwham
volcanos	walleyed	water ice	welldeck	whinchat
volitant	wallfern	watering	well done	whinsill

whipcord	wilfully	witch elm	woolsack	writeoff
whip hand	wiliness	witchery	woolshed	writings
whiplash	williwaw	witchety	woolskin	wrongful
whiplike	windburn	witching	woolwork	xanthene
whipping	windcone	withdraw	wordbook	xanthine
whipworm	windfall	withdrew	wordless	xanthium
whirring	windgall	withheld	wordplay	xanthoma
whiskers	windlass	withhold	workable	Xantippe
whiskery	windless	wizardly	workaday	xenogamy
whispery	windmill	wizardry	workfolk	xenolith
whistler	windowed	woefully	workings	xylology
whiteboy	windpipe	wolf fish	workless	yachting
whitecap	windrose	wolfpack	workmate	Yankeefy
whitefly	windsail	wolfskin	workroom	yarmulka
whitehot	windsock	womanise	workshop	yataghan
whitener	windward	womanish	wormcast	yeanling
whiteout	winepalm	wondrous	worm gear	yearbook
white tie	wineshop	wontedly	wormhole	yearling
whizbang	wineskin	woodbind	wormlike	yearlong
whizzing	wingbeat	woodbine	wormseed	yearning
whizzkid	wingcase	woodchat	wormwood	yeastily
whodunit	wingless	woodcock	worthful	yellowly
wholehog	wingspan	woodenly	worthily	yeomanly
whomever	winnable	woodland	wouldest	yeomanry
whooping	winnings	woodlark	woundily	yielding
whopping	winnower	woodlice	wrackful	yodelled
whoredom	wintrily	woodnote	wrangler	yodeller
wickedly	wiredraw	woodpile	wrappage	yoghourt
wide eyed	wirehair	woodpulp	wrapping	youngest
wideness	wireless	woodruff	wrathful	youngish
wifehood	wirework	woodshed	wrathily	yourself
wifeless	wireworm	woodsman	wreathen	youthful
wifelike	wirewove	woodwind	wreckage	Yugoslav
wigmaker	wiriness	woodwool	wrestler	yuletide
wild eyed	wiseacre	woodwork	wrestpin	zabaione
wildfire	wiseness	woodworm	wretched	zamindar
wildfowl	wishbone	wooldyed	wriggler	zaniness
wildlife	wishwash	woolfell	wristlet	zarzuela
wildness	wistaria	woollens	wristpin	zealotry
wildwood	wisteria	woolpack	writable	zecchini